Improving Educational Equity in Urban Contexts

An enduring educational concern that has plagued researchers and policy makers in a number of affluent countries is the endemic nature of educational inequalities. These inequalities highlight distinct differences in the educational skills, knowledge, capabilities and credentials between learners' demographic characteristics. They also point to issues of educational disadvantage that emanate from a combination of factors including family life, communities, the geographies of space and place, gender and ethnicity.

This book examines some of the causes and responses to educational inequalities, and focuses upon poor urban contexts where educational disadvantage is at its most concentrated, and where educational policy and practice has, over time, proliferated. It questions how wider inequities experienced by young people in urban contexts generate educational inequalities and disadvantage, detailing explicitly what an equitable approach to education might look like.

Included in the book is an innovative educational equity framework and toolkit with illustrative policy and practice case studies, bringing together unique scholarship and analysis to examine future educational policy in a holistic, comprehensive and equitable way. It will be valuable reading for postgraduate students, researchers and policy makers with an interest in education and educational equity.

Carlo Raffo is Professor of Urban Education at the University of Manchester, UK.

Improving Educational Equity in Urban Contexts

Carlo Raffo

Routledge
Taylor & Francis Group

LONDON AND NEW YORK

First published 2014
by Routledge
2 Park Square, Milton Park, Abingdon, Oxon OX14 4RN

and by Routledge
711 Third Avenue, New York, NY 10017

Routledge is an imprint of the Taylor & Francis Group, an informa business

British Library Cataloguing in Publication Data
A catalogue record for this book is available from the British Library

Library of Congress Cataloging in Publication Data
Raffo, Carlo.
  Improving educational equity in urban contexts / Carlo Raffo.
    pages cm
  Includes bibliographical references and index.
  ISBN 978-0-415-81747-9 (hardback)—ISBN 978-0-203-58421-7 (ebook)
  1. Education, Urban—Cross-cultural studies. 2. Educational equalization—
  Cross-cultural studies. 3. Children with social disabilities—Education—
  Cross-cultural studies. I. Title.
  LC5101.R352014
  370.9173'2—dc23
                                                                    2013012767

ISBN: 978–0–415–81747–9 (hbk)
ISBN: 978–0–203–58421–7 (ebk)

Typeset in Galliard
by RefineCatch Limited, Bungay, Suffolk

Printed and bound in Great Britain by
TJ International Ltd, Padstow, Cornwall

For Mandy – the love of my life

Contents

Acknowledgements

I would first like to thank the team at Routledge for believing in the book and providing professional guidance in its production. Secondly I would like to thanks Taylor & Francis for providing permission for a number of journal articles to be adapted for use in this book. Thirdly I would like to offer my sincerest thanks to Ruth Lupton and Bernard Barker for their detailed feedback on initial drafts of the book and to Patsy Hodson and Lynne Heath from Manchester Communications Academy for sharing with me their professional work on educational equity. I would also like to thank both colleagues in the School of Education, University of Manchester and those further afield who have, over the years, been an inspiration to my thinking and writing and have also provided me with invaluable support in my academic life more generally. In particular, and in no particular order, many thanks go to Helen Gunter, Alan Dyson, Dave Hall, Kirstin Kerr, Lesley Warr, Mel West, Mel Ainscow, John Smyth and Meg Maguire. Without their guidance and support this book would never have come to fruition. Needless to say, however, the views expressed in the book, and any errors or shortcomings it may contain, are entirely my responsibility.

Finally, I would especially like to thank my wife Mandy for her enduring love and support in the production of this book. It is her daily practice of educational equity in her classrooms that is my inspiration. In all ways she is truly a wonderful person.

Permissions

The author is grateful to Taylor & Francis for providing permission to adapt the following papers as chapters of the book:

Chapter 3 – Raffo, C. (2011) Educational Equity in Poor Urban Contexts – Exploring Issues of Place/Space and Young People's Identity and Agency, *British Journal of Educational Studies*, 59(1), 1–19. First published 15 December 2010 (iFirst).

Chapter 4 – Raffo, C. (2011) Barker's ecology of disadvantage and educational equity: issues of redistribution and recognition, *Journal of Educational Administration and History*, 43(4), 325–343.

Chapter 6 – Raffo, C. (2003) Disaffected young people and the work-related curriculum at KS4 – issues of social capital development and learning as a form of cultural practice, *Journal of Education and Work*, 16(1), 69–86.

1 Introduction

Improving educational equity in urban contexts

An enduring educational concern that has plagued researchers and policy makers in most affluent countries for perhaps as long as education has been available as a public good is the endemic nature of educational inequalities. These inequalities highlight clear differences in the educational skills, knowledge, capabilities and credentials between learners' demographic characteristics. They also point to processes of educational inequity that emanate from an intersection of factors that include learners' families, communities, the geographies of particular spaces and places, gender, ethnicity, material well-being, culture and the geopolitical developments inherent in globalisation. These factors interact with each other and with the individual characteristics and biographies of learners. Above all, they interact with the education system – with its structures, practices, values and expectations – in ways that result in educational injustices. The general theme of the book is about examining some of the causes and responses to these injustices. Specifically the book will examine issues of educational equity in those poor urban contexts in England, and internationally, where educational inequalities are at their most concentrated and where educational policy and practice has, over time, proliferated and been at its most focused. In so doing the context for this book is located in the more general arena of urban studies and in particular in what is increasingly characterised by a dichotomy in the field in and around notions of the 'urban' and 'urbane'. One element of this dichotomy is the urbane that is often reflected in ideas about cities and towns as 'glocal' informational centres gentrified by capital (social, cultural and economic) rich, mobile and powerful groups of people that harness the creative forces of such centres. This urbaneness is also commensurate with diversity of the metropolitan that brings a richness of experience, the locus of high culture, sophistication, and an area where this privileged population have the means to participate in what was once known as a 'cosmopolitan' way of life. Educationally this privileged population is stratified from the rest through the provision of either exclusive private education or via state schools located in expensive catchment areas. The contrasting element of the dichotomy is the mirror image signalled by the notion of the 'urban' that is suggestive of major challenges facing the very same towns and cities. Living cheek by jowl with the rich urbane panoply of social, cultural, economic, political and educational affordances and opportunities, are the many places in our towns and cities that contain profound pockets of urban poverty with commensurate levels of marginalisation and exclusion. Families living in such communities are faced with poor health, poor housing and infrastructure, high levels of crime and violence and high levels of unemployment. For young people in such communities the experiences of schooling and education are often blighted by their everyday experiences of poverty, exclusion and stigmatisation – experiences that are then compounded by the commensurate difficulties faced by urban schools in responding to such challenges. Hence it is in the poor urban neighbourhoods of our cities and towns that educational failure is at its most concentrated. It is a reality that has led some commentators to categorise such people and places as the 'urban outcasts' (Wacquant 2007) of our modern times. In addition high levels of social stratification and structural inequalities reflected in the urban-urbane dynamic and its 'outcasts', has generated tensions between and among communities with opportunities for enhanced community fragmentation and prejudice. Termed by some as problems of social exclusion, by others as constraining social mobility and by others again as examples of social injustice and racism, the urban-urbane problematic in its various guises has troubled educational policy makers in numerous ways and over a number of decades, and yet with little to show for the investments and interventions attempted over time. My take in responding to such a challenge is to take a different approach to many in the field who position themselves around juxtaposed perspectives that are either: (a) outwardly socially critical of current arrangements and explicitly focused on education for social justice, or (b) focus, conversely, on ameliorative, perhaps utilitarian equity improvements within currently constituted policy parameters. What this book attempts in the first place is a more detailed and philosophical scrutiny about the general notion of educational equity or fairness and how these terms relate broadly to different ideas about educational purpose and quality. As such the book is positioned more closely to what Broadfoot and Nisbet (1981) have termed the 'enlightenment' function of educational research in that it challenges existing and taken for granted conceptualisations of what educational quality and equity might mean. It also reflects Gewirtz and Cribb's (2006) position about the importance of explicit ethical reflexivity in orientating one's approach to undertaking social science research. My argument is that far too often implicit notions of purpose, quality, fairness, justice, equity, and equality are used, often interchangeably in relation to education but in ways that provide little precise detail about what is meant by such terms. This therefore creates confusion as what is desirable, possible and/or achievable. The specific aims of this book, therefore, are threefold. Firstly I want to articulate explicitly a normative understanding of the processes of educational equity and how this understanding might be linked to particular notions of educational purpose and quality. Secondly I want to then examine in more detail what it is about the urban-urbane paradox that provides explanatory potential for how and why these inequities materialise more frequently in poor urban contexts. Finally I want to examine how educational policy and practice in England and other countries have historically and more recently understood and then enacted notions of quality and fairness. My position is that being explicit and systematic about the normative dimension of educational equity, its links to purpose and quality and with a specific focus on the urban-urbane, requires a commitment to producing convincing arguments and understandings about why a particular state of educational affairs might be preferable and how things might therefore be improved. Although this may seem an obvious point to make, it is not an issue that has always been fully explored or articulated. For example, over the last 20–30 years research, policy and practice in many affluent countries has more often than not taken for granted notions of educational purpose, quality and equity. These have been utilitarian in their orientation and linked to the requirements of the economy and economic competitiveness. Quality has been associated with ideas about human capital and in particular maximising the number and level of educational credentials and attainments achieved by the greatest number of young people. Inequities have then been explained in terms of the inequalities that have permeated the education system, particularly in relation to those groups of disadvantaged urban young people that underachieve in relation to the attainment of those credentials. A list of multifarious explanations for these inequalities are then advanced, often located in discourses framed within existing perspectives about educational failure that discourage alternative approaches and that are more often than not focused on 'underperforming' schools and their teachers. Based on particular interpretations of research or 'best evidence' located within these mainstream educational perspectives, a plethora of, at times, unrelated strategies and resources for dealing with these educational inequalities are advanced. Partial successes are then applauded; however, the ongoing endemic problems of educational inequality remain unchallenged. My argument is that implicit assumptions about educational purpose, quality and equity do not engage systematically or analytically with detailed arguments about what an equitable education system might look like. Such an approach therefore makes it problematic to accept standard mainstream policy arguments about equitable education policies and their associated practices. Perhaps the challenge is best articulated by the philosopher and economist Amartya Sen when he posed the pertinent question 'equality of what'. And as Terzi cogently reminds the field:

> The under-specified status of the principles underpinning [the] policy is perhaps a crucial factor in the outcomes. Knowing more precisely what we mean by an equitable distribution – whether, for instance, it should be a fair distribution of resources in order to increase average achievement, or, conversely, in order to maximise the achievement of the lowest achieving students – would certainly make a difference to the policy design.
>
> (Terzi, 2008: 2)

What makes this book different to many in the field is that it starts by examining in some detail what is meant by educational purpose, quality and fairness. Based on this discussion I develop an Educational Equity Framework (EEF) that allows me to systematically review the nature of much educational policy and practice dedicated to educational fairness. As such, this approach falls in the tradition of applied philosophical writing on educational equity that has been a stuttering and yet recurring research focus for education writers over a number of decades. More recently there has been a renewed interest in such an approach that is particularly exemplified by writers such as Terzi (2008) in her work on educational equity and disabilities; Lynch and Lodge's (2002) work on the equity of school processes; Keddie's (2012) study of educational equity for indigenous people in Australia, and Tikly and Barrett's (2011) examination of social justice, capabilities and the quality of education in low-income countries.

Based on the EEF, I then provide explanations for educational inequities in the context of the urban-urbane paradox. Using the EEF and focused explanations for educational disadvantage and inequity much of the rest of the book then examines aspects of policy and practice that has been outwardly dedicated, in broad terms, to improving educational equity in such contexts. This is undertaken by providing the reader with a judicious mix of educational research that I have undertaken over the last ten years that has focused on such issues. At the end of the book, and based on this review and on a synthesis of the entirety of the work contained in the book, I develop an educational equity toolkit that provides policy makers and practitioners at different levels in the education system and beyond with a set of 'enlightened' rather than purely utilitarian questions against which they can judge the educational fairness of their policy and practice.

Nature and structure of the book

Given the broad introduction to the book and its parameters, what specifically will the book deliver to the reader? At one level the book draws on a central and important conceptual literature review on education and poverty and its links to educational inequalities that I, and colleagues at the University of Manchester, undertook and that was sponsored by the Joseph Rowntree Foundation (Raffo *et al.*, 2007). This review enabled an emerging categorising framework to be developed that provided significant clues about the vertical scope of analysis that are important in the field. This book makes significant reference to this work and in particular the use of the macro, meso and micro scales of analysis. At another level this book also draws on the conceptual ideas of educational equity that have been generated through my work with colleagues in the Centre for Educational Equity at the University Manchester. These deliberations convinced me of the central importance of articulating at the beginning of the book what educational fairness or equity might mean. In addition those discussions helped me to arrive at a clear position on such issues. As such this position rests on the idea that educational equity needs to not only engage with important relational issues central to young people's lives such as agency, identity and the cultural, but also with how such issues are mediated by constraining economic factors and the unequal distribution of resources more generally. It is also about how the 'voice' of young people is represented in the work of schools and education more generally.

Having articulated my approach to educational equity, the central part of the book then examines, in the main, aspects of English educational policy and practice in the light of these arguments. These cases do not necessarily represent the full array of initiatives developed over time to deal with educational inequities. Instead they are chosen to illuminate policy and practice at different levels of analysis. They include at the macro level of analysis national education initiatives and interventions – broadly classified as area based initiatives – that have attempted to provide additional resources for public service agencies, schools, families and young people in disadvantaged urban areas to work together to improve educational engagement and attainment. At the meso level the book contains case study research that examines how the practice of school leaders in 'challenging' urban contexts conceptualise and articulate educational equity and social inclusion for the most disadvantaged. The book, however, is not just about systems, schools, and contexts. It also provides an examination of the ways in which young people interact with systems, schools and context in their everyday lives. To exemplify this I provide a detailed case study of a micro level work-related curriculum project that attempts to re-engage 'disaffected' young people back into learning, but with limited success. In addition, and as an antidote perhaps, to much within mainstream urban education and schooling that appears to alienate many disadvantaged young people, the book also provides a case study example of a small-scale curriculum intervention that was successful in re-activating young people with learning. The evidence from this project exemplifies the importance of not only dealing with some of the distributional aspects of educational equity but also developing appropriate and relationally just pedagogical strategies that respect young people's identities and that are orientated towards what these young people value educationally.

Given the topics and research studies that inform the book, how is it to be structured and organised? In the next chapter I argue for a particular perspective on educational equity and related issues of purpose and quality. In order to provide a context to this thinking I first provide a brief overview of two main approaches that are located in: (a) the economic competitiveness/human capital, and (b) the personal development/rights-based traditions. I then examine general notions of equity and justice, assisted by Gewirtz's (1998) thorough mapping of the field. This is then followed by an exploration of the links between justice and the purposes of education and in particular how the broader thinking in the field helps illuminate what we might mean by educational equity. In detailing these arguments I draw on key ideas based on Sen's (1992) notion of capabilities and Fraser's (1996) perspective on distributional, relational and representational justice. Together these provide the foundations to my EEF that details a normative set of tools for examining both historic and current policy and practice on educational inequalities. The framework in essence focuses on the purpose of education being about personal development, that is linked to a rights-based agenda and that prioritises ideas about equity around young people's educational autonomy/agency to pursue educational capabilities and outcomes that they value and that are valued more generally by society. In so doing, however, it recognises that young people will adapt their educational preferences and choices according to what they know and what they think is possible for them. The framework will, therefore, examine those aspects of distributional and relational inequity that constrain this autonomy. It will do that by focusing firstly on broad processes of inequity that are beyond the school and that yet have a strong impact on young people's educational identity and agency. Secondly it will also examine those more specific school-based inequities in educational process that directly marginalise, psychologically constrain and/or discriminate against particular groups of young people.

Chapter 3 in essence is about documenting some of the key indicators of educational inequity as stipulated by the EEF and then exploring some of the reasons for how and why this inequity predominates in poor urban contexts. It starts by highlighting educational inequalities and in particular those groups of young people that have been documented by both researchers and policy makers as those most educationally disadvantaged. The chapter then builds on the philosophical conceptualisations about educational equity documented in Chapter 2 by developing a set of theorisations and explanations about how poverty/class, ethnicity and gender within urban spaces and places intersect with each other and with educational processes themselves to influence young people's educational identities and experiences and resulting inequalities. In so doing the chapter provides a set of integrated, multidisciplinary explanations for why inequities in educational autonomy and process exist for groups of young people in the urban.

The evidence documented in chapters 2 and 3 points to a complicated picture that includes issues of class, ethnicity, gender, urban space/place and the nature of the educational project itself. Educational policy over the last 40 years or so has tended to respond to educational inequality and disadvantage in predominately one of two ways that have, at times, operated simultaneously. The ongoing and main focus for improved educational equity has been attempts to raise standards across the system as a whole. This has included the development of a powerful mix of target-setting, national curricula and pedagogical development, and high stakes accountability (Raffo *et al.*, 2010). The underlying argument to such an approach is that all schools, no matter what the intake or where they are located, should be able to achieve broadly similar results with a broadly similar curriculum. However, educational data continues to suggest that although improvements can be made through the school system, these tend to be sporadic and inconsistent. Given these constraints, in Chapter 4 I utilise the EEF and conceptualisations for educational disadvantage developed in previous chapters to explore policy initiatives that have provided schools in disadvantaged urban contexts with additional compensatory resources to help improve outcomes. Given that the vast majority of educational failure is located (albeit differentially) in such contexts, the focus of this policy review will be on those interventions that over time have allocated additional resources to: (a) those disadvantaged urban contexts, (b) the schools located in those contexts, and (c) underachieving groups of young people and families who attend schools and/or live in those contexts – educational policies and interventions that have become known as area based initiatives (ABIs).

Developments in ABI policy and practice that are starting to be classified as 'new ABIs' will be examined and comparisons will be made with ABIs in other countries such as France's Zones d'Education Prioritaires, Portugal's Territórios Educativos de Intervenção Prioritária and the Harlem Children Zones in the US.

The focus of Chapter 5 is an examination of meso level school leadership rationales for improved educational equity and social inclusion for those young people and their families most disadvantaged. Given the importance of school leadership in much educational policy rhetoric, both in England and internationally, for bringing about educational change and improvement for those most disadvantaged (DfEE 1997, 1998, DfES 2004, 2005a) there are few studies (Muijs *et al.*, 2010; Stevenson, 2007; Walker *et al.*, 2009) that provide evidence for what these realities and rationales look like. What research there is appears to be both disparate and yet at the same time fork along two distinct lines of enquiry that either: (a) take for granted a somewhat vague understanding of educational equity linked to broad notions of social inclusion and instrumental school leadership practice; or (b) develop a social justice approach to schools and school leadership that are broadly critical of current educational policy and school leadership implied in that policy. In particular many studies in school leadership neither provide a rich understanding of what forms of equity are given primacy by schools and school leaders through their school policy and practice nor how these practices are both localised and linked into the national agendas. In addition there appears to be a lack of awareness in the literature about the leadership rationales that appear to underpin particular conceptualisation of educational equity and school leadership practice. Based on empirical research and evidence from other studies into school leadership and social justice, the chapter aims to respond to such challenges by providing evidence about various conceptualisations of educational leadership and how these conceptualisations link to broader notions of educational equity documented in earlier chapters.

Chapter 6 focuses on an area of educational policy development that has perhaps received growing attention in recent years in England and in other countries, particularly Australia. This policy arena, both nationally and internationally, contains curriculum initiatives that have attempted to re-engage disadvantaged young people into schooling and education more generally. In England many of these initiatives developed as a response to the relaxation of National Curriculum over the last five to ten years that enabled greater flexibility for schools to develop various curriculum initiatives to meet the differing needs of young people – particular those viewed as being educationally disadvantaged. The purpose of this chapter is to examine one such development broadly defined as a work-related curriculum initiative that has been used historically to meet the needs of 'less academic working-class students'. This chapter focuses upon one relatively large scheme that was used in the disadvantaged contexts of a large conurbation in the North West of England. In examining the initiative the argument I make is that such provision illuminates tensions between a continuing emphasis on 'narrowing the gap' in educational attainment through enhanced credentialism and the wider socio-cultural and relational dimensions that make up the lifeworlds of young people that orientate them to such provision. One of the consequences of these tensions is that young people participating in such schemes often become less willing to engage fully in what they see as the less relevant distributional (narrowing the gap) aims of school because they are given significant 'tastes' of relationally just workplace environments that go beyond school experiences and that reflect more clearly their own valued educational capabilities and aspirations.

Chapter 7 reports on a small-scale curriculum project that I, with colleagues and partners from across the city of Mellville, developed in response to the educational disengagement of some of our most disadvantaged young people. It was a vocational education programme with a strong mentoring component that aimed to provide opportunities for linking the valued educational capabilities of a group of young people to labour market opportunities generated by emerging economic developments in the city. It is an example of an educational intervention that attempts to focus equally on both distributional and relational issues of educational equity and that builds on engaging young people's autonomy through just educational processes.

In the final chapter I synthesise the main messages outlined in the preceding chapters of the book and detail an educational equity toolkit. The toolkit asks focused questions at the macro, meso and micro level of analysis that pertain to education, both in broad and specific ways, with the aim of helping policy makers and practitioners develop educational change that might impact more fully on the educational lives of those young people most disadvantaged in our society.

I hope that the book will provide guidance and inspiration to those dedicated to improving our knowledge about educational inequity. In addition I hope the book provides evidence for what a more equitable education system might look like and thus assist those responsible for bringing about that improvement through their everyday policy and practice.

2   What is educational equity?

Introduction

Far too often, writings dedicated to improving the educational outcomes of those least advantaged do so without being precise about what they want to try and improve and for what purposes. Researchers and policy makers often pronounce about such issues but do so in rather general and at times utilitarian ways that often lack clarity. In particular they lack what one might term systematic ethical reasoning to help articulate the nature of educational inequities. Perhaps a significant example of this type of undeveloped approach is provided by the important Organisation for Economic Co-operation and Development (OECD) report *No More Failures – Ten steps to educational equity* (Field *et al.*, 2007). What this report does is document a whole set of unequal educational outcomes that reflect the state of educational play in OECD countries. The report then argues that unequal improvements in educational attainments reflect educational unfairness in a whole variety of ways and for a whole number of different groups in society. In addition it suggests that certain groups of learners do not even achieve a basic minimum educational threshold, reflecting, perhaps, the multifaceted problems of inclusion within many education systems. Based on equity being understood, broadly and in rather general ways, as fairness and inclusion, the report then documents a whole series of steps to educational improvement. These steps are developed to respond to the descriptive failings documented in the report as specific educational inequalities but do so without any overarching and detailed sense of what improved equity might mean. This lack of clarity is redolent of Levin's views about equity:

> [A] commitment to equity suggests that differences in outcomes should not be attributable to differences in areas such as wealth, income, power or possessions. The question is then of what state or degree of inequality is acceptable. The answer to this question will always be a contested one, fought out in political arenas of all kinds on a continuing basis. The grounds of this struggle seem to have shifted in the last 30 years towards reducing the gap in outcomes between the top and bottom by helping those at the bottom move up. This may be unsatisfactory as a definition from an analytic

perspective but is workable from the standpoint of policy. The argument has been made about quality (Pirsig, 1974) that while we may not be able to define it, we know it when we see it. For equity, it may be that while we cannot define what it is, we know when we are far from it.

(Levin, 2003: 5)

In addition to issues of vagueness, education policy documents such as the OECD's further compounds the problem by failing to making explicit the connection between educational purpose, quality and fairness and notions of living the 'good life'. My argument is that without this clarity there is little possibility of knowing what the principles of education should be, thus making it difficult to know precisely what we need to understand and then do to make improvements. This chapter focuses on educational principles by examining the related ideas of educational purpose, quality and fairness and by making reference to broader concerns of equality, equity, and justice. In so doing I hope to respond to Gewirtz and Cribb's (2006) challenge about the need for educational research to be underpinned by a rigorous and reflexive examination of ethical values that engages with the realities of educational policy and practice.

What I attempt to do in this chapter is to argue for educational fairness to be prioritised around process notions of educational equity that relate to particular ideas about educational purpose and quality. In making the argument I develop an Educational Equity Framework (EEF) that prioritises the dynamics of educational fairness around young people's freedom to engage with valued educational capabilities. This framework is then used in later chapters when I examine particular examples of educational policy and practice that purport to be dedicated to improving educational equity. The centrality of my position on educational equity thus acts as the structuring framework for the book and allows me to: (a) detail discussions about where and why educational inequalities exist and how, in particular, economic and cultural disadvantage in urban contexts impacts on the educational experiences of young people and families in iniquitous ways, and (b) examine various equity oriented educational policy and practice responses that have been implemented over time to deal with educational inequalities. At the end of the book I will develop an educational equity toolkit that builds on the equity framework and empirical evidence documented throughout the book. The toolkit will provide policy makers and practitioners with a broad set of equity questions that will help them explore the extent to which their educational provision can be classified as fair. It will also provide a set of indicators by which the quality of that education can also be judged.

To start the process, and in order to provide a context to my thinking on equity, I will first provide a brief overview of certain key thinkers in the general fields of justice, equality and equity. These key ideas will then act as lenses through which to examine specific issues of educational equity, purpose and quality.

A brief discussion about justice, equality and equity

Let me start with some broad definitions. For me justice is about the fairness of social arrangements that individuals and different groups of people experience in their lives. A measure of justice can be articulated by examining the various social, economic and cultural indicators of equality or inequality that exist for different groups of people. Equity, on the other hand, might be thought of as a dynamic process of making things equal and fair.

For many the most important prerequisite for justice is economic justice; often referred to as the fair distribution of scarce resources between individuals in society. Inequalities occur when the distribution of those resources are clearly skewed in particular ways. For Marxists inequalities lie at the heart of capitalist society as the labour of working people is exploited by capitalists to earn them surplus gain. Fairness of economic distribution – a more equal society – may only come about with the demise of an inequitable capitalist system. However, libertarians suggest that as long as there is an equitable system of equality of opportunity – i.e. the existence of equal formal rights, equality of access, equality of participation, individuals, based on notions of meritocracy, should be allowed to exploit their greater talents or abilities to convert opportunities in ways that may result in unequal economic outcomes between people. Unequal outcomes (or inequality) can only, therefore, be really justified if everyone has access to an equitable system of equal opportunity to succeed. Inequitable processes that forcibly withhold the opportunities from individuals to engage in such activities would be viewed as a strike against individual freedom. For others, however, social justice is not just about fair economic distribution, it also about the general welfare of individuals and hence should be interpreted to mean that policies and institutions should be judged equitable according to the extent that they benefit the most disadvantaged (Rawls, 1972). Hence notions of what is fair, and what might act as the ingredients for social justice, can be interpreted in various ways, depending on the underlying ethical theory or ideology. In discussing such ideas, Sen in his theorisations about justice, equity and equality has correctly posited the question of 'equality of what' (Sen, 1992). In tracing the historic developments that focus on such questions, one might argue that western thinking about social justice was greatly influenced by utilitarianism—the idea, originally attributed to Bentham (1789), that the social goal should be to achieve 'the greatest happiness for the greatest number.' Although utilitarians were essentially unconcerned with the *distribution* of happiness (the equality of happiness), and enjoined societies simply to maximise the sum of utilities across all individuals, the approach has nevertheless earned the somewhat misbegotten reputation (at least among economists) of having egalitarian implications. Modern theories of social justice have largely moved beyond utilitarianism, in part because of its fundamental lack of concern with the distribution of welfare (equality of welfare). Most theories reject final welfare (or utility) as the appropriate space on which to judge the fairness of a given allocation or system. There is an acknowledgement that equity issues need to be associated with the important role of individual responsibility in moving from resources to final outcomes, including welfare. All prefer to see some combination of the set of liberties and distribution of resources available to individuals as the right space on which to form a social judgement and on which to examine justice. Gewirtz (1998) notes, however, that the theories that appear to have been most influential in much modern day thinking about justice relate to the ideas of Rawls (1972). For Rawls (1972:7) 'the subject matter of justice is the basic structure of society, or more exactly, the way in which the major social institutions. . . distribute fundamental rights and duties and determine the distribution of advantages from social co-operation.' Rawls argues further that for social justice to come about requires that two basic principles hold. The first principle 'demands the most extensive liberty for each, consistent with similar liberty for others' (Sen, 2000: 69). The second principle requires that opportunities – which he related to the concept of 'primary goods' – should be open to all members of society and, under the Difference Principle, proposes that the chosen allocation should be one which maximises the opportunities of the least privileged group. Rawls' ideas perhaps link most robustly to a more radical 'strong' version of distributional justice that is measured by equality of outcome which seeks to ensure equal rates of success for different groups in society through direct equitable and yet unequal interventions to prevent disadvantage. In summarising notions of distributional justice Gewirtz is clear that for a 'society to be perceived as just clearly cannot exist without a fair distribution of resources both material and non-material' (Gewirtz, 1998: 470). However, she also eloquently reminds the field that social justice is not just about distributional justice and equal outcomes but should be expanded to include what she terms relational justice that focus on equitable processes.

> The relational dimension of justice refers to the nature of the relationships which structure society. A focus on this dimension helps us to theorise about issues of power and how we treat each other, both in the sense of micro face-to-face interactions and in the sense of macro-social and economic relation which are mediated by institutions such as the state and the market.
>
> (Gewirtz, 1998: 471)

Gewirtz develops her thinking about relational justice by contrasting it to Rawls' notion of distributive justice. She argues that for Rawls justice is about equality: the distribution of rights, duties and the social and economic goods accruing from social co-operation. It does not appear to about equity or the processes of social co-operation itself. Relational conceptions of social justice refer to developing an equitable political/relational system within which the distribution of social and economic goods, rights and responsibilities take place. She argues that it is 'about the *nature* and *ordering* of social relations, the formal and informal rules which govern how members of society treat each other both on a macro level and at a micro interpersonal level' (Gewirtz, 1998: 471).

This relational dimension of justice incorporates what Fraser (1996) refers to as the politics of recognition that focuses on the cultural and that emphasises equitable processes. Fraser argues that although issues of redistribution and equality are important as indicators of social justice, a focus on the politics of recognition targets cultural injustices which are rooted in inequitable social patterns of representation, interpretation and communication.

> Examples include cultural domination (being subjected to patterns of inter-pretation and communication that associated with another culture and are alien and/or hostile to one's own); nonrecognition (being rendered invisible via authoritative representational, communicative, and interpretative prac-tices of one's culture); and disrespect (being routinely maligned or dispar-aged in stereotypic public cultural representations and/or in everyday life interactions).
>
> (Fraser, 1996: 7)

Fraser suggests that the remedy for this type of injustice involves equitable pro-cesses of revaluing disrespected identities and the cultural products of maligned groups. Rather than being classified as class-like entities, the politics of recogni-tion see the victims of injustice by the relations of recognition and in particular the lesser esteem, honour and prestige that they enjoy relative to other groups in society. The politics of recognition is clearly associated with the cultural and is suggestive of a focus on individual diversity and identity. As Gewirtz notes social justice based on a politics of recognition favours an 'immanent universalism' that arises from struggles for recognition by those groups most disadvantaged. She also notes that it is about a commitment to equitable processes that avoid the power of surveillance, control and discipline upon others. In developing these arguments she draws on Young who suggests that these processes reflect a 'universality in the sense of the participation and inclusion of everyone in moral and social life' which does not leave 'behind particular affiliations, feelings, commitments and desires' (Young, 1990: 105).

Based on notions of social justice which are both 'individualistically, atomisti-cally and materially distributional and also essentially holistic and being concerned with the interconnections between individuals and society' (Gewirtz, 1998: 482), how can relational and distributional perspectives – or issues of equity and equality – be reconciled? For Fraser a polarisation between distributional and relational justice is a false antithesis, since she argues that justice requires both. In order to deal with what she maintains is a false opposition, Fraser proposes a 'bivalent' conception of justice, which encompasses both concerns, without, reducing either of them to the other. The normative core of her framework is the notion of parity of participation, which 'requires social arrangements that permit all members of society to interact with one another as peers' (Fraser, 1996: 30). As Terzi (2008) notes in her application of Fraser's work to issues of educational equity and disability, two conditions are necessary for participatory parity to be accomplished: an objective precondition, which states that material sources should be distributed to ensure individuals' independence and voice; and an intersubjective condition, stipulating that cultural and social arrangements should express equal respect for all and ensure equal opportunity for achieving self-esteem (Terzi, 2008: 176). This is about addressing the complex nature of justice from egalitarian distributive and equitable relational/recognition positions. However, in examining how such ideas might be operationalised Fraser and others are clear that the unit of the analysis should be at the individual level. This is not saying that structural, political, economic and cultural issues are not important merely that these dynamic inequities in process should be understood through the way they inform the heterogeneous agency of individuals. In examining how a framework for operationalising distributional and relational notions of justice at an individual unit of analysis could be developed I, in a similar vein to Terzi, have found the capability approach developed by Sen (1985) most useful. Central to Sen's concerns about justice is the equity concept of 'agency freedom' by which he means the ability for individuals to pursue rational goals that they value, that are important for the life they wish to lead, and that contribute to democratic and civic improvements in society more generally. Agency freedom and processes of becoming and doing are, therefore, about valuing the autonomy of individuals in all their diversity and difference and yet recognising that autonomy as being part of a broader civic responsibility that some commentators have referred to as the guiding principles of democratic ethics and values (Biesta, 2012; Fielding and Moss, 2011). These ethics and values recognise and give primacy to individual diversity and difference but do so within the broader parameters of a democratic civic life that, thereby, constrains an individualistic cultural relativism associated with 'pure' notions of autonomy and choice. However, since agency is central to Sen's ideas of freedom to engage with what is valued, a lack of agency or a constrained agency equates to inequitable processes of social injustice and ultimately to constrained forms of the civic. An evolving notion of ethical individualism therefore integrates securing and expanding intrapersonal and interpersonal freedoms (individual agency and social arrangements). Individuals and their opportunities should therefore not be seen in isolated and individualistic terms but instead seen in relational holistic and interconnected ways. As Walker notes (2006) a person's agency depends on individual circumstances, the relations a person has with others and the social, cultural and economic conditions and contexts within which potential options (freedoms) can and should be achieved. Individual freedoms, as Sen points out, depend also on egalitarian social and economic arrangements and on democratic political and civil rights. So, for example, inequalities and inequities of gender, race and class affects one's abilities to convert the resources we have into the capabilities to function. Thus the egalitarian distribution of resources is only part of the story; what matters for Sen is a politics of recognition that focuses on the extent to which each person has the equitable social and cultural process and opportunities to convert his/her bundle of resources into valued (both individually and collectively), rationally chosen, doings and beings. It is not that Sen thinks that the distribution of resources does not matter; of course it does. But his concern is with processes of equity and human diversity and their effects on the conversion of resources into particular outcomes. Developing this thinking further Nussbaum (2000) argues explicitly that subjective preferences and choices are shaped and informed by society and public policy so that unequal and inequitable social, political and economic circumstances lead to unequal chances and inequitable capacities to choose. The external material, social and cultural circumstances 'affect the inner lives of people: what they hope for, what they love, what they fear, as well as what they are able to do' (Nussbaum, 2000: 31). People adapt their preferences and subjective well-being or choices according to what they think is possible for them, or following Foucault (1975), how individuals are subjectivated through their constitution in and by the discourse of power.

Developing ideas about educational equity

Building on ideas about justice or fairness highlighted above, what I want to state at the outset is that for me educational fairness is predominately bound up with ideas about educational purposes, quality and equity. The reason for this is that a consideration needs to be made as to what counts as educational purpose and quality, so that how this purpose and quality are made available to young people in equitable ways can then becomes a clearer focus for analysis. In other words, without detailing what is understood by educational purpose and quality, trying to make education fairer becomes meaningless. Purpose, quality and equity are therefore interlinked with one presupposing the other in terms of how they are understood and then enacted. Thus by making such connections one can then start to appreciate different orientations to educational fairness and also recognise more explicitly the directions and challenges for educational policy and practice in developing such orientations to fairness.

If we start with ideas about educational purpose and quality, we are reminded by James and Pollard (2011) that within contemporary western democracies three major strands of philosophical and political thinking have been established. The first concerns linking education to economic productivity – and has taken various forms historically as labour market needs have evolved. The second concerns social cohesion and social inclusion of different groups within society – a concern that continues to be an issue given the continuing inequities experienced in our diverse communities. The third concerns personal development, fulfilment and expression – with a contemporary manifestation perhaps in the terms 'well-being' and the educational rights of individuals. However, I would argue that although in principle these three strands reflect distinct ideas about the purpose and quality of education, education for social cohesion and inclusion could be accounted for within either the economic competitiveness strand or the personal development strand. Thus from one perspective social cohesion and inclusion can be viewed as the extent to which educational provision promotes the economic integration and the meaningful participatory access of different social groups and individuals into the mainstream economic life of society. Individuals are socially included through their engagement with the core life activity of employment and this employment provides a stake in the cohesion of mainstream social life of communities. From a different perspective it can also mean the way diverse individuals and groups are given recognition for who, and what, they are through the education they receive. This latter perspective shifts the lens from a situation where there is an interest in education for economic engagement and related issues of cohesion and inclusion to one that examines how cultural diversity is recognised and valued by society and in particular in the way that young people experience their rights in, and through, education. Inclusion and cohesion from this perspective comes about through a respect for diversity and heterogeneity.

Once purpose and quality are understood then understanding what makes for equitable educational processes and outcomes becomes more apparent. Perhaps one of the most explicit links to be made between educational fairness, purpose and quality and issues of justice is provided by Popkewitz and Lindbland (2000) who argue that there is a potential 'equity problematic' for education around broad notions of the economic and cultural.

Economic competitiveness and the human capital approach to educational purpose/quality – issues of distributional equity and economic inclusion and cohesion

Equity problematics from this perspective focus on the purpose and quality of education being linked to economic competitiveness and to human capital development. Quality is defined by the development of appropriate functional skills (such as numeracy and literacy), subject discipline capabilities (redolent of the academic school curricula of many international education systems) and vocationally oriented skills that reflect the needs of business and society. It is measured by the level and distribution of attainment levels and credentials generated throughout the education system. The central rationale for investing in education from a human capital perspective lies in the contribution that education can make to economic growth and social mobility. At a general level, human capital approaches have provided policy makers with an important economic rationale for a focus on educational equity. The argument presented is that schooling, through improved levels of attainment at every stage of education, should, on transition to the workplace, promote fairer distributional access and success in the economic field thereby delivering greater levels of social coherence, inclusion and justice. To put it another way, justice is enhanced by enabling a fairer distribution of academic attainments and credentials that will act as passports to improved educational and labour market opportunities for more young people. Educational equity from this perspective is a therefore defined as being about narrowing the distributional gap (equality of outcomes) between those more and less advantaged at each stage within the education system. In other words it is about finding ways of equalising an unequal educational playing field. In many respects both current and recent education policy in England and in many other developed countries focuses on these measures of quality and equity (see for example Programme for International Student Assessment indicators of educational quality and equity). The approach to improving outcomes then tends to focus on technical educational issues of input, process and outcome. Much of the educational research dedicated to making technical improvements in educational quality defined in such terms is reflected strongly in the literatures of school improvement and effectiveness (see for example Creemers and Kyriakides, 2012). Rogers (2012) reminds readers that such literatures reflect MacIntyre's (2001) distinction between effectiveness and excellence in education. For MacIntyre effectiveness is where education as a good is primarily seen as external to practice. This is contrasted to excellence in education that he sees as integral to practice. Using MacIntyre's distinction suggests that school improvement strategies linked to enhanced achievement of credentials is perhaps more about effectiveness than excellence.

Personal development and a rights-based approach to educational purpose/quality – issues of relational equity and cultural inclusion and cohesion

Here the relational equity problematic relates to both representation and stereotyping, and the institutional rules, processes and discourse that may culturally exclude some groups from mainstream social life. Equity issues for education vis-a-vis relational equity focus on a whole number of issues that can be exemplified in a number of ways, for example:

- a focus on the lived identities and lifeworlds of young people and what they bring to education from outside;
- the nature of the representation and recognition of gender, class and ethnicity in the curriculum;
- teachers' discourses about cultural plurality in classrooms;
- inclusion in mainstream classrooms of young people with special educational needs;
- educational affordances given to the valued educational functioning of young people and their families and communities that reflect diverse class and ethnic backgrounds;
- the civic dimension in school, curriculum and pedagogy and appeals to democratic engagement.

In many respects the issue of cultural injustice can be aligned with what Tikly and Barret have articulated as a set of educational purposes and quality that, in contrast to the human capital approach, advocates a personal development approach underscored by a moral and democratic rights-based perspective. A personal development approach to education is therefore about respecting an individual's democratic rights to an appropriate learning environment that enables engagement with the social, cultural, political, economic and civic domains of one's life (Subrahmanian, 2002; Unterhalter, 2007). These moral and democratic rights include for example celebration and nurturing of learner creativity, use of first languages in schools, and pupil participation in democratic structures and debate. Hence, teaching approaches that are broadly identified as learner-centred, democratic school structures that provide student voice and a civic curriculum that encourages notions of responsibility are promoted within the personal development and rights-based approach. At the macro level is also about the distribution of power though appropriate mechanism of representation that enable authority and control over resources that, together, aid the development of cultural recognition. An emphasis on cultural and relational justice through the processes of power and control of education is exemplified by projects such as the Porto Alegre experiment in Brazil (Gandiñ and Apple, 2002) and the radical education and 'common school' proposals advocated by Fielding and Moss (2011). At a different level of analysis the work of Smyth and colleagues in Australia also resonates with these approaches as they examine schooling from the viewpoint of the lives, experiences, interests, aspirations and communities from which young people come, and within which they are embedded (Smyth *et al.*, 2010). In addition the work of Susan Hart and colleagues suggests that the rights of individual students should not result in them categorised as having innate and fixed educational capabilities or aptitudes but that schools and teachers instead should develop inclusive and transformative learning environments that 'create learning without limits' (Swann *et al.*, 2012). These examples point to what MacIntyre (2001) terms as excellence inherent to educational practice. Building on these ideas, Rogers (2012) reminds readers that it is not just technical skills that make schooling approaches effective but the excellence that underpins the ethical way in which teaching and learning is developed and deployed and which recognises a duty to the educational rights and personal development of students (Carr, 2006).

So how do these equity problematics and their relationship to educational purpose and quality relate to educational policy and practice? As I argued above, at one level, educational purpose, quality and fairness can be aligned to policy developments that focus on maximising human capital development through providing equality of educational opportunity. This is where schools are provided with similar resources to allow young people to attain core educational credentials based on their perceived individual talents. In many respects the 1944 Education Act and the development of comprehensive schools in the early 70s were underpinned by this approach. However, educational equality from a human capital perspective can also be interpreted in line with Rawls' Difference Principle highlighted above (Rawls, 1972) and mean that educational policies and schools should be judged according to the extent that they benefit the most disadvantaged. This later perspective suggests that the chosen allocation of educational resources should be one which maximises the opportunities of the least privileged group – in other words that there is a clear focus on the maximisation and equalisations of educational attainments between different social groups. Here the focus is on compensatory distributional measures to make up for disadvantages that young people may experience both inside and outside school. In many respects aspects of Labour government policy between 1997 to 2010 in the UK, building on policy ideas such as the Educational Priority Areas of the 60s and early 70s, focused on the redistribution of resources to schools via policies such as

Educational Action Zones, Excellence in Cities, the City Challenge and many others (see Chapter 4 for extended discussion on these ideas)

In many respects, however, distributional approaches to educational purposes, quality and fairness that focus on educational credentials have perhaps failed take into account Sen's (1985) central observation that different young people have different 'conversion factors' from educational resources or inputs to educational actions and outcomes. Or to put it another way, notions of educational fairness might instead need to be based on a politics of recognition where educational purpose and quality is enacted and measured through the way schools advocate a cultural heterogeneity that recognises the different educational priorities, orientations and aspirations of different groups of young people. These ideas reflect Perrenoud's view (1998) that:

> [P]upils do not have the same abilities nor the same way of working. An optimal situation for one pupil will not be optimal for another . . . one can write a simple equation: diversity in people + appropriate treatment for each = diversity in approach.
>
> (Perrenoud, 1998: 94)

The argument here suggests that attempts to equalise inputs or provide additional compensatory levels of input to generate similar outputs may in fact result in much the same – a rejection by young people of educational practice because of its failure to recognise fully and authentically their specific educational needs and desires. Therefore, in order to understand more fully young people's educational 'conversion factors' one needs to acknowledge and understand young people's different educational agency and autonomy. Based on Sen's important conceptualisation of equity (2000, 1992) central to my views about educational fairness is the concept of 'agency freedom' (Sen, 1992). Educational fairness is then judged by the extent to which young people are provided with the autonomy to develop a diversity of educational capabilities and to pursue educational processes and goals that they value, that are rationally important for the life they wish to lead and that are also generally regarded as being important to lead the 'good life' in society. These capabilities and outcomes will be age related and will reflect the particular stage-specific processes of engaging with different knowledge domains. As young people grow older, these capabilities and outcomes may start to include processes of vocational skills development. At every stage of learning they are likely to also reflect aspects of personal, social and emotional development, issues of democratic civic engagement and skills associated with the body. The important point to make, therefore, is that these subjective valued educational capabilities and outcomes are not static and do not occur in a social, cultural and economic vacuum. Instead they are dynamic and reflect an ongoing set of interrelationships within, and beyond, schools. Hence educational equity should recognise the role of a quality educational project in ensuring that young people are enabled – or provided agency freedom – to experience authentically and openly the plethora of important powerful knowledge, skills, personal, social and civic domains from which this choice of capabilities and outcomes is made (White, 2011) – one that is more broadly person-centred as opposed to narrowly individualistic. Given this, and since agentic freedom is required to engage appropriately with education, a lack of agency or a constrained autonomy, I would argue, represents the epitome of educational inequity. In the context of education young people's educational preferences and choices are adapted according to what they know and what they think is possible for them – choices and preferences that can be constrained in all sorts of inequitable ways. So for example, Walker notes 'are girls, or black children, or disabled children, or mature learners equally able to convert resources into valued educational opportunities, and are they recognised socially and subjectively as having equal claims on such resources and opportunities' (Walker, 2006: 167). Furthermore, are young people who have been labelled as bottom set learners in their schools enabled to aspire to academic success? Do approaches to pedagogy and curriculum development that fail to build on the experiences and understandings of young people provide them with the autonomy or agency to engage fully in classroom learning? Hence, I would argue, comprehending how contexts, both inside and outside school, constrain agency, autonomy and aspirations vis-à-vis what might be valued by young people is central to understanding educational equity. A sophisticated appreciation of how engagement with valued capabilities and outcomes evolve and develop is provided by Gottfredson's *Theory of Circumscription and Compromise* (1981; 2002), which gives primacy to the ways in which individuals circumscribe their preferences in accordance with their perceived social identity. In a similar vein to Walker, she argues that young people's educational identity and agency is increasing defined by an appreciation of the intersection of social class, race and gender roles, as well as self-assessments of ability. Circumscription describes the progressive elimination during secondary schools ages of least favoured options in accordance with perceived roles and prestige, while compromise describes the progressive relinquishing of most preferred preferences in accordance with perceived compatibility with life circumstances. As Gutman and Akerman (2008) suggest, it is this final process of compromise, where young people dismiss highly desired options, where notions of 'expectations' come to the fore. It is not just the self-assessment of cognitive ability (that is often a strong reflection of school expectation and labelling of pupils) that sets 'realistic expectations' but also iniquitous societal and educational processes that together circumscribe and compromise young people's agency freedom to pursue what they might value educationally. These circumscriptions and compromises generate a constrained set of educational expectations that then lead to a particular and constrained set of final educational outcomes and trajectories. I would suggest that it is these very exogenous and endogenous factors that constrain autonomy and agency that are at the heart of educational inequities. In making such a statement, I recognise that I am, therefore, making a plea for a focus on educational purpose and quality that represents the personal development and educational rights of young people. Educational equity issues are therefore about examining how these developments and rights are mediated by material, cultural, social and psychological experiences both within and beyond school. So an investigation of the distribution of educational outcomes is only relevant to educational fairness if it points to areas of educational purpose and quality that appear to constrain the opportunities and freedom of individuals to pursue educational capabilities, outcomes and aspirations that are valued rationally, individually and collectively, and that reflect educational rights.

An associated and complementary way of thinking about my ideas of educational fairness are also provided by Unterhalter's notions of educational equity that focus on what she terms the above, below and the middle. For Unterhalter equity from below entails:

> [S]ome acceptance of a space of negotiation in which particular concerns of groups or individuals on say curriculum content or the form of assessment or the treatment of girls and boys or the approach to management are negotiated not on the basis of majority rule, or the intensity of one person's view with regard to another, but through a process of reasonableness and reflection that considers each person participating in the discussion has a valuable opinion, but what is most valued is the process of establishing the considerate and fair relationships that support negotiation, questioning and discussion.
>
> (Unterhalter, 2009: 418)

Equity from below aligns with an emphasis on agency, process freedoms and resulting aspirations. Her argument is that social, cultural, economic and psychological conditions that foster equity from below support the development of agency and process freedoms in education for diverse individuals and thus enhances the range of real alternatives and aspirations that very heterogeneous young people can consider in expanding and developing their educational capabilities. The focus is then on the way that family members, teachers, communities and various other institutional personnel interact at the micro level with young people in ways that support agentic freedom and the opening up of aspirations and opportunities.

For Unterhalter, educational equity from above suggests that there are educational rules or normative educational capabilities that have been decided as fair and reasonable by a widely recognised body of opinion. Issues for regulation in this way might, for example, be how many years of instruction constitute an acceptable level of education that provides lives of value for all children across widely differing contexts. Seeing equity in terms of reasoned (and potentially revisable) rules implies young people have rights to particular levels of schooling, to perhaps to an agreed set of base educational capabilities and perhaps, more radically, to particular educational processes that require core engagement or representation from young people such as school governance arrangements. This requires educational policy to satisfy these rights and to put in place procedures for ensuring their delivery in diverse contexts. Equity from above and the appeal to rules and notions of public good resonate with concerns in the capability approach about instituting conditions for positive freedoms (Vizard 2006; Deneulin *et al.*, 2006).

Finally equity from the middle in education for Unterhalter is associated with the movement of ideas, time, money, skill, organisation or artifacts that facilitate 'investments' in the learning of young people. Equity from the middle is not in itself fair or just without an articulation with equity from below and equity from above. Thus meanings of equity as educational regulation and societal expectations (equity from above) and as participation among equals (equity from below) confer on the new word (equity from the middle) a sense that the social arrangements that make up the flows that facilitate education and learning must be fair. In supporting the development of educational capabilities policy and practice would need to be attentive to redistribution, particularly when forms of diversity and their history have in the past entailed discrimination. Just giving equal shares of time or money will not mitigate the unfairness of existing social arrangements with regard to education, in the many societies where the consequences of the past are written in the present.

The Educational Equity Framework (EEF)

Although the ideas above are important in providing a sense of what educational purpose, quality and fairness might mean, what they fail to provide is an explicit framework for scrutinising the extent to which education and its associated outcomes and processes are fair or equitable. In attempting to develop such a tool or framework I have been particularly inspired by Tania Burchardt and Polly Vizard Equality Measurement Framework (2009) that was developed for the Equality and Human Rights Commission and that was based on Sen's capability approach. Their approach to the Equality Measurement Framework was based on the concept of inequality around the notion of substantive freedom, which encompasses three aspects:

- Inequality of outcomes (central and valuable things in life that individuals and groups actually achieve).
- Inequality of autonomy (empowerment, independence in decision-making, choice and control).
- Inequality of processes (unequal treatment, discrimination, lack of dignity and respect).

Based on that framework, on further development of Sen's ideas (particular the work by Unterhalter) and on the broader issues of distributional and relational equity and their links to educational purpose and quality highlighted above, I wish to propose my own EEF. The framework in essence builds on the concepts highlighted above and prioritises ideas about educational purpose, quality and equity that focus on young people's educational autonomy/agency to pursue educational capabilities and outcomes that they value, that are valued more generally in society and that reflect young people's evolving and supported aspirations.

However, in recognising that young people will adapt their educational preferences and choices according to what they know and what they think is possible
for them – their expectations if you will – the framework will examine those
aspects of distributional and relational inequity that constrain autonomy and
aspirations in relation to capabilities and outcomes – their agency freedom if you
like. In so doing it will focus on both broad processes of inequity that are beyond
the school and that yet have a strong impact on young people's educational
agency and also in those related inequities in educational process that directly
psychological constrain, culturally marginalise and/or discriminate against young
people. In effect such an approach examines different manifestations of power
with respect to social relations between young people and others that reflect
aspects of the cultural, social, economic and psychological. Data about inequalities in educational inputs, process experiences and outcomes between different
groups of young people provide the evidence for these manifestations of power in
the educational sphere, if not how such processes of power operate. Adapting and
building on Vizard and Burchardt's work (2009) the EEF, therefore, captures
three distinct aspects of educational inequality and inequity:

1. The distributional inequality of educational inputs, process experiences and outcome indicators

The focus in the first part of the framework is on the inequality of educational
inputs, process experiences and outcomes that individuals and groups of young
people actually face in education. So although not focused on the dynamic processes that generate these inequalities, knowing about the educational inequalities
that exist provides a locus of attention. In many respects this part of the framework refers to Unterhalter's equity from above in that equity is defined in terms
of reasoned (and potentially revisable) rules with implications for young people
rights to particular levels of, and approaches to, schooling and perhaps rights to a
normative set of valued societal educational capabilities (particularly at primary
level). The first part of the framework therefore provides the evidence for which
groups of young people attain their rights within education and also how these
different groups achieve or attain more or less within the education system. It
focuses on educational inequalities per se rather than the inequitable educational
processes that generate those inequalities. Examples of inequalities are not just
related to the distribution of educational credentials but also emerge from
Burchardt and Vizard work (2009) to include the distribution of broader educational opportunities and experiences. One way of examining these inequalities is
to consider indicators of how individual students and groups of young people
experience aspects of schooling that reflect the resourcing of education (e.g.
school infrastructure, educational resources, number and quality of teachers, etc.)
and that also include:

> curriculum differentiation, discipline, measured achievement, and educa-
> tional attainment and progression . . . [these] cover students' positional

placement, treatment, and achievement, all of which are important aspects of education.

(Lucas and Beresford, 2010: 40)

Curriculum differentiation reflects the division of a domain of study into segments and/or the division of students into groups. This could include ability groupings, special education placements, gifted and talented education programmes, and English language-learning programmes, vocational versus academic programmes. All these are phenomena that require curriculum differentiation and inequalities may exist in relation to particular groups of young people predominately residing in particular segments or divisions.

Discipline is most often measured through numbers and levels of school exclusion. Evidence clearly points to exclusions resulting in other forms of educational inequalities including measured achievement in terms of grades and test scores and progression onto further and higher education. Once again inequalities need to be examined in relation to those groups of young people that are predominately excluded from schools.

Educational attainments reflect the highest credential achieved and inequalities can then be examined by comparing the differences on these attainments for diverse groups of young people. In addition data on the stratified progression into higher education and employment that reflects the achievement of particular educational outcomes provides broader evidence of levels of human capital development and economic inclusion as a potential indicator of social inclusion and equity.

Together these input, process experience and outcome indicators – indicators that are readily and publically available – provide evidence for the extent and range of educational inequalities. However, as stated above, care needs to be taken to ensure that the indicators do not become the sole arbiters of educational fairness and quality which might then marginalise the more important process equity issues associated with personal development and a rights-based approach to education. As Boyle and Charles (2011) reminds the field, standardised tests and other objective measures of excellence are meant to enable policy makers and practitioners to compare individuals from different demographic, geographic and social cohorts and to strategise equitable policies accordingly and not to be used as the 'primary gatekeeper to upward mobility' (Guinier 2003). Although the focus is useful, what these indicators do not explain is why these inequalities exist. In other words the evidence does not explore the extent to which these inequalities are either fair or iniquitous. This latter challenge requires an examination of the fairness or otherwise of educational processes, both broadly and specifically articulated, that have resulted in unequal educational inputs, process experiences and outcomes. As I have argued above, in order to examine whether inequalities are fair or unfair there is a need to explore the extent to which individuals and groups of young people are supported to freely convert educational resources into a variety of educational capabilities and outcomes of which they have been made aware and which they value and are valued. There is therefore a need to examine those factors that appear to either aid or constrain agentic freedoms. I would argue that this first strand of the EEF should become less important as policy and practice becomes more attuned to the equity issues where standards of educational quality become more qualitative in nature and focused more on process issues rather than outcomes. The second two parts of the EEF are therefore less concerned with inequality of outcomes and more concerned with the broad and specific equity processes that generate those outcomes. This part of the EEF therefore is located more strongly in the personal development and rights-based approach to educational quality and equity. It is also, I would suggest, the central component of the framework as it deals explicitly with Sen's question about 'equality of what'.

2. *Broad inequities and their impact on educational autonomy*

Broad inequities refer to those general economic and cultural processes that impact on the independence, choice and control that individual or groups of young people have to both understand and then make decisions about educational capabilities and outcomes, their educational aspirations and, more generally, what they value educationally. This relates to two main educational equity process arenas. The first relates to the distributional material circumstances of young people that constrain their ability to engage in educational autonomy, choice and control. This is demonstrated, for example, by how a lack of resources can generate financial pressures on families and young people that result in a whole number of hardships – economic, cultural, personal and social – that explicitly and implicitly impact on educational experiences. For example, economically, parents may struggle to pay bills, may have limited space in their homes for shared living, may need to undertake two or more jobs to try and make ends meet and may battle to provide the basic essentials for their children including heating, clothing and food. The social, cultural and psychological consequences of economic hardships are then equally compelling. These may range from family strife and conflict emanating from not being able to cope financially to a lack of self-respect and dignity about living in poverty in a society that apparently has so much to offer and which the media glamorises as being open to all sorts of possibilities. The concentration of poverty in certain communities also has the effects of fragmenting relationships and networks of support, distancing people ever more from potential developments in their localities and stigmatising those areas and people in those areas as 'unsafe' and at times 'not worthy' of society's support. Poor areas are also sites that attract those who take advantage of the vulnerability that people can feel when made poor – whether these be loan sharks or those peddling drugs to provide and apparent 'relief' from the daily grind of poverty. This scarcity can make for a dispiriting existence which impacts on a whole set of core capabilities that include self-confidence, self-esteem, self-efficacy and the ability to see further than one's locality and perhaps those immediately around. It is the material, social, economic, cultural and psychological conditions of poverty and their impact on educational autonomy and aspiration that is the focus of this part of the framework and in many respects refers to Unterhalter's equity from the middle where a lack of ideas, time, money, skill, organisation or artifacts can constrain 'investments' in the learning of young people. In supporting the development of the educational autonomy of young people, educational policy would need to be attentive to redistribution, particularly when forms of diversity and their history have in the past entailed discrimination. So care must given in relation to the redistribution of resources as just giving equal shares of time or money will not mitigate the unfairness of existing social arrangements with regard to education where the consequences of the past are written in the present.

In addition to distributional inequalities and living in scarcity and their impacts on educational freedoms, the second broad educational equity process arena refers to those relational social, cultural and political inequalities of power that generate constraining discourses or institutionalised arrangements that affect the inner lives and autonomy of disadvantaged young people. Examples of these include the power of essentialising deficit discourses that often underpin the view of media, employers, educationalists, policy makers and others in position of authority about the cultural dispositions and capabilities of disadvantaged young people and their families and communities – labels that often generate psychological self-fulfilling prophecies and constrained expectations in the educational lives of young people. So, for example, Bauder (2002) examined the ideological underpinnings of the discourse of deficit neighbourhood effects that permeates much dominant educational discourse about the challenges that schools in such contexts face. He suggested that the language of deficit neighbourhood implies that the demographic context of poor neighbourhoods instils 'dysfunctional' norms, values and behaviours into youths, thus triggering a cycle of social pathology that creates educational disengagement and disaffection. The problem is that these essentialist conceptions (fixed traits that do not allow for variations among individuals or over time) then imbue the way that schools and teachers think, act and react to young people in such contexts that then further contribute to the neighbourhood effects phenomenon. In addition relational inequalities that constrain agency can also reflect Unterhalter's equity from below in the way family, communities and institutional personnel interact at a micro level in constraining the agentic freedom of young people to engage and to aspire educationally.

3. Inequities in educational processes and their impact on educational autonomy

This third part of the framework refers to those specific educational inequities in treatment that are based on: (a) a lack of appropriate educational resources to support particular groups of young people to engage fully with education, (b) misrecognition and cultural injustices for particular individuals or groups of young people and families in educational settings, and (c) a lack of representation of young people and their families in the processes of education. Taken together these inequities speak to the way individuals or groups of young people are both educationally and institutionally silenced and marginalised and psychologically constrained through a misunderstanding or disrespect of their values and orientations and through the application of institutionalised power differentials. These inequities come about as of result of the use of power, discrimination and/or disadvantaging processes by other individuals and groups in schools, or by schools and educational systems. For example Lawson's study (2003) in the US addressed teachers' and parents' perceptions of the meanings and functions of parental involvement in children's education. Lawson found that in many respects teachers' prevailing orientations towards disadvantaged parents were based on deficit perceptions that portrayed them as having poor parenting skills and poor supportive capacities with regards to education. This approach contributed to what Lawson argued was a systematic silencing of the strengths, struggles, and 'communitycentric' worldviews evident in the parents' perspectives. He argued that parental involvement is a limited and limiting concept in low-income ethnically concentrated communities because the notion is largely the power domain of teachers that hold a narrow 'schoolcentric' view. In addition the work by Hart *et al.* (2004) examined powerful classroom processes that stigmatise and label young people's educational abilities. They argue for a different approach that is based on a view of transformability located in a discourse of 'learning without limits'. This perspective developed from research on teachers who worked with young people's cognitive, affective and social domains in order to help them engage and develop valued educational capabilities and outcomes. In many respects these arguments refer to both Unterhalter's equity from the middle and from below in that they examine the level of educational resource in conjunction with the way teachers and other educational personnel interact at a micro level in schools.

How might my thinking about educational equity be summarised? I have argued that much mainstream international policy approaches to educational purposes, quality and fairness often focus on credentials and human capital perspectives and on distributional educational inequalities of attainment. These approaches often fail to consider personal development and rights-based approaches to education that focus on relational inequities in educational autonomy and opportunity (Who did the choosing, were young people given the opportunity to develop valued and aspirational educational capabilities and did circumstances aid or constrain autonomy?) and inequities in educational processes (Such as cultural discrimination/exclusion, a lack of educational resources or other aspects of unequal treatment and power, that result in a lack of efficacy, choice, dignity, respect and representation in the educational experiences and lives of young people.). What these questions suggest is that disadvantaged groups of young people do not operate in isolation but are part of a wider configuration of relationships and institutional arrangements, some of which can constrain the ability of individuals to meaningfully engage with education. This means that atomistic and individualistic attempts at the redistribution of educational outcomes that focus on resource issues and/or cultural deficit factors both inside and beyond the school are likely to fall short in generating educational fairness because these strategies fail to understand fully equitable process issues that focus on relational issues of educational autonomy, agency and aspiration. In many respects my framework reflects Meuret's (2001) important review of educational equity principles produced through his work with members of an *ad hoc* group focusing on equity issues within the International Education Indicators Project of the OECD. At one level he argues that equity principles must help citizens and those who govern to judge the quality of the system, but it must also identify, for the sake of those who govern, the opinions of citizens on the equity of the educational system and the criteria that form the basis of those opinions. My development of the EEF, with its focus on a personal development perspective and the rights of individual young, parallels that approach. Secondly he suggest that indicators must measure not only inequalities in educational results (measured by categories, deviations among individuals and the proportion of individuals falling below a minimum threshold – part 1 of the EEF) but also the more immediate inequalities related to life in school and in the way students are treated by the institution and its agents (part 2 of the EEF). Thirdly he suggest that it is important to measure not only inequalities in educational results and processes, but also inequalities at the source of the educational system that affect the teaching process itself – inequalities that I suggest stem from a focus on academic credentials and a human capital approach that by their very nature are predisposed to class-based positional activity and that do not prioritise personal development. Fourthly he suggests that among the benefits distributed by the educational process, priority must be given to those that are most important to individuals and for the democratic life of the country – a suggestion that educational equity reflects educational rights that are associated with cultural diversity, inclusion and personal development. And in a clear reference to issues of constrained agentic freedom, a further educational equity principle developed by Meuret pertains to those variables of life experience from which the individual struggles to escape and that includes the debilitating effects of poverty and the marginalisation of voice through deficit discourses of the powerful. The sixth principle suggest that equity indicators must permit discussion between the concern for equality and other values that underpin the education system – a discussion that I have argued requires issues of purpose, quality and equity to be predicated on each and integral to each.

In order to start the process of developing a practical understanding of the framework (and Meuret's associated principles of educational equity), I now wish to use the framework to help explain the potential educational inequities experienced by three different hypothetical young people. Adapted profiles of these young people were developed by myself and colleagues at the Centre for Equity at the University of Manchester and are detailed in Ainscow *et al.*'s recent book on developing equitable education systems (2012). These cases provide illustrations of the kinds of equity issues that schools frequently encounter. In documenting these cases, and then examining them briefly via the EEF, what I hope to do is provide the reader with an opportunity for some initial engagement with the ideas detailed in this chapter before I develop the EEF more fully in subsequent chapters. Call it an appetizer if you like.

> *The case of Henrik* – Henrik is an 8-year-old boy who has made a successful and happy start to his school career in his home town in central Europe. However, the country he comes from is relatively poor and there are few well-paid work opportunities. His father, therefore, decided to move the family to England so that he can find work, at least in the medium term. They have moved to a particular urban context where there is a shortage of men with his particular skills and have found some cheap accommodation close to a number of other families that have moved from their home country.
>
> Having been enrolled in the local primary school, Henrik can make little sense of the lessons since he speaks almost no English. The school does not have a member of staff who can speak Henrik's language. The best that it can offer is to sit him next to a classmate who comes from the same country and speaks a little more English than he does. Together, they try to find their way through the lessons, but Henrik's educational progress has come to a halt, and he is now very unhappy at school.
>
> (Ainscow *et al.*, 2012: 2)

Understanding Henrik utilising the EEF framework

The first part of the framework is used to focus attention on inequalities in educational outcomes and experiences. Henrik's case clearly points to a lack of progress in his learning. His learning has stopped. The question then becomes one of examining the extent to which this is because of broad and/or specific educational equity processes that appear to constrain his educational autonomy. Broad inequities in educational autonomy refer to general economic and cultural processes that impact on the independency, choice and control that Henrik has over his educational experience. The case suggests that he has no such problems with these issues when based in central Europe. And one might argue that his move to England does not generate immediate constraining general equity issues. He has moved to an area in England where other families from his native country have located and where there is employment for his father. Of course there are cultural constraints in relation to what he and his parents may know about the education system and there does not appear to be any support structures to assist in this process. However, there does appear, at least, an informal support infrastructure in the community. What is more problematic is the lack of resources in the school to help him engage meaningfully in teaching and learning. A lack of a language resource is clearly constraining his freedom to engage with the educational capabilities that he valued back in central Europe. He cannot speak English and there is no provision to support English language acquisition. He cannot, therefore, engage with the curriculum and he does not make progress. He becomes alienated from the school as the lack of equity in educational processes impact on his educational development.

The case of Julie – Julie is a 13-year-old girl who has grown up on a poor social housing estate on the outskirts of a major city. Her family is described by her as somewhat chaotic. Her father left long ago and her mother has had a succession of boyfriends, some of whom mistreat her and the other children. Julie's older brothers are at times in trouble with the police and drug misuse is a feature of home life and is common in the area. Her educational attainments in secondary school are low, but despite this, she enjoyed her time at primary school. Although she could in principle have chosen any one of a number of secondary schools in the area, the reality was very different from this. As far as she and her mother were concerned, the other schools were ruled out because they were for 'posh kids', or were full of children from ethnic minorities, or were faith schools. It never really occurred to either of them that Julie should go anywhere other than to the school on the estate – the same school that her mother had attended.

Julie's time at her secondary school was a mixed affair and was not without its problems. [She enjoyed certain classes and teachers but also missed a lot of schooling, and at times ended up in fights with other students, or in quarrels with some of her teachers. She often described her schooling experience as 'boring' of 'no use' to her. Despite these challenges, the school attempted to support her and with her tutors developed a personalised curriculum that included a creative multimedia course delivered by the local FE college for part of the week. This course in addition to certain classes – 'Miss Jones, my English teacher is great. She really respects us and involves us in lessons' – are clearly valued and enjoyed and act as a refuge from what she described as a somewhat turbulent home life]. However, the school itself was in difficulties because of the challenges of achieving benchmark academic results, the problems it had in retaining staff, and its declining roll as other, more apparently successful schools competed for students. Eventually, the local authority decided to close the school down. Julie and her mother were offered a choice of other schools to attend and chose the one some of Julie's friends also chose, a few miles away. Unfortunately, from her perspective she received little of the support in her new school that she had previously enjoyed, and she found herself being bullied by some of its existing students. That, together with the long bus journey to get to school, impacted on her attendance, which became very erratic. In effect, she had ceased to learn anything in school, and did not feel comfortable in the home, and spent much of her time walking round the estate with a group of other girls whose attendance was equally poor.

(Ainscow *et al.*, 2012: 3)

Understanding Julie utilising the EEF framework

Julie has made little progress in her school and appears to be heading for few educational qualifications. In addition, because of lack of engagement with her current school she is also likely not to develop other educational capabilities that the school has to offer and which Julie might value. Her case clearly points to both broad and school-based inequities that are constraining her educational autonomy. However, it also details some aspects of her school experience that would appear more equitable and enabling. Her conditions of everyday living provide challenges for school engagement with her home life described by her as chaotic, with drugs are seen as a perennial problem on the estate and strife between family members endemic. Added to this are relational inequities that are referenced by the lack of power and autonomy her family/community have to keep the local school open, which is then compounded by a lack of awareness about possible educational options. Her new school does not engage with her in an appropriately relational way resulting in forms of misrecognition and this, together with use of power over her by bullies, alienates her from school life. And yet at the same time there are aspects of this case where her educational aspirations and valued educational capabilities are catered for within the educational processes of her first secondary school. These include the additional resources allocated to set up the multimedia experience and the relational approaches of respect, pedagogical inclusion shown by her English teacher that have resulted in valued educational experiences for Julie.

The case of Linda – Like Julie, Linda is 13 years old. Like Julie also, her family have relatively little money. However, Linda describes family life as stable where home is a safe place. She also says that she has always been encouraged by her parents to try her best at school. However, over time her aspirations have waned as she has come to realise through her experience of school that her attainments are nothing very special. She expects not to achieve a great deal in term of educational attainments. She has no obvious difficulties, but neither does she, as she puts it, 'shine at anything'. She recognises that she is a shy girl who does not like to draw attention to herself. At primary school she liked her class teacher, who made a point of spending time with her and who went out of her way to tell her parents how she was doing. [She was confident and in her eyes succeeding, achieving similar or at times better attainments in national tests than her class mates.]

At secondary school things are different. The school operates a policy of grouping students by levels of attainment and, for most subjects, Linda is in one of the lower sets. Some of her friends get taken out of lessons for extra help, but Linda does not. Instead, she goes from lesson to lesson and keeps her head down. Some of the boys in her classes take up most of the teachers' attention, and there is little opportunity for Linda to get to know her teachers, or them to get to know Linda. She is content enough at school, but she is making little progress. Her parents know little about what her school life is really like, and are happy that she appears to be keeping out of trouble and has no obvious problems.

(Ainscow *et al.*, 2012: 4)

Understanding Linda utilising the EEF

Linda's parents are poor and yet at the same time are generally supportive of Linda and her experiences of school. They are not, however, particularly well informed of her specific progress and are generally happy that Linda does not have any obvious problems. One might surmise that Linda's experiences of home and community life are not particularly constraining with regards to her educational autonomy, although issues of material well-being are likely to have their usual impacts. The education process that appears to have had the greatest impact on Linda's educational autonomy and aspiration is the labelling of abilities in secondary school and the ensuing lack of care/focus/attention from teachers. This has led her to make little progress and there is clear evidence that her educational expectations as she progresses through school will harden around a set of school-to-work trajectories that lie closest to hand and that reflect a material and cultural reality redolent of her neighbourhood, gender and class.

An analytic approach to using the EEF

The chapter so far has provided a detailed examination of what I mean by educational equity and how links can be made broadly with ideas about educational purpose and quality. What I have argued is that educational policies in many country contexts have attempted to reference issues of equity and fairness but often have done so in rather general ways that lack clarity of argument and purpose. In response to this gap I have developed an EEF that is a synthesis of a number of philosophical arguments about educational fairness but that has at its core notions of agentic freedoms for young people to develop and achieve valued educational capabilities and outcomes. I have provided a few hypothetical worked examples of how the EEF might be applied to individual circumstances. However, in order to provide analytical power to some of these ideas and also as means of providing a sense of coherence and direction for the forthcoming chapters of the book what I propose in this section is a diagrammatic exposition of the framework that links empirical research and explanatory conceptualisations of educational inequity to educational equity policy and practice interventions developed over time (see Figure 2.1, page 34). The diagram then leads to a final synthesis that provides the foundations for an educational equity toolkit.

Let me now provide a bit of detail to the diagram. The diagram starts with what I understand by educational equity. As I have argued without a clear normative exposition as to what is understood by such an idea there is then great difficult in arguing what one needs to do to bring about improved fairness. In addition it is also difficult to explain what the purpose and qualities of a good education system are without understanding the equity issues that pertain to that system. So purpose, excellence and equity are interrelated and are not irreconcilable to each other, as is sometimes argued in parts of the educational excellence and equity literatures (Valverde,1988). Following MacIntyre (2001) it is my view that one cannot develop an excellent education system with excellent outcomes without that system and its outcomes being responsive to the diversity and heterogeneity of students and what they value (i.e. excellence in the internal workings of teaching and learning as opposed to effectiveness in the outcome measures external to teaching and learning). One also cannot develop appropriate purposes to education without these being responsive to both the general needs of society and to the specific needs of different young people that make up an integral part of that society and that are, in essence, core to the educational project. Purpose, quality and equity are therefore interrelated and inseparable.

Having documented what I understand by the notion of educational equity and its links to purpose and quality it then becomes paramount to know which groups of young people seem to be inequitably constrained in their experiences of education. This requires a clear examination of indicative data that can provide important evidence as to the educational 'state of play'. Hence in the first part of the next chapter I review this data. Based on the evidence, I suggest that there is a strong relationship between socio-economic disadvantage, gender, ethnicity, the place where young people live and educational attainments and experiences more generally. In addition it suggests further that young people who experience the greatest levels of educational inequity tend to be concentrated in the poorest of urban neighbourhoods. At the same time, however, evidence also points to differing aggregate educational outcomes for young people in equally poor contexts that suggests that there may also be varying socio-cultural neighbourhood effects, over and beyond poverty, that also impact on young people's educational engagement and attainment. As the diagram suggests this therefore requires explanatory argument and evidence that focuses on those processes in schools and neighbourhoods more generally that create inequitable educational outcomes for different groups of young people. The second part of Chapter 3 in essence undertakes this challenge. However, what makes Chapter 3 different to many in the field is that the explanations and evidence are informed by the normative perspective of the EEF. As Benadusi (2001) has argued cogently, most explanations for educational inequality and inequity, particular those located in the discipline of sociology, often take for granted what is understood by such inequalities and inequities and then develop explanations for why things are as they are and how things might be done differently. In other words normative understandings of equity are implicit rather than explicit. What is important in Benadusi's work, therefore, is that he makes explicit the normative dimensions of educational equity in sociological thinking. He starts with the classic and still widespread concept based on the principle of equality of opportunity for students belonging to different types of social groups (class, stratum, race, gender, local community, etc.) and where educational outcomes are independent of ascriptive or background variables. He highlights how this conception has appeared in two different versions. The first he terms equal opportunity with merit that is generally supported by functionalist sociologists such as Talcott Parsons (1961) and falls more clearly within the meritocratic tradition. Such a concept essentially coincides with the 'liberal equality of opportunity' depicted by Rawls as I have noted above. The second version is currently the most widely adopted by sociologists

What is do we understand by educational equity?

- Educational equity can be summarised as the processes that enable young people to demonstrate agentic freedom (or purposeful free actions) to develop, and succeed in, a variety of educational capabilities and outcomes that they value and are valued by society more generally.

Which groups of young people experience educational iniquiies?

- Which educational indicators demonstrate particular groups of young people experiencing constrained agentic freedom in relation to valued educational capabilities and outcomes?

What are the explanations for the processes of educational inequity?

- Research that focuses on both broad processes of inequity that are beyond the school and that have a strong impact on young people's educational identity, agency and aspirations and also those inequities in educational process that directly constrain, culturally marginalise and/or discriminate against young people.

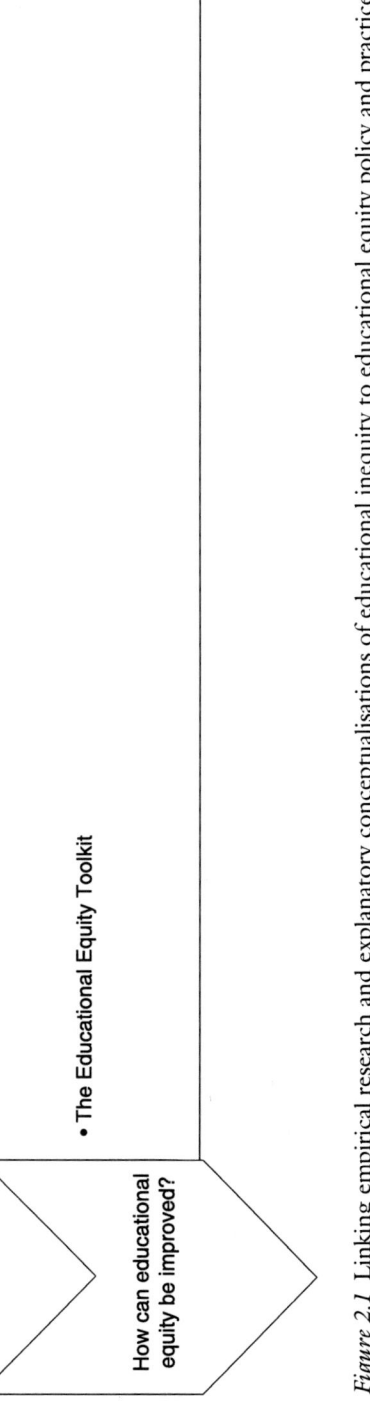

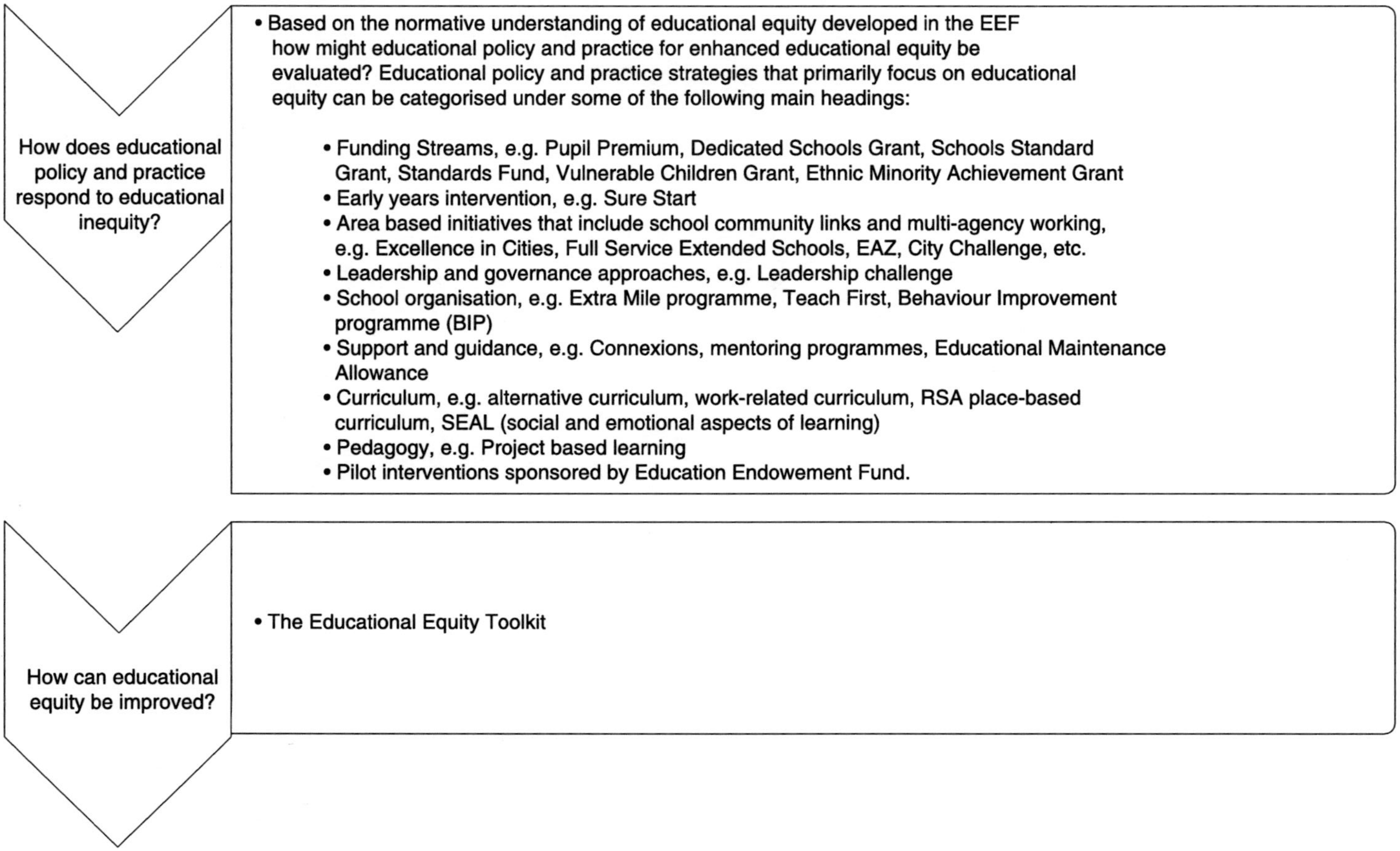

How does educational policy and practice respond to educational inequity?

- Based on the normative understanding of educational equity developed in the EEF how might educational policy and practice for enhanced educational equity be evaluated? Educational policy and practice strategies that primarily focus on educational equity can be categorised under some of the following main headings:

  - Funding Streams, e.g. Pupil Premium, Dedicated Schools Grant, Schools Standard Grant, Standards Fund, Vulnerable Children Grant, Ethnic Minority Achievement Grant
  - Early years intervention, e.g. Sure Start
  - Area based initiatives that include school community links and multi-agency working, e.g. Excellence in Cities, Full Service Extended Schools, EAZ, City Challenge, etc.
  - Leadership and governance approaches, e.g. Leadership challenge
  - School organisation, e.g. Extra Mile programme, Teach First, Behaviour Improvement programme (BIP)
  - Support and guidance, e.g. Connexions, mentoring programmes, Educational Maintenance Allowance
  - Curriculum, e.g. alternative curriculum, work-related curriculum, RSA place-based curriculum, SEAL (social and emotional aspects of learning)
  - Pedagogy, e.g. Project based learning
  - Pilot interventions sponsored by Education Endowement Fund.

How can educational equity be improved?

- The Educational Equity Toolkit

Figure 2.1 Linking empirical research and explanatory conceptualisations of educational inequity to educational equity policy and practice.

and focuses on educational attainment and social mobility. It distinguishes itself more clearly from the pure meritocratic hypothesis, formulating its own definition of equality of opportunity (synonymous with equity) as total independence of educational attainment from background variables. Conceived in this way, equality of educational opportunity is a central prerequisite of social fluidity; that is, of inter-generational mobility. Although central to much work in the sociology of education, Benadusi notes that many sociologists within this tradition have regarded the equality of opportunity principle more as a citizenship right than as a requisite of just meritocracy. This line of thinking suggests that citizenship rights require the need to establish the minimum threshold of instruction and competencies to be guaranteed to all citizens as a basic social right. Any variance from this rule would then be considered unfair. In contrast to much writing that focuses on equality of educational opportunity linked to ideas of meritocracy (Parsons, 1961), social mobility (e.g.; Bowles and Gintis, 1976; Bourdieu and Passeron, 1977) or rights (Foster, Gomm, Hammersley, 1996), a fair respect for differences is perhaps the most recent concept to have emerged within the sociology of education particular from those writers of a more strongly post-modern tradition (Spindler, 1997). It holds that all social groups and all individuals – whether expressed mainly in communitarian or individualistic terms – have equal rights to be given instruction (including state-financed instruction) modelled on their own particular ways of perceiving and constructing their educational needs – a line of thinking that is perhaps closest to the ideas developed in this chapter.

Perhaps what is most important in Benadusi's work is that he argues for what I am advocating in this book – the need to develop explanations of educational unfairness that are predicated on explicitly argued normative understandings of educational equity backed by supporting empirical evidence. Hence my normative EEF, and associated explanatory conceptualisations and evidence documented, provide the framing device for making sense of educational policy and practice. As the diagram suggests policy and practice interventions to deal with educational inequities are numerous and multifaceted in that they have been developed to meet a whole array of specific and more general educational need – from funding streams to curricular and pedagogical developments. They are also multi-level in that they span the whole spectrum of educational provision, from early years schooling (e.g. Sure Start) to post-compulsory sectors of the educational system (e.g. Educational Maintenance Allowance and Widening Participation strategies). My approach in this book is not to attempt to cover all of these approaches, interventions and levels of analysis. Instead my aim is to focus on detailed examples of policy and practice and subject them to an appropriate critical analysis using the EEF. So in Chapter 4 I examine educational area based initiatives that have been developed and implemented over the last 15 years to help improve schools in areas of disadvantage. In Chapter 5 I review approaches to educational leadership in disadvantaged urban schools and in Chapter 6 and 7 the focus on the work-related curriculum and aspects of project based and placed based pedagogy and mentoring.

Finally in Chapter 8, and based on the preceding EEF, research evidence and explanations and review of policy and practice, I derive an educational equity toolkit that provides policy makers and practitioners with a set of equity questions for examining and then delivering improved educational equity.

Summary

The manner in which concepts of educational purpose, quality and equity are understood is generally informed by wider debates about the educational project and social justice. I have argued that these issues relate to equity concerns that reflect distributional outcomes, relational justice, economic and cultural justice and issues of capability and aspiration. In order to examine purpose, quality and equity more fully I have developed an EEF that synthesises these key ideas into an overarching normative tool for analysis. A diagrammatic representation of the analytical power of the EEF was then presented. In the next chapter I examine the evidence as to the nature and extent of inequities of educational outcomes and experiences. In addition I provide a set of explanations for how issues of constrained educational autonomy, aspiration and process play out for young people in those disadvantaged urban contexts where educational outcomes and experiences are at their most problematic.

3 Disadvantaged urban contexts and educational equity

Introduction

The philosophical conceptualisations about educational purpose, quality and equity documented in Chapter 2 point to a complicated picture that reflect notions of redistribution and relational issues of recognition and representation and also issues of agency, autonomy, aspiration and the educational process itself. These ideas have been synthesised and operationalised into what I have termed the Educational Equity Framework (EEF). In the first part of this chapter I will comment on large scale statistical data sets that focus on educational inputs, process experiences and outcomes and that provide evidence for the first part of the framework. However, as I argued in Chapter 2 what this evidence does not provide is a set of theorisations or explanations for why this is the case. This chapter undertakes this task and hence focuses on those processes that seem to impact on the autonomy, freedom and agency of young people to engage with education.

Part 1 of the EEF – The distributional inequality of educational inputs, process experiences and outcomes

This initial section of the chapter focuses on the first part of the EEF highlighted in Chapter 2 and documents an array of proxy indicators for the inequalities of educational inputs, process experiences and outcomes for different groups of young people and that include curriculum differentiation, discipline, measured achievement, educational attainment and progression.

Firstly in terms of educational inputs, schools in disadvantaged areas in England through various complex weighting funding formulae are generally, if differentially and inconsistently (Freedman and Horner, 2008), more generously resourced through mainstream funding than schools elsewhere, although this can in many respects depend on the nature of how funds from central government to local authorities is then allocated to schools in those authorities. Equitable educational funding arrangements in other affluent countries do not hold to any particular model. For example in the US funds available for schools are based on tax revenues of the district. For disadvantaged districts this has the perverse effect of reducing funds to schools located in such districts, even though these schools are likely to have additional needs. In an attempt to ameliorate this position Title I ('Title One') of the Elementary and Secondary Education Act in the US attempts to distribute federal funding to schools and school districts with a high percentage of students from low-income families. To qualify as a Title I school, a school typically has around 40 per cent or more of its students that come from families that qualify under the United States Census's definitions as low-income. Schools receiving Title I funding are regulated by federal legislation, including the No Child Left Behind Act. Title I funds may be used for children from preschool through high school, but most of the students served (65 per cent) are in grades 1 through 6; another 12 per cent are in preschool and kindergarten programmes. In contrast in many Nordic countries the level of public funding for comprehensive education is above the EU mean and generally more fairly distributed (for example in Finland each school educates children at the same per pupil rate). Although these various funding mechanisms may say much about the historical developments of education in different countries what they all demonstrate is an equity commitment to the public funding of education for all too at least upper secondary level.

In examining educational process experience indicators, and in particular curriculum differentiation issues, there is clear evidence that different curriculum programmes, particularly the variety of academic and vocational course in schools, tend to be predominately inhabited by different groups of students, with, for example, students from lower socio-economic status families being over-represented in vocational studies programme (see Chapter 6). In addition, the use of ability grouping – such as setting, streaming and broad-banding – is also known to reinforce social inequalities because pupils from lower social classes (especially boys) and particular ethnic groups are most likely to be placed in lower sets or bands (Harlen *et al.*, 1999). In terms of discipline, there are also clear differences between the exclusion rates for different categories of young people. For example, the Equality and Human Rights Commission point out that boys are more likely than girls to be excluded and that many of these have been categorised as having one or more special educational needs (SEN) and are more likely to be in receipt of Free School Meals (FSM), a proxy poverty indicator. Ethnic minority students are less likely to achieve higher degree qualifications or attend selective universities (such as the Russell Group in England) and there is still proportionally a low level of young people from disadvantaged backgrounds entering higher education.

However, where the evidence for educational inequalities appears most profound and compelling is in the area of educational outcomes. For example, international data from the Programme for International Student Assessment study of Organisation for Economic Co-operation and Development (OECD) countries (OECD, 2008) shows that this is a widespread problem with deprivation having a negative impact on attainment across all OECD countries. Those young people who live in conditions of poverty, however defined, are more likely not to enrol or be retained in education, are more likely to achieve poorer educational outcomes and in many other ways are likely to demonstrate lower levels of general educational capacity than young people living in relative affluence. In addition the problem is exacerbated for poor young people that live in more unequal and yet affluent societies (Wilkinson and Pickett, 2009). Conversely those not enrolling or being retained in education and those achieving low educational outcomes in either narrow attainment terms or in more general terms of educational well-being are also more likely to then experience poverty. In England Cassen and Kingdon (2007) found that eligibility for FSM is strongly associated with low achievement. In addition these findings are shown to be consistent from one generation to the next (Bynner and Joshi, 2002). In addition, other research has demonstrated the link between schools serving poor communities and some of the lowest levels of aggregate educational attainment to be found in those areas (Mortimore and Whitty, 1997; Demie *et al.*, 2002; Bell, 2003). For example, in England the Social Exclusion Unit (SEU, 1998) found that five times as many secondary schools in 'worst neighbourhoods' had 'serious weaknesses' than was typically the case, and children drawn from poorer family origins were more likely to have been in the lowest quartile of attainment in educational tests compared to their counterparts in other quartiles. Evidence from the Department for Children Schools and Families (Schools Analysis and Research Division, Department for Children Schools and Families, 2009) in England highlight that deprivation as measured by FSM and the Income Deprivation Affecting Children Index (a neighbourhood poverty index) is strongly associated with poorer performance on average, at every stage of a pupil's school career. For example at the Foundation Stage (from age 3 to Reception class) in 2007, only 35 per cent of pupils in the most deprived areas reached the expected level of attainment, compared to 51 per cent of pupils in other areas.

At a different level of analysis the focus is less on economic factors and more on the link between particular socio-cultural and capability characteristics of different groups of young people and their educational attainment. For example the research by Cassen and Kingdon (2007) has not only shown the link between socio-economic status and educational attainment but also documents how nearly half of all low achievers are white British males and how boys outnumber girls as low achievers by three to two. In addition their data suggest that white British students on average – boys and girls – are more likely than other ethnic groups to persist in low achievement. Furthermore, that Chinese and Indian pupils are most successful in avoiding low achievement and Afro-Caribbean pupils are the least successful. In addition looked-after children and those with SEN often do not get the support they require to achieve educational success. In contrast to economic data, this data suggest that there is something significant about the socio-cultural and cognitive characteristics of young people that influence educational attainments.

At face value, this data would tend to suggest a disparate set of economic, social, cultural and cognitive variables impacting on the educational outcomes and experiences of different groups of young people. Although this may appear to be the case, geographers have highlighted convincingly how these disparate variables intersect and are spatially concentrated in particular places. The argument made is that although educational outcomes and experiences are differently influenced by young people's class, ethnicity and gender, what provides a commonality of context is the spatial concentration and intersectionality of these factors. What the evidence demonstrates is the strong correlation between the geographical spread of poor aggregate educational attainments and the disadvantaged urban neighbourhoods of major cities and de-industrialised coastal and former mining towns. However, in terms of intersectionality, fine grained urban geo-demographic research highlights that although educational failure is concentrated in poor urban contexts, there is a nuanced difference between the socio-cultural make-up of different contexts, with some equally poor urban neighbourhoods demonstrating differentially better or worse educational outcomes and levels of progression onto higher education (Corver, 2005; Webber and Butler, 2007). For example, according to Webber and Butler (ibid.) neighbourhoods characterised by inner-city social housing pupils consistently do much better at GCSE than would have been anticipated on the basis of the poverty index of their home neighbourhoods. A similar pattern is evident in neighbourhoods of Asian owner-occupiers, where GCSE results are much higher than would have been anticipated on the basis of socio-economic factors alone. By contrast, some of the neighbourhood types with the very worst GCSE performance are characterised by predominantly white pupils living on very large overspill housing estates in England's larger provincial cities. Such neighbourhoods, although struggling academically, are not identified as being acutely poor or disadvantaged. What this suggests is that economic, cultural and historic factors influence the ways places develop which in turn shape the agency and identities, including the educational agency and identity, of young people and what they aspire to and value.

Part 2 of the EEF – Broad inequities and their impacts on educational autonomy

In examining the educational autonomy of young people in poor urban neighbourhoods, what the evidence of geodemograhic researchers suggest is that a major focus of research should be on the various ways in which educational autonomy, aspiration and valued educational capabilities are constrained and/or enabled by the intersection of distributional and relational circumstances of particular place. In other words what becomes important to examine is young people's structured agency and autonomy about the external decisions they make with regards to education and in particular how that agency develops through the material lifeworlds they inhabit and the social relations that make up that world. To be able to do this requires an understanding of how educational autonomy and aspiration is linked to identity formation and development. Lee and Anderson elegantly remind the field of the importance of focusing on young people's identity in thinking about educational equity:

In educational contexts, questions of identity are especially critical because the development of educational practice and policies are grounded in different ways of understanding who learners are or should be. How students interpret and develop their identities in a given context is shaped by self-perceptions, desires, hopes and expectations as well as salient aspects of social context, such as sociopolitical ideologies, histories and structures that are often beyond the control of an individual.

(Lee and Anderson, 2009: 181)

Although a much contested notion, my understanding of identity formation and agency is shaped by Lee and Anderson's ideas. I argue that identity formation and agency should be viewed as processes enmeshed in interaction that comprise not only individual interactions at the micro level but also larger material realities and cultural imaginaries linked to neighbourhoods and society more generally. This approach requires an examination of the way young people's identity and agency is linked to wider distributional and relational issues associated with structural, environmental and socio-cultural constraints and affordances as well as the micro relational network realities of family and neighbourhood life. What makes this perspective interesting is that its theoretical focus is spatial, including space that is both close and at a distance from individuals and space that is both enabling and constraining. Hence young people's external educational autonomy, identity and agency can usefully be located in the recent 'spatial turn' in educational theory and research (Gulson and Symes, 2007) that has started to influence theorisations about educational disadvantage.

In reviewing this 'spatial turn', most commentators see space as not fixed or absolute, but as socially produced: a social construct not a physical entity (Lebfevre, 1991). Therefore space is not seen as existing independently of human activity, since its meaning is produced by the social relations of people within and outside it, through the ways that they use it and imagine it. As Lupton argues (2010) space produces particular forms of activity and sets of relations by configuring the identities and understandings of people who occupy it. In this sense, particular places cannot be thought of only in physical and locational terms as a backdrop to human activity. Nor can they only be thought of as containers in which people are gathered and in which they interact. They are actively implicated in and made sense of by human activity and are thus also dynamic and relational. What it means for young people to be disadvantaged or poor, what constitutes valid and useful knowledge, and how their educational experiences appear to either alleviate or reinforce inequities are all understandings that are constructed in and through space. And yet at the same time I have also suggested that it is the peculiarities of particular places that appear significant in influencing the identity formation of young people. Following writers such as Massey (1994) I therefore see space and place being theoretically intertwined so that place is seen as an 'articulated moment' (or 'space/time moment') in spatial relations (Massey, ibid.: 115). Massey conceptualises space as 'a complex web of relative domination and subordination, of solidarity and co-operation' (Massey, 1993: 81) within which place becomes a tightly constrained local pattern. For McDowell (1996) places have a particular structure of feeling that can be seen as nestling inside spaces, providing significant meanings for individuals and groups. 'Spaces and places are not only sets of material social relations but also cultural objects.' (McDowell, 1996: 32)

Such conceptualisations of space and place are central to my thinking in relation to issues of educational equity. It is in poor urban places – places that are physical manifestations of articulated moments in spatial relations – that poor educational outcomes are concentrated, with particular poor neighbour-hood types being more closely associated with the poorest of educational outcomes (Webber and Butler, 2007). This suggests that the spatial relations in particular urban places or neighbourhoods are both similar and yet different to spatial relations in other poor urban places. This implies that the development of broadly articulated educational autonomy and identities of disadvantaged young people and their educational aspirations and expectations are place-based and reflect particular manifestations of spatial social relations where 'place and identity are inexorably linked' (Thrift, 1997: 160) In various cultural and ethnographic studies of community and family life in disadvantaged neighbour-hoods (e.g. Reay and Lucey, 2000; Power, 2007) there is both empirical data and theoretical explanations about how particular places are implicated in forming and influencing the gendered, classed and ethnically informed autonomy and identities of young people. However, much spatial educational analysis has either examined general socio-economic and political processes that generate educational inequality in particular places (Anyon, 1997; Lipman, 2004) or the demographics of disadvantage and the schooling/educational challenges associated with such demographics (Brighouse and Fullick, 2007). Neither of these broad approaches appears to have simultaneously focused on the histor-ical, relational and dynamic socio-cultural aspects of particular places (Morris, 2004) and the way these influence individual young people's educational autonomy, identity and aspiration. Gulson and Symes (2007) edited collection provides a strong counterbalance to this situation but there is still a clear need for further elaboration of key ideas associated with the spatial turn in education. This suggest a continuing need to examine how aspects of place and space become implicated in the way groups of young people develop their educational identities and autonomy and then how these are recognised, credited or valued by the educational processes of school life. As Reay and Lucey (2000) have argued forcibly:

> [O]ur argument is not simply that more attention should be paid to social class in studies of children and space and place. Rather space needs to be made for working-class understandings of locality and place within academia in order to counter the hegemony of middle-class versions. Otherwise we will never be able to move very far from representations of deficit and pathology in relation to the urban poor.
>
> (Reay and Lucey, 2000: 425)

In order that proper consideration is given to how the distributional and relational circumstances of urban place and space are implicated in young people's broader educational autonomy, agency and aspiration I will now focus on theorisations about the urban *in* education. In order to do this I start with a concise historical overview of urban education provided by Gerald Grace (2004), one our foremost thinkers in the field. During the 80s and 90s he suggested that the field of urban education appeared to reflect, with varying emphases over time, some or all of the following interconnected themes:

- A strengthened focus on urban education policy during periods of urban crises.
- An overemphasis upon cultural deficits as an explanatory category and an underemphasis upon the structural.
- A mode of enquiry dominated by various forms of micro-institutional studies that focused on schools, pedagogy and local educational systems.
- An inadequate sense of the historical in the understanding of urban phenomena.
- Limited conceptualisations of power and resource utilisation.
- Bracketing out of socio-political references and a positive concentration upon the technical and immediately realisable issues.

More recently Campbell and Whitty (2007), in their introduction to the UK section of the International Handbook for Urban Education, note that, although the general field of urban studies has evolved and become more multifaceted and diverse, the specific field of urban education in the UK has developed little since the 80s and has rarely met the challenges highlighted by Grace above. This is reflected in scholars from different knowledge domains (e.g. school improvement and effectiveness, critical policy, etc.) at times locating themselves in the urban but doing so through a 'contextual rhetoric' that focuses on education in the urban rather than a 'substantive emphasis' (Grace, 1984: 12) where the focus is on the urban *in* education. However, although Campbell and Whitty set out a challenge for urban educational research to be more substantive and integrative, what is interesting about the chapters that make up the UK contribution to the book is how many of them only partially respond to such a challenge, with some repeating similar failings that previous writers in previous generations had demonstrated. Few chapters, and perhaps only Thomson, Riddell and Grace in any detailed sense, examine how the micro detailing of schooling are located in the interpenetration of the urban macro and meso.

What I hope to do in the rest of this section of the chapter is to use the work of a number of current urban scholars and ethnographers to help develop a more robust set of ideas about the urban in education in order to deal with these limitations. In order to do this I will focus on a macro, meso and micro scale of theorisations (Taylor, 2009; Raffo *et al.*, 2010) of the urban that are imbued with notions of the historical, structural, cultural and political and that reflect the type of approaches exemplified by the work of Thomson (2007) and the writings of researchers from the US such as Mirón and St. John (2003) and Noguera (2003). In so doing I aim to show that theorisations about the urban can provide an appropriate methodology for exploring disadvantaged young people's educational identities and constrained autonomy (McDermott *et al.*, 2009). Although not denying the importance of schools (their impacts are detailed in the examination of cultural injustice and relational inequities of educational process later in the chapter) what I will argue is that their influence in such matters has to be understood as an element or subset of urban neighbourhood and family social relations. It is these latter variables that I will argue are the major harbingers or foundations of educational identity formation and hence educational autonomy and aspiration for young people.

Let me now move onto theorisations about the urban as a way of making sense of young people's educational identities and autonomy. Macro theorisations that have examined the shifting fortunes of the urban in affluent countries over the last 20–30 years have tended to focus on issues of globalisation and the difficulties that many western economies are experiencing competing on the basis of exploiting natural resources or on the basis of low-cost, high volume manufacture (Brown, 1999; Lash and Urry, 1994). I do not wish to provide an extended commentary of such issues as these can be found elsewhere (Raffo, 2006). However, Wacquant (2007) has neatly summarised the effects of globalisation on the urban through his conceptualisation of 'urban outcasts'. For Wacquant urban outcasts result from the macro structural that generate advanced distributional marginality in many industrial towns and parts of industrial cities. These circumstances of increased urban marginality are reflected in increased unemployment and increased social instability and life insecurity; a disconnection from macro-economic trends where communities are not linked into major service sector growths of cities; isolation and stigmatisation of particular poor and excluded communities; a dissolution of 'place' with concomitant reduction in feelings of home and relative security; a loss of hinterland including kin, cliques, trade unions and the church and social fragmentation with a decomposition of class in these areas. Wacquant's broad categorisations of urban re-structuring provide a powerful macro analysis of what at the meso and micro level communities, families and young people in the poorest of urban contexts have had to endure. They demonstrate how global capital has distributionally transformed the urban landscape over the last 30 to 40 years decimating particular neighbourhoods and communities and the lives of families and individuals (Byrne, 2005). However, what these types of studies do not provide are in-depth relational analysis of how both social change and preservation occurs at the meso and micro level. In other words these studies provide little evidence for the way different and particular urban contexts have responded or changed in response to these structuring forces or of how micro level family, peer and community relations interact with both meso space/place dynamics and macro structural changes. Studies, such as Seaman *et al.*'s (2006) and Power's (2007) research on parenting and children's resilience in disadvantaged communities, are required that provide evidence of the way communities and families have evolved various forms of resilience in spite, or because, of the onslaught of these structural changes.

Recent developments in urban theory that focus on the meso and micro, and that parallel some of the neighbourhood writers highlighted above, are perhaps most compellingly provided by Sanchez-Jankowski's (2008) study of the meso level structural and cultural contours of poor neighbourhoods and the associated micro social dynamics. His longitudinal study of endemically poor neighbourhoods in Los Angeles and New York provides a rich and detailed set of theorisations about how the everyday lifeworlds of inhabitants of those neighbourhoods reflect value orientations that emanate from sub-cultures of distributional scarcity and that support particular behavioural orientations and identities. He demonstrates how the life of the poor is influenced relationally by different institutions that operate in those neighbourhoods, and particularly in the difference between neighbourhood oriented and enterprise oriented institutions. Furthermore he explains how communities can be both relationally contested and fragmented, depending on ethnic flows and migrations and the level of settledness in any particular neighbourhood at any particular time. Of importance in these neighbourhoods is the way individuals recognise their position, status and a sense of belonging – their place specific identity if you like – that reflects the nature and type of relational networks to which individuals belong (Raffo and Reeves, 2000; Seyer-Ochi, 2006). The values underpinning these networks generally reflect the orientations that are imbued in the daily interactions of institutions, families, neighbourhoods, particularly in relation to gendered, class and race issues. And young people use these relational networks to develop practices that assist in the daily navigations of living in their neighbourhoods. An example of such placed based activities and networks is provided by Gunter and Watt's (2009) study of British urban working-class youth's autonomy with regards to transitions, cultures and leisure practices in a multi-ethnic East London poor neighbourhood. Their research suggests that the particular local neighbourhood has an enduring significance on youth autonomy, aspiration and transition expectations that are:

> . . . formed by the interaction of paid work opportunities with youth cultures and leisure practices ('road' and 'grafter' cultures), ethnicity, gender and social networks. Even within a single deprived and stigmatised neighbourhood such as Manor, a number of transitions could be identified. These include 'grafting' at manual, masculine 'dirty work' in the construction industry; going to college allied to 'clean', service sector work; and an 'alternative' route of 'working on road' by undertaking a variety of low-level, illegal money-making activities.
>
> (Gunter and Watt, 2009: 515)

In addition to some of the socio-cultural dynamics of living in poor urban contexts, Spicker (2001) also points to environmental conditions that reflect particular aspects of material distribution and that are reflected in a lack of area based resources that exacerbate the social experiences of living in such areas. He includes urban stressors such as inadequate housing and estate designs, noise pollution, environmental pollution and dirty living conditions, inadequate local resources and infrastructures. These stressors increase the wear and tear on the body and mind and hence in one's freedom to aspire to, and achieve, valued educational capabilities, all of which clearly reflect Power's acute observations that 'cities can be cruel places' (Power, 2007: 1).

By combining both distributional and relational conceptualisations of inequality that reflect macro structural, meso cultural/environmental and micro ethnographic accounts of poor urban neighbourhoods one can start to develop a historically pertinent understanding of the influences on young peoples' autonomy in terms of who they are and the orientations and aspirations they have towards educational capabilities and outcomes. In this respect I align myself to work by Gardner, Dillabough and McLeod (2004) who see youth identities and hence educational autonomy and engagement as both 'a response to, and a connection between, macro and micro forces of social change' (ibid.: 11). By taking such an approach we can start to understand the interpenetration of urban place with educational identity, autonomy, aspiration and expectation and hence the challenges and opportunities that face schools in such places. It is in particular places that young people are both actors and acted upon and are therefore both socialised through these structuring structures and socialise others through their structured structuring – forms of socialisation that become manifestations of what might be termed a 'neighbourhood-informed habitus'. And yet at the same time I would not want to overstate the determinism in such arrangements, a view reflected in Thompson's concerns about 'an impoverished conception of self in which the self is the product of an external symbolic system' (Thompson, 1995: 210). Young people can and do operate at the boundaries of any particular symbolic system, opening themselves to new and different experiences that go beyond the immediate locale (Raffo and Reeves, 2000; Raffo 2006) and that provide different ways of thinking about self and in demonstrating autonomy. However, taken together, structural, socio-cultural and environmental accounts of the urban provide important indicators of how different groups of young people develop their identity and educational autonomy in such contexts. And it is precisely the nature of this identity and autonomy that many schools have difficulty in understanding, often accrediting choices and behaviours of young people within schools to forms of cultural deprivation experienced in communities rather than seeing these choices and behaviours as a complex set of often rationally chosen actions based on culturally and economically situated contexts (Hatcher, 1998)

Part 3 of the EEF – Inequities in educational processes and their impact on educational autonomy

In the previous section I have argued how distributional and relational issues in the urban constrain young people's general educational orientations, autonomy and choice. In this section I want to explain more fully how the specific educational processes of schooling in poor urban contexts often results in iniquitous impacts on educational autonomy, identity and aspiration.

Although external distributional and relational worlds help to develop the foundations for educational autonomy and identity of disadvantaged young people, it is in educational domains where specific notions of choice, independence and autonomy play out. As Riddell notes (2007), notions of educational autonomy play out, for example, in the quasi-markets of educational choice and in the choices individual young people have with regards to both the curriculum and key transition points. In reality, however, these choices favour particular classes over others. For example there is clear evidence of middle-class families entering as skilled choosers of schools because of the knowledge of the system they bring to the market process (Power, Edwards, Whitty and Wigfall, 2003). In addition their economic capital means they are able to purchase private education or a house in the catchment area of favoured schools (Bell, 2007). Working-class parents and young people tend not to be market players at all (Ball, Bowe and Gewirtz, 1995). The result is that the quasi-market in education favours the middle class, and particularly so in urban contexts (Riddell, 2005). In addition educational choices about the curriculum in schools and also choices about key transition points between schools and between schools and colleges by young people also reflect classed, gendered and ethnically informed experiences of the urban. For example, Hatcher notes that the 'choices concerning transition to higher levels of education differ according to class position, even when there is no difference in level of achievement' (Hatcher, 1998: 8). This evidence is complemented by Micklewright's (1989) research that states that family background and experience influence not only the likelihood of young people leaving school early but also the take up of vocational instead of academic pathways pre and post-16. Various ethnographic studies have also outlined some of these choices. For example Willis's study of Learning to Labour (1977) illuminated one distinctive urban cultural orientation, the choice of 'lads' to reject the school–work exchange. Hollands' study (1990) of urban youth on a Youth Training Scheme showed how the majority wanted to leave school at 16 because they disliked the social relationships of schools and the academic character of the curriculum. In summary, disadvantaged young people in poor urban contexts are more likely to choose to leave school early, not progress onto higher education and take vocational as opposed to academic courses than similarly able middle class counterparts in more affluent areas. At the same time however, the specific nature of these choices are also, as I have argued above, influenced by the gendered, classed and ethnically informed experiences of young people who live in particular urban contexts and neighbourhood types.

Throughout the chapter I have argued that young people from different poor urban neighbourhoods, although not totally limited by such contexts, will tend to develop educational autonomy and particular orientations to schooling that may reflect particular networks of influence suggestive of a placed based identity or neighbourhood-informed habitus. Young people enter schooling from different structural positions, associated with differing social habitats, wherein they embody distinctive and different qualities of cultural disposition, or 'habitus'. I have argued that these are affected, but not completely so, by urban placed based networks of social relations, distributions, structures and cultures. These dispositions in turn operate selectively in schools as 'cultural capital' of stronger or weaker species (Bourdieu, 1986). Bourdieu (1998) summarises his longstanding concern with the problem of schooling that reproduces social stratification:

> The educational system . . . maintains the pre-existing order, that is, the gap between pupils endowed with unequal amounts of cultural capital. More precisely, by a series of selection operations, the system separates the holders of inherited cultural capital from those who lack it. Differences in aptitude being inseparable from social differences according to inherited capital, the system thus tends to maintain pre-existing social differences.
>
> (Bourdieu, 1998: 20)

In schools, young people's educational dispositions acquire greater or lesser 'capital' value depending on how near or far they stand in relation to 'standard' cultural codes that dominate in mainstream schooling in such things as curriculum, pedagogy and assessment (Bourdieu and Passeron, 1977). In many, if not all, poor urban communities the cultural habits brought to school by significant proportions of students are not utilised or scaffolded to traditional school learning methods and contents. Simply put, their 'virtual schoolbag' (Thomson, 2002: 1) is not unpacked. Rather, their lack of fit with the culturally arbitrary selections that are valued by school become localised and internalised as 'failure'. As Riddell states:

> Some young people . . . *will* have a background of rich learning in community, but *transfer* may be weak if the school's expectations and environment cannot "recognise" the learning and its conventions, particularly if the dominant ones are of a different type from those in school.
>
> (Riddell, 2007: 1033)

To put it bluntly, too many young people living in disadvantaged communities feel relationally 'misrecognised' (Fraser, 1996) by schools and teachers, resulting in a array of 'status injuries' (Fraser, ibid.) that young people experience. Feeling devalued within a social system can lead to the development of strategies of resistance (Mac an Ghaill, 1988) and this may partly account for the limited educational achievement of many poor urban young people. The cultural disjuncture between neighbourhood and school life is likely to contribute to alienation and obviously has a role to play in communicating a sense of inferiority (Mac an Ghaill, 1988). In addition, Teese and Polesel (2003) are explicit in their argument about how the reproduction of social stratification occurs in schooling. Students whose embodied capital does not match the cultural of much schooling miss out in two significant ways. First, the curriculum too often makes no connection with their learning in their community contexts and the educational capabilities they may have come to value, so that there is no intrinsic value to engage them in the educational experience. Second, as a result of this lack of connection, students often miss out on the codified knowledge of the curriculum (Young, 2008) that gives access to further education, training, and employment. In addition Hatcher (1998) points to many discriminating processes in schools that can disadvantage poor urban students further, particularly in the way students are provided no choice but are directed to particular curriculum options.

Summary

In thinking about how evidence, concepts and ideas associated with educational disadvantage illuminate the EEF documented in Chapter 2, it is clear that resources, both materially and symbolically, that are available for developing authentic educational autonomy, identity and aspiration for the young people are often limited. The net result is that the skills, knowledge and the vernacular developed within particular networks of influence tend naturally to emphasise survival issues and often restrict educational choice and engagement. My arguments also suggest that the prospects of engaging effectively with schooling and education more generally seem limited, with young people experiencing the schooling process in ways that generate status injuries and of being culturally excluded by the experience. However, not all evidence points to a deterministic negative picture. There are examples of inclusive educational processes that demonstrate how educational autonomy and choices can be influenced by: (a) additional resources, (b) emerging and evolving networks of influence, and (c) relationally just pedagogical practice. In providing my own example of such approaches, Chapter 7 demonstrates how living in disadvantaged urban contexts does not necessarily preclude young people from developing educational autonomy, aspiration and engagement. In addition, in the final chapter of the book I provide a case study of a school that, although not providing a panacea for all the structural and stratified pressures in the education system, clearly attempts to engage with equitable educational processes that might ameliorate some of the real challenges facing some of our most educationally disadvantaged young people.

Given the arguments and evidence highlighted above, the next chapter examines how educational policy and practice has evolved to meet the challenges of improving educational purpose, quality and equity.

4 Educational policy for educational equity

Introduction

As I articulated in chapters 2 and 3, education systems in many industrialised countries are characterised by marked inequalities in educational outcomes and experiences as well as inequities in educational processes. These differences relate – albeit in complex ways – to social class, ethnicity and gender and also to a spatial dimension, with access and outcomes being distributed differently across more and less affluent parts of the country. Over the last decade or so English educational policy, in line with many other developed countries (in particular the US), has focused heavily on conceptualising educational purpose, quality and fairness in human capital and distributional terms associated with credentialism and narrowing the attainment gap between different groups of learners. Education inequality is then understood as the comparative poor educational attainments of disadvantaged groups of young people in relation to the rest of the more advantaged population. These poor attainments are then related to broader concerns of economic well-being. Low levels of educational attainment are associated with low levels of human capital acquisition that, at an aggregate level, then result in lower economic productivity and increased levels of social and economic polarisation – what the previous New Labour government in the UK referred to as social exclusion. Quality and fairness in educational attainment is therefore seen as a core driver for enhanced economic equity, both of which are equated in much policy rhetoric with notions of social inclusion, mobility and justice. As Michael Gove, the English minister for education has recently commented: 'Schools should be engines of social mobility – the places where accidents of birth and the unfairness of life's lottery are overcome through the democratisation of access to knowledge' (Gove, 2010).

Although past and current policy endeavours have sought to ameliorate the situation, the reality of endemic distributional educational inequalities continues to blight the purported functional purpose of education, resulting in continuing debates about the shape and direction of educational policy and in particular the nature of specific additional educational interventions geared towards improving the situation. This chapter explores these interventions but does so by examining the extent to which they have more broadly engaged with different components of the Educational Equity Framework (EEF) developed in Chapter 2.

Education policy responses

Over the last 40 years or so educational policy in many affluent countries, and particularly in England, has tended to respond to educational inequality in predominately one of two ways that have, at times, operated simultaneously. The ongoing and main focus for improved educational fairness has been attempts to raise educational quality for all by raising outcomes across the system as a whole and by improving the distribution of such outcomes. In England, this has included the development of a powerful mix of target-setting, national curricula and pedagogical development, and high stakes accountability (Raffo *et al.*, 2010). The underlying argument to such an approach is that all schools, no matter what the intake or where they are located, should be able to achieve broadly similar results with a broadly similar curriculum. However, educational data continues to suggest that although improvements can be made through the school system, these tend to be sporadic and inconsistent. The continuing difficulties that schools in poor contexts face in improving educational outcomes has resulted in a plethora of interventions that have provided additional compensatory resources to those schools and their contexts. Given that the vast majority of educational failure in most affluent countries is located (albeit differentially) in disadvantaged urban contexts, internationally educational policy has, over time, allocated these additional resources to: (a) those disadvantaged urban contexts, (b) the schools located in those contexts, and (c) particularly underachieving groups of young people who live and attend schools in those contexts. In England, these educational policies and interventions have, over time, become known as area based initiatives (ABIs) and their aim has been to 'acknowledge and seek to remedy the effects and impact of social exclusion' (Barker, 2010: 21). Although these ABI policies in England and other countries have been of many kinds, frequently emerging and disappearing within the space of a few years, they can perhaps be best categorised under four main foci:

- ABIs targeted at schools in disadvantaged areas.
- ABIs co-ordinating policies in disadvantaged areas across education, health and social welfare.
- ABIs in particular cities where poverty is heavily concentrated.
- ABIs that focus on area regeneration initiatives that include an education component.

This typology is far from perfect, and there is a good deal of overlap between these different foci. Nonetheless, it is a useful way of making sense of what otherwise might seem to be a chaotic policy scene. Given this typology of interventions what do these policy strands of ABI look like? In undertaking this analysis, most of the examples are drawn from the English educational policy scene. However, important and specific examples of ABI development are also drawn from French, Portuguese and US policy contexts.

ABIs – schools in targeted areas

Given the link between urban areas marked by poverty and low educational achievement many ABIs have been targeted at concentrated areas of disadvantage where learners are at risk of underachievement. Although one can point to examples of ABIs in England as long ago as the late 60s and early 70s, and in particular Educational Priority Areas initiative (Smith, 1987), more recent articulations include the Excellence in Cities (EiC) programme in England that was developed from the earlier Education Action Zones. The programme was launched in September 1999 to raise standards and promote inclusion in disadvantaged inner cities and other urban areas. It focused on providing additional resources to support leadership, behaviour, and teaching and learning. Initially just based in secondary schools, the programme quickly expanded to include primary schools. The programme attempted to tackle underachievement in schools through specific strands targeted at underachieving or disadvantaged groups. So: Learning Mentors worked with underachieving students in schools; Learning Support Units were established to provide for students at risk of exclusion from school for disciplinary reasons; a gifted and talented pupils programme was developed; and City Learning Centres were established to enhance adult learning opportunities (particularly through information technology) for local people. Additional resources were thus provided to the poorest urban areas to assist schools help engage young people and their families improve their educational attainments. Area targeted approaches have not only been important to English education policies but have also been central to both France and Portugal. France's Zones d'Education Prioritaires (ZEPs) were established in 1982 in order to support the work of schools serving areas of disadvantage through: (a) the targeting of additional resources into schools in those areas, (b) the development of local initiatives and new educational methods, and (c) an attempt to strengthen local involvement in educational decision-making and practice. The development of area approaches in Portugal was developed in 1995 and termed Territórios Educativos de Intervenção Prioritária (TEIPs) – Priority Intervention Education Areas in English. They took the form of a central designation of disadvantaged areas in which educational interventions were called for in order to enhance learning conditions for students in disadvantaged areas, and so combat social inequality. TEIPs shared some features in common with ZEPs and EiC.

Although the above initiatives date back a number of decades, a complementary major thrust in current education policy discourse from the UK coalition government is the proposed redistribution of educational resources through the introduction of a pupil premium into the school funding system in England. These proposals aim to increase the targeting of resources at schools with a high proportion of disadvantaged pupils, and to reduce the disincentive to attract hard-to-teach pupils. The suggestion is that the resources themselves would: (a) provide opportunities for targeted support for young people in schools, (b) reduce the social segregation in schools, as schools would be incentivised to attract poorer pupils thereby impacting on achievement through peer effect, and (c) provide incentives for new schools to be developed. Although not an ABI in its truest sense, the pupil premium proposal would result in additional funds going to schools located in the poorest areas.

ABIs – co-ordinating initiatives across education, health and social welfare

Sure Start centres, and more latterly Children's Centres, were set up in England to enhance the functioning of children and families living in disadvantaged areas by providing additional services in local programme areas. In many respects these centres emulated the work of programmes such as Head Start in the US. These interventions were aimed at providing additional resources to disadvantaged preschool children with the purpose of delivering programmes and services that would prepare preschool children for elementary school. Typically services included parenting support, access to health provision and child care and educational facilities for young parents. Sure Start/Children Centres were strategically situated in areas identified as having high levels of deprivation and were designed to enhance the life prospects of young children in disadvantaged families and communities. By virtue of their local autonomy, Sure Start/Children Centres did not have a prescribed curriculum or set of services. Instead, each programme had extensive local autonomy concerning how it fulfilled its mission to improve and create services as needed, without specification of how services are to be changed. The underlying principle, however, was about providing additional resources for public agencies to support poorer families in disadvantaged contexts. In particular it was about supporting parents to develop their parenting skills so that their children would be school ready and also better supported during their school lives.

Community-oriented schools under the guise of Full Service Extended Schools (FSES) in England, constituted focal points at which strategies for raising educational standards overall were supported by additional resources for targeting support to schools serving disadvantaged populations, and strategies for tackling neighbourhood and family problems. In England the detailed guidance from the Department of Children Schools and Families on FSES at the time proposed no fewer than 23 possible outcomes from community-oriented schools, ranging from improved access to childcare and ICT, through reductions in health inequalities and the number of unemployed people, to better school security and improvements in students' behaviour. In other words, FSES were expected to intervene in the multiple problems which beset children, families and communities living in disadvantage. However, at the heart of these interventions was a commitment to education as the pathway to achievement and hence to employment and social inclusion – and to raised expectations as a necessary precondition of raised achievement. The FSES therefore initiative focused on both the educational development needs of young people and enhanced family and community engagement via parenting classes, crèches and skills development programmes. In addition there was a recognition of the need for a more integrated approach to delivering certain core public services via a multi-agency strategy located in the school. Once again this ABI was about diverting funds to schools and other agencies to improve integrated support for disadvantaged young people and families' engagement with education.

Perhaps one of the most developed and holistic intervention programmes that has attempted to integrate and co-ordinate initiatives across health, social care and education in particular places of deprivation is the Harlem Children's Zone (HCZ) in the US. The Zone is a geographically based non-profit organisation. It currently serves around 100 blocks in Harlem, New York, which is predominantly home to low-income black families. It offers them access to an interlocking network of education, health, family, and social welfare services. These are not simply wrap-around services, but have been designed to create a 'pipeline' of support for children from cradle to career. To this end, HCZ has established an integrated package of programmes to support children's education in early childhood, elementary school, middle school, high school and college contexts, and it runs its own charter schools called Promise Academies. HCZ's wider programmes of family and community support are built around this education-oriented pipeline. The HCZ offers a range of interventions that makes up its 'pipeline to success' and its wider network of support. Early years interventions include the *Baby College* that provides a series of parenting workshops for parents of children aged up to three living in the Zone. Designed by early childhood experts, the college aims to help parents to provide a nurturing and stimulating home environment. Early years interventions also include the *The Three-Year-Old Journey* programme that concentrates on how best to promote children's language and learning skills, *The Harlem Gems* is an all-day pre-kindergarten programme for three-year-olds where the emphasis is on school readiness. During school year the HCZ runs two Promise Academy charter schools, catering for elementary, middle and (increasingly) high school students. These have an extended school day, including after-school and weekend tutoring, and a wide range of enrichment activities. Students are given freshly prepared meals and have onsite access to medical, dental, and mental health services. Fifth to Twelfth Grade students also have access to case managers who track students' individual progress (academic, social and emotional), creating and implementing a support plan for every student. Students are also supported through college preparation and employment via the *HCZ Employment and Technology Center* that promotes technology skills as well as academic support for high school students. The *Learn to Earn programme* helps high school students improve their academic skills as well as prepare for college and the job market and the *College Success Office* supports students with all aspects of college access, from financial aid applications to academic issues and time management. Finally the HCZ contains wider family and community programmes. These include the *Parenting support programmes* where activities range from parent reading groups to cooking classes and support with managing their children's chronic health conditions – for example, the HCZ asthma initiative. In addition there is the *HCZ Community Pride programme* that aims to support and energise tenant and block associations to improve living condition and the *Family Development Program and Family Support Center* that focus on strengthening at-risk families and run foster care prevention programmes. Finally the HCZ supports the *Peacemakers programme* that employs young adults to work in public school classrooms as teaching assistants and run after-school programmes and *Beacon Community Center* that create a shop front for access to all of HCZ's support services. All those resident in the Zone have the opportunity to access the HCZ full range of school- and community-based provision. HCZ is similar to other ABIs but more developed in that it recognises that inequalities in outcomes cannot be tackled unless the causes of those inequalities in family and community contexts are also tackled. The system for addressing these inequalities is focused on a particular local area, seeking to understand and tackle the dynamics of disadvantage in that area, and to meet the diverse and multiple issues facing the children and families who live there. In addition it is doubly holistic, working with children *over* time to develop a cradle-to-career 'pipeline' of support, in the wider context of the families and communities in which they live. It is also able to act strategically for children and families in the area. HCZ is funded, governed and led in such a way that it can concentrate all its energies on the single task of improving a wide range of outcomes for children and young people, can do so in a strategic and integrated way, and can sustain this over time.

ABIs – city initiatives in education

Whereas many of the initiatives highlighted above provided additional resources to targeted areas, the London Challenge was an example in England that recognised the distinctive difficulties facing schools in large metropolitan cities – in terms, for instance, of low levels of achievement, high levels of disadvantage, the problems and benefits of a multi-ethnic population, and the balkanisation of governance of London education, which is divided between a large number of local authorities. The Challenge deployed a range of strategies to address these issues, including targeted intervention with low-performing schools, programmes aimed at increasing teacher recruitment and retention, a gifted and talented programme, developments in vocational education and support to local authorities in managing their education systems (see, http://www.dfes.gov.uk/londonchallenge/). Similar programmes have also been set up in other major cities. The focus of all the city challenges has been about by diverting additional funds to schools in those cities in order to enhance the above strands of activity that, together, might raise educational attainment for young people most disadvantaged.

ABIs – regeneration initiatives

In England concerns with area-focused interventions have historically been repeated across many aspects of government social policy. Schools and early years centres in disadvantaged areas participated in interventions that were developed by government departments and agencies other than the Department of Education. For instance, the early experiments with extended schools arose out of the cross-departmental National Strategy for Neighbourhood Renewal (Social Exclusion Unit, 1998). Likewise, the Single Regeneration Budget and the New Deal for Communities managed by the Department for Communities and Local Government had dedicated education strands that were often a source of additional funding for schools and early years centres.

Evidence of impact

There seems little doubt that ABIs of the sort described above have been effective in some ways in raising attainment and in focusing attention on particular groups, areas and institutions, and in stimulating activity in relation to them. Excellence in Cities (Kendall *et al.*, 2005), Full Service Extended Schools (Cummings *et al.*, 2005) and Sure Start seem to have acted as catalysts for considerable activity on the ground. These policies have generated some of the improved outcomes at which they were targeted. For instance, test and examination performance increased in EiC schools, as did attendance. These increases were often modest and variable, but they did tend to be greater than in other schools (Kendall *et al.*, 2005; Blanden and Machin, 2007). Moreover, there were more marked improvements in some schools and for some groups of young people targeted by the programme. Melhuish *et al.* (2005) in their review of Sure Start suggests that there were benefits to the programme; however, it produced greater benefits for the moderately disadvantaged than for the more severely disadvantaged and resonated with other evaluations of such interventions (e.g. Early Head Start; Love *et al.*, 2002) and in particular how particular groups are better placed to make use of current resources and can acquire further resources of support through their engagement with networks. As regards FSES, there was some evidence of positive outcomes with regards to raised attainment, increased pupil engagement with learning and a growing trust and support between home and school. There was also improved multi-agency working that brought some benefits to children and their families (Cummings *et al.*, 2005). Cummings *et al.* (2005) suggest that these initial data provide some evidence for a partial intervening to break the cycle of disadvantage in some of the areas that they serve. According to Dyson *et al.*'s report (2012) examining the implications of HCZ for the English context, there is some evidence to suggest that academic attainments have improved in the Zone. They quote a study by Whitehurst and Croft (2010), that found that students attending Promise Academy schools do 'impressively better than students of their backgrounds attending a typical public school in New York City'. They also focus on another study by Dobbie and Fryer (2010), that claims that gains made by Promise Academy students were enough to 'reverse the black–white achievement gap', at least in some subjects and for some age groups. Both studies suggest that at individual programme level there is some evidence of positive impacts across the HCZ's wide remit. At the level of these wider effects, however, Dyson *et al.* suggest there is far less evidence available. The two independent evaluations, by Whitehurst and Croft (2010) and Dobbie and Fryer (2010), although focusing on attainment outcomes also tried to explore whether the other services provided by the Zone had any impact on attainment. Since other charter schools in New York do as well as the HCZ Promise Academies, and since children who do not receive additional services seem to attain as highly as those who do, they conclude that there are no cumulative effects from these services, and that it is the schools alone that make the difference – challenging HCZ's underpinning theory of action.

Overall, however, although there have been modest improvements based on the various investments in ABIs in differing national and local contexts, the basic premise still holds in most countries that the more disadvantaged an individual's background the less well he/she will achieve in education (Chitty, 2002) and the more that social hierarchies are reproduced through generations (Blanden and Machin, 2003). Given the evidence highlight above, why have ABIs only had a differentially limited impact on educational equity?

ABIs and educational equity

In order to examine some of the reasons for the partial success of ABIs the chapter reflects on the discussion and analysis of educational purpose, quality and equity documented in chapters 2 and 3 and articulated through EEF.

I start by reminding ourselves of the issues. Redistributional educational equality is about educational quality for all and hence focused on narrowing the educational gap and ensuring a fairer distribution of educational attainments across classes, ethnicities, gender and places. More often than not the underlying notion of educational purpose associated with such an approach derive from ideas of human capital development. The main focus for interventions, therefore, is about ensuring that resources are appropriately apportioned to enable this to occur. However, in examining ideas about resource allocations, Fraser reminds the field that the spectrum of any form of resource redistribution can range from the affirmative to the transformative. Affirmative redistribution seeks to redress maldistribution by altering patterns of allocation without disturbing the underlying mechanisms that generate them. In contrast to affirmative redistribution, transformative redistribution seeks to redress injustices by altering the underlying framework that generates them. Almost all of the ABIs highlighted above can be categorised as examples of affirmative redistribution. As I have shown in the preceding descriptions, educational ABIs have provided a framework for enhanced funding for schools in disadvantaged and challenging urban contexts. In addition ABIs such as FSES, Sure Start/Children Centres and HCZ have redistributed additional resources for out-of-school support for families and parents through, for example, parenting classes, improved crèche facilities and health and other social facilities. Furthermore certain ABIs have been linked into the wider regeneration of areas where educational developments have been planned alongside wider redistributive activities such as enhanced economic opportunities and support for young people and their families and communities. However, at whatever level of redistribution, the underlying core perspective underpinning ABIs is economic and is linked to ideas of human capital development. Firstly ABIs are economic in the sense that economic resources are being redistributed in particular ways to support poorer schools, young people, families and communities achieve higher levels of educational attainment. Secondly they are also economic in that the ensuing aim of narrowing the educational gap is about generating a fairer distribution of human capital and thus enhanced levels of economic activity, social mobility and enhanced social inclusion for those most disadvantaged. One might argue, therefore, that much of what is badged as educational ABI policy focuses on ideas about purpose and quality that are concerned with enhancing educational outcomes as a way of improving economic equity and minimising economic marginalisation and social exclusion. What educational ABI policies focus on in different ways and to varying extents are the distributional aspects of life and their impacts on young people's educational agency both inside and outside school. These policies recognise that many disadvantaged young people do not engage because there is an inadequate level of resource for families and communities beyond school and for school leaders and teachers within schools to enable these young people to access, engage and then achieve within the education system. ABIs recognise the distributional part of the EEF framework, and hence the resource impact on young people's educational autonomy. However, as this and previous chapters have documented, these approaches have only been partially successful in achieving their aims. Based on the arguments that I developed previously I would argue that at one level a major reason for the comparative and historic limited success of ABI policies both in England and abroad is due to their continued focus on meso and micro level aspects of affirmative, and perhaps wholly inadequate, levels of redistribution. Clearly certain ABIs, and in particular the HCZ, have provided greater levels of resource at different levels of activity and in more or less integrated ways. However, without a full recognition of the way distributional factors operate simultaneously within the micro, meso and macro (Raffo *et al.*, 2010), no strand of ABI activity is likely to succeed in combating the economic factors that impact on educational inequality. As Anyon (2005) notes, while educational policy interventions need to address the response of the education system to the academic challenges posed by learners living in poverty, they also need to tackle what she calls the 'macro-economy'.

However, although issues of redistribution, whether affirmative or transformative, are important I would argue that, in themselves and at whatever level they are pitched, they are insufficient to bring about educational equity. In line with the EEF, I suggest that an emphasis on issues of autonomy and agentic freedom, both broadly defined and also more specifically focused on educational processes, provide a different and yet complementary focus for the way in which ABIs need to develop. As I documented in Chapter 2, issues of equity associated with autonomy and agentic freedom are relational issues that focus on what Fraser terms the politics of recognition that target cultural injustices rooted in social patterns of representation, interpretation and communication. In terms of education, the politics of recognition illuminates the many cultural injustices associated with aspects of poverty, class, gender, ethnicity, and disability that different groups of young people and their families experience through their engagement with the educational system. In Chapter 3 I suggested that educational injustices occur because of the way these groups of young people and their families have their autonomy, funds of knowledge, and educational aspirations silenced by dominant educational discourses or paradigms that operate both at the state and school/neighbourhood level (i.e. from above and below). I suggested that the remedy for this type of injustice involves revaluing disrespected identities and the cultural products of maligned groups. Although ABIs are avowedly dedicated to improving the educational outcomes of young people in the most disadvantaged of urban contexts, there is very little in most ABI policy formulation, nationally and internationally, that recommends engagement with neighbourhood discourses about area based provision of education. In fact, quite the opposite. Even in relation to the integrated and double holistic HCZ programme, there is very little recognition of the importance of engaging with young people and community members as partners in the development and implementation of the programme. Compounding these educational inequities of recognition and their constraining influences on young people's educational autonomy are broader recognition injustices that young people's families and communities are likely to experience with educational ABIs. These inequalities in educational processes reflect examples documented in Lawson's (2003) study in the US which addresses teachers' and parents' perceptions of the meanings and functions of parental involvement in children's education. His analysis revealed that teachers and parents can have different perceptions of parental involvement. In his study of schools and families in one low-income, urban community, the author suggested that parental involvement can mean different things to teachers who tend to be more 'schoolcentric' as opposed to parents who can be more 'communitycentric'. In many respects teachers' prevailing orientations towards parents suggested that they were seen as having poor parenting skills and capabilities with regards to education. This orientation contributed to a fairly systematic silencing of the strengths, struggles, and 'communitycentric' worldviews evident in the parents' explanations. The author argues that parental involvement is a limited and limiting concept in low-income ethnically concentrated communities because the notion is largely the domain of teachers within a narrow schoolcentric view. Lareau's (1987) study also in the US asks similar questions, particularly in relation to what schools ask of parents and the variations in teachers' expectations of parental involvement in elementary schooling. Their research suggests that there are a variety of factors that affected parents' participation in their children's education – parents' educational capabilities, their view of the appropriate division of labour between teachers and parents, the information they had about their children's schooling and the time, money and other material resources available in the home. Lareau argues that 'the differences in social, cultural, and economic resources between the two sets of parents help explain differences in their responses to a variety of teacher requests to participate in schooling' (p. 81). As schools tend to favour the school–family relationship model more likely to be accessed by the middle-class parents, those parents have an advantage over working-class children and parents. If schools were to promote different types of school–family relationship, maybe 'middle class' ways of doing things may not act as a 'social profit'. Middle-class relations according to Lareau are not intrinsically better; rather they are just tied more closely to the school's aims and objectives. Lareau argues that the standard of a school's expectations should be problematised as not neutral. She states that 'these results suggest that social class position and class culture become a form of cultural capital in the school setting' (p. 82) and argues that it is unfair that all schools ask the same from all parents regardless of social class and yet not all cultural resources are valued equally in contributing to this.

These broad inequities in educational process in schools in disadvantaged contexts (the third strand of the EEF) are compounded by broad inequities in geographical forms of exclusion (Sibley, 1995) that are emerging both in terms of where people live and where children and young people go to school and which more broadly, therefore, impact on the educational autonomy of young people. These forms of geographical exclusion result in children and young people who live in areas of poverty as being constructed as abject and/or considered out of place in specific contexts and in specific schools. Bauder (2002), for instance, uses the notion of cultural exclusion as a way of highlighting how young people from disadvantaged urban neighbourhoods with different reputations (based in part on the ethnic and class make-up of these neighbourhoods) are steered towards particular training and educational opportunities in education. Likewise, Gulson has suggested that particular forms of urban neighbourhood redevelopment, linked to various area based educational interventions that have focused on developing aspiration towards careers afforded by these developments, have had a debilitating effect on the educational identities of young people and communities in poorer surrounding areas. At the same time, other social groups, which possess the necessary personal resources, are able to do well out of the new situation, selling their skills for ever-increasing amounts on the labour market. Inevitably, they too congregate in certain parts of the city, contributing to an overall polarisation which is compounded by further divisions along ethnic grounds. In addition Bauder (2002) approaches the idea of educational ABIs by reference to the ideological and relational underpinnings of neighbourhood effects. He suggests that the idea of neighbourhood effects implies that the demographic context of poor neighbourhoods instils 'dysfunctional' relational norms, values and behaviours into young people, thus triggering a cycle of social pathology. In addition neighbourhood effects are part of a wider discourse of inner-city marginality that stereotypes inner-city neighbourhoods. In effect, this leads to what Bauder sees as essentialist conceptions (fixed traits that do not allow for variations among individuals or over time) of neighbourhood culture among employers, educators and other institutional officers that then further contribute to the neighbourhood effects phenomenon. These essentialising discourses are then suggestive of solutions that focus on remedying the 'problems'.

By reflecting on the relational aspects of the EEF, what the research high-lighted above suggests is how both historic and current approaches to ABIs have given very little import to inequities in educational autonomy and process that have resulted in the cultural identities, agency and viewpoints of disadvantaged young people, families and communities being essentialised and pathologised by educational professionals and policy makers, and society more generally. So what would ABIs look like if they were underpinned by relational notions of equity that enhanced young people's educational autonomy and their experiences of equitable educational processes?

As I highlighted in the EEF documented in Chapter 2 relational equity gives primacy to young people's educational identity and agency and the freedom to pursue educational processes and outcomes that they value. In that sense they reflect Sen's shift of attention away from material deprivation per se towards the freedom and ability to convert resources into valued achievements or 'function-ings' (Sen, 1999: 71) – in other words a move from issues of redistribution to ideas about recognition. As I argued in Chapter 2, Sen's (1992) equity concept of 'agency freedom' (p. 57) is key to developing this analysis. What therefore becomes important for educational policy is to recognise what it is about social relations that young people experience that influence their valued educational capabilities and agentic freedoms. As I argued in Chapter 3, the intersection of space and place with issues of class, ethnicity and gender, impact in the way disad-vantaged young people's educational capabilities and outcomes are brought into existence. In order for ABIs to recognise young people's agentic freedoms to pursue valued educational capabilities and outcomes, schools, colleges and other educational institutions need to understand in a detailed anthropological way the manner in which educational identities of young people are relationally formed and developed. This would require developing an understanding of young people's agency and in particular the placed based social networks of influence on young people's identity formations. What this means in practical terms is that schools and teachers need to engage in the development of area or placed based curricula that reach out and enable the different 'funds of knowledge' (Gonzales *et al.*, 2005) of young people and communities to be respected and utilised in schools. It is about bringing the community into schools and about developing curricular and pedagogical relationships in the classroom that give voice, choice and independence to young people (Hattam *et al.*, 2009) and their identity narra-tives (Goodson, 2008). It also about ensuring that teachers move beyond a 'pedagogy of indifference' (Lingard, 2007) in order to create appropriate bridges from young people's narratives and informal learning experiences into the codi-fied curriculum knowledge of schools and the wider experiences of life. This will enable young people to develop skills and capabilities to operate effectively and appropriately at both the global and within the local (Gruenewald and Smith, 2008; Raffo, 2006). In essence ABI educational policy needs to ensure that educational provision is aligned to meet the needs of local communities that reflect the identities and aspirations of young people from those communities. Policy, therefore, needs to engage with issues of recognition and agency so that schools move from being what Sanchez-Jankowski (2008) defines as enterprise oriented institutions delivering centralised bureaucratic educational targets that potentially misrecognise communities and young people to being neighbourhood oriented that appropriately respect those communities and give democratic voice and governance back to those communities. In many respects these suggestions reflect Barker's analysis (2010) and recommendation for overcoming disadvantage where he outlines the transformative importance of strong democratic links between schools and communities that: (a) enables teaching and learning to increase the self-esteem and self-efficacy of both parents and young people, and (b) increases the emphasis on personal growth and enhances young people's own interests, creativity and expression. The relational aspects of the EEF require that ABIs focus on educational purpose and quality that is reflected and privileged in a personal development and rights-based discourse rather than one that assumes a hegemonic human capital approach.

Given current economic difficulties, one might argue that a re-working of educational policy around the relational equity aspects of the EEF could be viewed is a cost effective way of embracing the diversity and identities of disadvantaged young people and their families within educational policy and practice. This would result in a loosening of ties with a neo-liberal educational policy agenda that views educational purpose and quality in terms of educational credentials that have little meaning in the lives of many poorer young people and their families. It would provide opportunities for the way schools 'should work with their communities, aiming to facilitate mutual relationships that develop people and create conditions that build confidence and commitment. This is how schools and teachers can enrich, improve and even transform lives' (Barker, 2010, 172).

However, although relational approaches to educational equity provide a different lens for the way ABI policies might engage with young people and their families and the type of curriculum and assessment regimes that might enhance learning and progression, what these approaches fails to recognise is how educational values, orientations, identities, agencies and capabilities are influenced by the economic conditions within which young people live. As I have documented throughout the EEF, and clearly highlighted in the empirical evidence about disadvantaged young people in Chapter 3, agency is restricted by disadvantage with, for example, aspects of educational access and aspirations/expectations limited in what young people may value. As Sen notes, agentic freedoms to pursue valued educational capabilities are important but are not real freedoms if constrained by material poverty and disadvantage. ABIs have to reflect an understanding of the way economic factors impact on the autonomy and agentic freedom of disadvantaged young people, families and communities in pursuing what they value. At the macro level, for example, ABIs needs to be aware of how increased levels of globalisation supported by neo-liberal economic policies have had deleterious impacts on many urban communities, particularly in relation to high levels of family and environmental poverty. They also need to be aware of the way that disadvantage has indirect influences on educational outcomes because of the way factors such as low levels of economic resources, inadequate housing and estate designs, noise pollution, environmental pollution and dirty living conditions, inadequate local resources and infrastructures mediate young people's identity and engagement with educational processes. The impact of these economic and environmental factors suggests the need for ABIs to, not only embrace relational justice, but to align itself at the macro level to general redistributive public policy on poverty eradication. Brady (2009), in his international comparative analysis of welfare reform, suggests that poverty eradication is most successfully brought about through focusing on the widespread improvements in welfare benefits and the structural improvements in employment and neighbourhood renewal. This is about investing in places through improved health and transport infrastructures, the development of neighbourhood employment opportunities and the re-imagining of assets in the community. It is about re-energised attempts at reducing child poverty statistics through the appropriate combination of welfare and tax reforms. It is also about ensuring that places, families and young people are not stigmatised by poverty but instead are provided with the assets and resources to help engage in civic aspects of life, including education, with dignity and pride.

Conclusion

Although ABIs might gain considerably by focusing on relational issues of educational autonomy documented in my EEF, my argument is that favouring any one particular approach over another is problematic for educational equity. What I have argued is that most groups of educationally disadvantaged young people are so positioned because they are disadvantaged both economically and culturally that is reflected in the totality of the EEF. My argument is that given the effects of socio-economic maldistribution and cultural misrecognition on poor young people, ABI educational policy cannot be informed solely by either a politics of redistribution or a politics of recognition but instead require both to operate simultaneously in order to bring about fundamental shifts in the way young people are both motivated and enabled to engage freely with education in ways that they value. ABIs therefore need to reflect all three strands of the EEF

But what are the probabilities of this happening? Rees *et al.* provide a clear rationale for why ABI policy is unlikely to engage in aspects of a more radical oriented set of interventions:

> Once social and economic disadvantage is redefined as an aspect of the wider inequalities which are characteristic of British society, then these limitations become apparent. The state is not in a position to engage with issues of social inequality, structural shifts in the organisation of economic activity and their consequences, except at the margins. The kinds of redistribution which would be necessary to do so simply do not appear on the policy agenda. ABIs and the conceptualisations of disadvantage on which they are based reflect this. They provide a means of presenting the promise of 'active

government', but within the highly restricted policy repertoire which in reality is available.

(Rees et al., 2007: 272)

Rees *et al.*'s analysis of the need for government to continually develop and re-implement ABIs reflects Fraser's perceptions that partial forms of redistribution results in the state needing to make surface reallocations again and again. And given also that much of the past and current ABI repertoire draws from a neo-liberal project – a project which protects the market and the accumulation of capital, that sees education as supporting the needs of capital and yet at the same time requires education to 'fix' the social and educational problems that the project then generates – underlying structural inequalities are unlikely to be accommodated in the policy theorising of these initiatives. Educational policy developments in England around pupil premiums may provide some additional redistribution through increased funding to schools attracting poor students, but it will not compensate for all the additional cuts and increased levels of unemployment that poorer families are likely to now experience during these difficult economic times. The limited nature of these redistributed measures are also highlighted by the fact that part of the pupil premium is likely to be funded by previous affirmative redistribution policies such as City Challenge and Educational Maintenance Allowances that are now to be cut.

Given this situation what are the likelihoods for a relational politics of recognition that focus on both broader and more specific issues of educational autonomy and process informing changes in educational ABI policies? Once again national and international educational policy rhetoric does not seem to bode well for such changes. Much of the blame in international policy discourse for educational failure does not seem to focus on the lack of a credible curriculum and/or set of appropriate credentialising strategies that recognise the choices, identity and autonomy of disadvantaged young people. Nor do policy announcements suggest new ways in which schools might engage with communities and neighbourhoods in more democratic, inclusive and relational ways. Instead the explanation focuses on the paucity of schooling in generating appropriate levels and type of educational credentials in our most disadvantaged areas and where the remedy is to be found in organisational solutions based on the practices of the free market and the workings of new managerialist approaches in particular types of academies, Free schools and charter schools.

So how would I sum up the prospects for ABIs? Clearly what I have provided in this chapter is not a particularly hopeful analysis. And yet at the same time my arguments are not just a policy scholarship critique without any positive suggestions for change. I do highlight what could or perhaps should be done and these are developed more fully in Chapter 8. However, the questions posed by my analysis ask whether policy makers really do want to respond to the EEF in its entirety and:

- give power back to schools and communities to develop educational ABIs that might engage with the choices, identities desires and autonomy of those most disadvantaged;

- side with those least well off economically and financially to enable them to access appropriately that provision and hence engage with wider societal opportunities.

In terms of what might be done, I document in the final chapter of the book examples of schools working with local authorities and their communities and neighbourhoods in ways that reflect the totality of the EEF and that show how some young people and families can benefit from education. These hard fought victories for educational equity should be supported and applauded and the initiatives and interventions that underpin them developed further. However, given much of what I said in this chapter and in previous chapters it may be difficult for these relatively minor initiatives to inform major strands of educational policy that appear to be wedded to a human capital focus on educational quality and an ameliorative notion of redistributed educational equity. One can only hope that continuing failures of such a general approach linked to detailed equity articulations documented in this book and beyond, and supported by equitable practice in particular places, may yet help the cause.

5   Leading schools to promote educational equity

Introduction

As I have documented throughout the book, one of the key and ongoing aims of much national and international educational policy is on enhancing the human capital agenda through improving the educational attainments for all children, regardless of personal circumstances and family background. To a great extent mainstream policy discourse has suggested that the removal of barriers to engagement for disadvantaged young people should enable them to participate and succeed in educational life. As I documented in the previous chapter, over the last ten years, as well as mainstream school effectiveness and improvement developments, there have been numerous educational area based initiatives (ABIs) that have attempted to support this agenda, resulting in schools being more outward looking with a focus on working with partners to provide a range of services to support children, families and communities. In addition many national and international research studies have focused on the nature and efficacy of ABIs. However, although much of this research has focused on systemic and organisational issues, little emphasis has been placed on systematically examining, categorising and synthesising the way school leaders working in disadvantaged context (many working within ABIs) view the interrelated issues of educational purpose, quality and equity (studies by Stevenson (2007) and Walker *et al.* (2009) are perhaps the exception to the rule). Given the importance of school leadership in much educational policy rhetoric for bringing about educational change and improvement (DfEE 1997, 1998, DfES 2004, 2005a, b) it seems rather strange that this is the case. What research there is appears to be both disparate and yet at the same time fork along two distinct lines of enquiry that either: (a) take for granted a somewhat vague normative understanding of educational purpose, quality and equity linked to broad notions of economic inclusion, the human capital agenda and instrumental school leadership practice; or (b) develop a social justice approach to schools and school leadership that are generally critical of current educational policy and bureaucratic forms of school leadership implied in that policy. In particular many studies in school leadership neither provide a rich understanding of what forms of purpose, quality and equity are given primacy by schools and school leaders through their school policy and practice nor how these practices are both localised and linked into the national agendas. Likewise there appears to be a lack of awareness in the literature about the leadership rationales that appear to underpin particular conceptualisation of educational equity and school leadership practice. In this chapter I aim to build on the evidence of Dean *et al.* (2007), Stevenson (2007) and Walker *et al.* (2009) to provide appropriate conceptualisations of educational leadership and then examine how these conceptualisations link to notions of educational equity documented in previous chapters – in particular how they relate to the Educational Equity Framework (EEF) developed in Chapter 2.

Rationales for school leadership and equity

Building on the educational leadership and equity research studies documented above, I intend in this section to provide three rationales for school leadership and equity in play within policy. Later in the chapter I will provide empirical evidence for how these rationales play out in the practice of school leaders and perhaps more importantly how these rationales and practice link to the EEF. The three rationales I develop in this chapter are based on work with colleagues at the University of Manchester (Dean *et al.*, 2007) and are termed delivery focused, localising and democratising.

1 Delivery focused   School leaders have their work and purposes developed to ensure the efficient and effective management of the school and public resources. They are known as transformational leaders who can build the commitment of others to the policy vision, and deliver national reform locally. They concern themselves with setting broad strategic directions and enduring the delivery of this strategy. These strategic directions are in many respects underpinned by educational policy that reflect government perspectives and rationales for education such as a focus on human capital accumulation and the redistribution of educational credentials. School leaders see the delivery of particular and policy privileged educational forms such as narrowing the gap as the sole remit of schools and their systems, structures and processes. Generally, delivery focused school leaders rarely examine in any detailed way factors beyond the school that might constrain educational engagement. In many respects these leadership rationales are underpinned by government inspection frameworks that focus on educational outcomes and with leadership effectiveness reflected in an input, process, output model and advocated by many school improvement/effectiveness literatures.

2 Localising   School leaders develop their work and purposes as being about 'making things work here'. There is some evidence of policy discourse shift currently that appears to be focusing on abandoning total control of the design and delivery of public service provision directly and instead fostering a 'new localism' which makes services more responsive to local conditions. School leaders bring to bear, therefore, their detailed knowledge of the school and its communities in ensuring that national frameworks are customised and elaborated in ways that meet local needs and priorities. Educational equity then becomes about school leaders understanding some of the cultural and economic factors impacting on the local community and hence on educational outcomes and how these might be ameliorated through particular educational practice. This practice may include working on reducing barriers to learning that emanate from outside school and that may require multi-agency work with other professionals and community organisations. The main focus however, is on enhancing local strategies to meet national human capital agendas.

3 Democratising People have become alienated from traditional democratic institutions which seem remote from their lives. A democratising rationale is, therefore, a relational form of educational justice whereby people can once again develop their agentic freedoms and autonomy to engage with decisions which affect them directly. In this case, school leaders understand their work and their purpose as stimulating opportunities for local democratic participation, and ensuring that the school is run in ways that involve and meet the wishes of local people. Educational equity is about giving recognition to and empowering young people and local people to take charge of the educational project for their own needs. It is about fostering educational autonomy, aspiration and engagement. It is also about working in transformative ways with other agencies and local economic development to improve the holistic lives of families and communities.

As I have already stated, the previous New Labour governments in England attempted to intervene in various ways to promote educational quality and equity through policies that focused on the redistribution of educational attainment by narrowing the attainment gap. Its main focus was on standards, the reform of educational structures and practices, the growth of the private sector in the design and delivery of public education, and the creation of a culture of performativity. Put simply, education systems should be made more effective through outcome measures so that particular 'standards' could be driven up in those parts of the system serving variously disadvantaged groups. If this improvement could be accompanied by other policies to address the range of barriers experienced by these groups, then there was no reason why educational equity could not be improved. The focus was on the functioning of schools generally, with extra attention paid to those serving disadvantaged urban areas and disadvantaged communities of learners. These schools were targeted with extra resources and support, they were subject to incentives and their leaders were given autonomy, encouragement and training on the assumption that, at some point, they would be able to make the breakthrough with their students. These previously disengaged, underachieving children and young people would, under the right circumstances, begin to switch on to learning, re-discover their 'will to win' and go forward to a brighter future.

In many respects this policy approach to improving schools in disadvantaged areas is suggestive of our first rationale of school leadership that has as its core rationale notions of efficiency and effectiveness and where the school with additional resources, and generally working in isolation, can make the difference through strategies of continuous improvement. Dean *et al.* (2007) have termed this *delivery leadership* and it reflects in many ways what is currently the status quo with regards to the roles and responsibilities of school leaders. Leadership in these terms is both functional and instrumental and is about ensuring effectiveness of the organisation regardless of local conditions and for ensuring that central government policy on maximising credentials and cultural integration are translated into effective and efficient local practice. The instrumental styles of leadership adopted however, may vary from heroic and transformational approaches (the school leader as hero in times of difficulty) to forms of distributed leadership where the school agenda for reform delivery is shared between role incumbents at all levels of the school. The reform agenda, however, is restricted to developing leadership and managerial systems, structures and processes within the boundaries of the school as a means of managing the operation of the quasi-market and providing improved redistribution of educational credentials.

As I highlighted in Chapter 4, other major streams of New Labour government policy on educational equity were suggestive of a more holistic distributional approach to education that reflected notions of economic and cultural inclusion and recognised the importance of the school's context. The Every Child Matters agenda, operationalised in the Children Act 2004, promised to take a broad view of the needs of children and families and to create area based integrated structures and services aimed at meeting those needs in a coherent and co-ordinated way. As I documented in Chapter 4, the example of Extended and Full Service Extended Schools (DfES 2005b), offering a range of services to children, families and communities, and acting as the base for other community agencies, seemed to offer a new model of schooling which was much less narrowly focused than its immediate predecessors and which required different forms of school leadership.

In many respects this type of schooling, that clearly links to local areas, points to leadership approaches that attempts to contextualise the work of schools in order to meet the needs of young people and the community – they are area based in their approach. Dean *et al.* have termed this *localising leadership* in that school leaders are seen as a means of ensuring that the service is fitted to the local context. Here the argument is that the delivery of education through schools cannot be left to central government because they have to be shaped to area based local conditions and the role of school leaders in such contexts is to make this happen which implies that school leaders need to know about the local context and area. This does not necessarily imply local democractic leadership but it does suggest that the way schools should be run is nested in the interplay between professionality and realities of the context. Leadership strategies may therefore include consulting with local communities. It is also likely to include working collaboratively with other professionals through multi- or inter-agency partnerships. However, although the leadership approach is localising, its primary focus is on developing localised leadership strategies for improving the performance of schooling and education as they are centrally constituted by government policy.

In other words the localising agenda is not about a commitment to supporting the agentic freedom of young people to engage in education that they value. Nor is it explicitly about an agenda that gives democratic voice to young people, families and communities in relation to the educational processes that are enacted on their behalf. Instead it is about socialising, cajoling and enabling young people to commit to a human capital agenda of enhanced educational attainments.

Other aspects of government policy, particularly with regards to citizenship, neighbourhood renewal and community empowerment are suggestive of greater relational levels of equity requiring local people to be consulted and to have a direct say over the approaches and type of public service provided at the local level. And in a sense this brings us to the localism agenda suggested by the previous Labour government's Office of Deputy Prime Minister (ODPM) and by the current coalition government policy approach. In their report for the ODPM Aspden and Birch (2005) focused on the way local government can work with service users to look at ways of improving the design and delivery of services so that they can take into account decentralised and better local decision-making, revitalised democracy and enhanced civil and community renewal. In essence their report was fundamentally interested in the extent to which local people demonstrate the agentic freedom to participate in and have, or feel they have, control over the services and environments which they value and that have a direct impact on their lives. The authors examined evidence that focused on ways of effectively working with local people, ways to improve partnership working, the different models of participation and perhaps most radically an examination of the relational impact of more direct partnership initiatives that linked to notions of capacity building, mainstreaming and maintaining representativeness. Although improved forms of consultation and sounding out of communities by local authorities were explored perhaps the examination of direct participation provided some of the strongest evidence of levels of user engagement, delivery and decision-making. What Aspden and Birch found was that:

> . . . overall satisfaction and performance levels in situations where users are delivering a service tend to be at least as high, and often higher than local authority provision . . . . There are broader community benefits from more direct user involvement, for example, Tenant Management Associations acting as a local focus for social and community development activities and successfully promoting improved security . . . . There is evidence that closer working between local authorities and users, and the latter being more actively involved in both consultation and delivery, can be positive in delivering better quality and value for money services
>
> (Aspden and Birch, 2005: 8)

They also recognised that in order to engage local people with service design and delivery there was a need for service users and other partners to develop key skills and competencies in a variety of areas including managing performance. In addition there was a requirement to enhance capacity not just at the level of the individual but also at an area and authority-wide level to ensure continuity, coverage and representation.

Aspden and Birch also suggest the need for initiatives to be mainstreamed to avoid the possibilities of sidelining opportunities. In order to achieve this there was a suggestion that users get involved at the early stages of planning and decision-making in relation to the service delivery with requirements for a coherent strategy of promoting the organisational development of service user groups/forums across a local authority. There was an additional task of enhancing representativeness so that forums and boards were appropriate and not recruited from too narrow a band of people. All of this suggests an active engagement by local people in more relational forms of school leadership that not only deal with efficiency and effectiveness issues and the need to take into account local needs but have at their core the notion of democratic renewal through relationally just user engagement in service delivery and decision-making. In many regards it represents aspects of co-production that is becoming ever more developed in the literature on public service delivery. As Stoker (2006) argues: 'local devolved institutions need to build around an often complex and layered sense of identity: we need a local government system that enables us to act in our neighbourhoods and that has the strategic capacity to frame our local response to globalization' (p. 177). This is therefore suggestive of the third school leadership rationale as a public service that has the central notion of co-production via user engagement in service delivery and decision-making. Dean *et al.* termed this *democratising leadership.*

Democratising suggests the equal valuing of local people, and in particular young people, in decisions where they are resourced and decide on all aspects of rationale, strategy and definition of what the school should offer. As Ranson (2000) argues there is evidence from 'Learning Cities' where 'the key to regeneration lies in creating the conditions for . . . reflexive and dialogic learning communities to emerge' (p. 266). In such situations school leaders may recognise that an inability to improve educational quality may only be achieved if the community democratically control the school to bring about this agenda. However, a more common manifestation might be that giving democratic control to local communities may result in the delivery of different types of educational processes and outcomes that are reflective of a personal development and rights-based agenda. These processes and outcomes may be reflective of more biographical and complex forms of leadership, or perhaps approaches to leadership that are critical of mainstream educational policy. Whatever the style adopted the rationale for this democratic approach is about issues to do with the power gap and the desire to ensure more local control over public services. It is therefore about relationally empowering disadvantaged groups to engage more fully with education and to control its direction in order to meet particular needs. This suggests a relational and communal form of leadership (Foster, 1989) and one where those working to resolve problems understand that they are not their problems alone and they may not be directly responsible for causing them. Problem posing is vital to the process of 'answering back' to the wider systemic causes of advantage and disadvantage.

The analytical tool developed so far in this chapter provides an approach for exploring various links between educational policy, equity and school leadership. At one level it asks which conceptualisations of educational equity a school and its leaders tend to favour. It then focuses on examining the leadership rationales being adopted to bring about this equity. In order to examine these rationales and approaches to school equity more carefully I now provide evidence for how school leaders working in challenging circumstance reflect and act on such issues.

Educational equity and the practice of school leaders

Evidence about how school leaders conceptualise educational purpose, quality and equity is provided through a study sponsored by the National College for School Leadership and Children Services that was undertaken by myself and colleagues at the University of Manchester (full details of the research can be found at http://www.nationalcollege.org.uk/docinfo?id=17161&filename=ecm-leading-under-pressure-full-report.pdf) and by evidence from leadership research undertaken by Stevenson (2007) and Walker *et al.* (2009). In this chapter I will outline some of the key findings from these research studies.

I start with the study that I, and colleagues at Manchester, undertook for the National College. The study adopted a qualitative case study approach to interrogate issues of leadership and the interrelated issues of educational purpose, quality and equity. A case study approach was adopted as the intention of the study was to collect data on processes occurring in schools which were best collected through interrogating a range of data sources in-depth. It was also felt that the exploratory nature of this study meant that it was most appropriate to not overly structure our research and data collection methodology, and allow different perspectives and viewpoints to emerge.

Six case studies were conducted that contained the following elements:

1   Developing accounts of leadership practices – Qualitative evidence was collected within each of the schools, based on interviews and focus groups with head teachers, students, staff, local authority officers and families. This enabled us to gain rich data on leadership practices across the organisation. As well as this group we interviewed a focus group of parents in most schools and a focus group of pupils in all schools, in order to get a fuller picture of equitable education in the sample schools. The interviews were semi-structured, to enable us to clearly focus on the key research questions while allowing sufficient flexibility for our experienced research team to react to relevant emerging data.

2   Analysing individual cases – The evidence for each school was analysed in order to determine possible links between contextual factors, leadership practices and student outcomes and experiences, using a coding system corresponding to emerging themes (Miles and Huberman 1994).

3   Cross-case analysis – a cross-site analysis of the six accounts of practice was undertaken in relation to the overall research questions. A central strategy

here was the use of 'group interpretive processes' as a means of analysing and interpreting evidence. These involved an engagement with the different perspectives of team members in ways that are intended to encourage critical reflection, collaborative learning and mutual critique (Wasser and Bresler 1996). In this way, conclusions were reached that were both valid and relevant.

It is important to stress that the six schools that were investigated were not selected on the basis of assumed good practice. Rather they were seen as instructive cases, in that the existing knowledge of the schools suggested that they were varied in terms of the nature of the communities they served, their stages of development and the styles of leadership noted. What was also known was that all these schools had an interest in and a commitment to educational equity, in whatever way it was defined by them. The districts and two schools in each district were chosen to be representative of different types of socio-economically disadvantaged contexts common in England (although the schools themselves were all located in the North West). Both primary and secondary schools were included (one each in each district), as were a variety of school types (e.g., comprehensive, faith schools, academies).

In summary, the districts had the following features:

District 1: A town with high levels of economic deprivation, 'hidden' in a large rural county that is generally well off. The population of the town is almost entirely white.

District 2: A town that has a large enclave in which families of Asian heritage live. Schools are noticeably segregated on ethnic lines and there are selective schools at the secondary stage.

District 3: An inner-city area that houses a complex and diverse population, where there are high levels of crime. There is a range of school 'choices' at the secondary stage, including faith schools and an academy. Attendance and disciplinary exclusions are areas of considerable concern.

In terms of conceptualising educational purpose, quality and equity, what became clear from the case studies was that, though all were concerned with these issues, schools and schools leaders differed substantively as to what they understood by such concepts. In particular schools' notion of educational equity was differentiated around three main concerns:

1   Improving attainment and qualifications for all social and ethnic groups.
2   Overcoming barriers to learning that exist within particular groups.
3   Enhancing other capabilities, skills and aspirations of children from disadvantaged groups.

It was clear that schools did not focus solely on any one of these three areas. Achievement and attainments in particular was a focus for all the schools, as any school neglecting this aspect would soon find itself in serious weaknesses in relation to government inspection regimes. Similarly, no school totally ignored attempts to overcome barriers to learning. However, what we did find was that schools differed in the extent to which they focused on these different aspects, with some showing a very strong orientation towards achievement and little attention to enhancing broader educational capabilities, skills and aspirations, while others saw these as almost as central as achievement. Schools focusing mainly on attainment we labelled as type I schools. Those which, in addition to a focus on attainment, took a strong interest in overcoming barriers to learning we called type II schools, while those which, in addition to attainment, were oriented towards enhancing other capacities, skills and aspirations we called type III schools. It is important to keep in mind here once again that elements of all three perspectives were present to some extent in all schools, and that the typology is therefore a matter of degree rather than one of exclusion of particular elements. It is also worth pointing out that none of the three main types were typified by schools working in similar contexts. For example, both type I and type III contained schools in ethnically homogeneous areas, as well as those that were serving heterogeneous communities. There were no significant differences between any of the schools on other intake characteristics, and all were performing well in relation to intake, with none in an 'OFSTED category' such as Notice to Improve or Special Measures.

Type I school – delivery focused rationales and instrumental narratives for educational equity

Improving attainment was a goal that was of major importance in the case study schools. An emphasis on attainment as one of the means to enhancing educational equity was not questioned. Indeed, for some schools this was clearly very much the primary goal: 'Educational equity is about learning and attainment, because that's what our job is. We're educators; we're not social services.' (Deputy head teacher). This view was at times linked to ideas about educational equity that reflected an awareness of the heterogeneity of the student intake: 'It's not about everyone doing the same thing, but about everybody being able to do what is right for them. It's about access to the curriculum, letting everybody achieve and the right to not having those opportunities taken away from them.' (Deputy head teacher). A similar view was expressed by a primary school head teacher, who saw educational equity as: 'Taking each child and doing everything possible to allow the child to gain access to a curriculum and hopefully, into society.'. Background and social problems were of course acknowledged in these schools, but, as one teacher commented: 'It's tough love, we have to say: no excuses.'. Within the school all pupils are expected to achieve, and the school is there to provide the safe and learning-oriented environment that allows them to do that. Saying this, it was clear that in the contexts of social disadvantage these schools faced there were limits to what an intensification approach around standards could achieve. In schools where the emphasis was very strongly on attainment as the means to enhancing educational equity, this dilemma was solved through staff taking actions on a problem-by-problem basis, contacting individual parents or organisations where necessary. As one head teacher said: 'Sometimes you have to intervene in the home . . . . You've got to blur your responsibility between education and the pastoral.'. These schools, however, did not have a formal policy or formal structures for conducting community work or work with parents. Although there was at times a nuanced understanding about equity, the primary focus of these schools was clearly delivery focused and strongly linked to human capital perspectives about quality. The narratives used were often instrumental with few head teachers engaging in biographical issues or linking their ideas about education to relational issues of social justice or democratic engagement.

Type II schools – localising rationales and instrumental narratives for educational equity

In other schools, while attainment remained a key goal, there was a stronger emphasis on overcoming the disadvantages the specific backgrounds of pupils presented. The educational equity leadership rationale for many head teachers in these types of schools was localising. Head teachers talked about collaboration with other agencies that intervened in health and social problems, and through work with parents to help them to develop their own skills in supporting their children. In one school, for example, a senior leader described educational equity as, 'including everyone, regardless of background, income, disability, being gifted and talented . . .' It has, she said, to: 'encompass the child's background and involve other agencies.'. Preparing parents to help their children was often a part of the approach to educational equity in these type II (localising) schools: 'There is a lot of parental involvement. The parents know how they can help right from the word go. They get a booklet in nursery how they can help, then in Reception, Year 1, Year 2 and so on. So every year they know how they can help the child and reinforce the learning at home.' (Classroom teacher). This emphasis was evident in one secondary school serving a white working-class community, which works extensively with outside agencies. There was an emphasis on catering to pupils' social, emotional and health as well as academic needs, and there was a clear identification of educational equity with the pastoral, as evidenced by the choice of interviewees presented to us. The emphasis on overcoming barriers was clear in this school: 'if they don't have their basic needs seen to, they are not going to come to lessons and learn. So we have to meet those basic needs as well.' (Head teacher). The head teacher therefore feels that with Every Child Matters: 'we win hands down. Because we've always had to do that.'. While in type I (delivery focused) schools involvement with parents and pupils' social issues was *ad hoc*, in these schools it was a key part of school policy. The standards agenda and Every Child Matters were therefore intertwined. Interviewees consistently argued that they saw their academic, social inclusion and general equity work as closely interrelated. As one middle manager put it: 'Without the social inclusion policy, the academic side of the school would fall apart.'

Type III schools – localising and cultural inclusion rationales and biographical narratives for educational equity

In type III schools educational equity was strongly linked to enhancing the cultural inclusion of young people attending the school. As well as attaining qualifications, educational equity was seen as involving a lot of work on social skills, attitudes and self-esteem: 'educational equity is about more than just attainment, it's about how they move out into the wider world and interact with others around them' (Head teacher). Cultural inclusion was therefore explicitly at the heart of what this kind of school wanted to do. In a primary school serving a predominantly Asian community, for example, a key goal was helping pupils to learn 'what it means to be a British Asian' (Inclusion manager). The head teacher defined this as: 'as a British Asian you need good results, but you also need the interpersonal skills. You need a rounded education.' This concept was linked to values by the head teacher:

> . . . if you look at the host culture being British, then there is a set of values that British people will have, there is a set of values that Asian children born in Britain will have that they take from their parents, and my philosophy is that what we have to do is integrate, one set into a common set in the middle. You pick out the best of your own culture, but you also pick out the best of British culture.
>
> (Head teacher)

In another school, social aspects are likewise emphasised:

> . . . we're talking about people leaving the school literate and numerate, but also being able to speak with people from different backgrounds and cultures and not feeling humiliated. They all leave with a confidence and high regard for themselves. I think if we do that they will hold down jobs in the community.
>
> (Head teacher)

School types and leadership strategies

These different rationales about school leadership and educational equity resulted in the use of somewhat different strategies for educational quality and equity. In type I (delivery focus) schools, the main aim was to ensure access to the curriculum and an atmosphere oriented towards learning and achievement. An illustrative quote is: 'the first thing we had to do was to create a sense of normality, of "schoolness" about the place' (SMT member). Consistency in teaching methods and behaviour policies was seen as key: 'we are trying to bring structure into their lives at school, and equal opportunities, and that means treating everyone the same' (Middle manager). In another school, attainments are emphasised throughout, and pupils spontaneously mentioned the 'work hard, play hard' motto of the school to us.

Where overcoming barriers was a major orientation of the school (type II schools), work with parents and booster classes for specific groups of children seemed to figure strongly. One school emphasised adult literacy and computer classes, in some cases with parents learning alongside their children. In another primary school, the head teacher commented that parents are illiterate in their own language. With this in mind, the school produced a DVD for parents that introduce the work of the school, explaining its overall approach and addressing the sorts of difficulties that newly arrived families may face, such as what to do if a child is ill or is likely to be absent for a sustained period. This DVD was available in five languages. In type III (localising, cultural inclusion) schools, there was a stronger emphasis on non-academic skills and enrichment alongside academic attainment. Enrichment activities focused on widening pupils' experiences were seen as key. In one primary school serving a largely Asian community, the school organised international visits, such as school trips to demonstrate traditional dancing, while staff also took the children to watch the local football team out of hours. Providing these experiences was seen as important in the light of the limited experiences that many children may have had in their home environment: 'we want to provide these experiences, which may be other children, schools can take for granted. We have to make sure that we make up for that through the type of trips and activities we organise.' (Classroom teacher). Every year group went on several trips a year, which were then linked to cross-curricular work in the school.

The main factor impacting on leadership in all these schools was the extreme pressure schools were under. In these schools, the standards and accountability agenda combined with the social disadvantage in the area meant that pressure to perform at adequate levels was unrelenting and high stakes. It also meant that schools constantly faced dilemmas, such as the tension between the standards agenda and wider notions of equity. It was noticeable that in some schools where head teachers were more localising in their leadership rationales, they shared some or many background characteristics of that community, while head teachers who came from very different professional and personal contexts (such as having previously led a middle-class school) more often employed deficit language when talking about the community and pupils. As was the case with views on educational equity and inclusion, schools had different attitudes and relationships with their communities. At one extreme there was the 'fortress model', where the school saw its role as education, and itself as a beacon to, but also standing somewhat outside, the community. 'The school here, it is really like a cathedral in the Middle Ages. For our kids it is the most impressive building and calmest environment they have seen. And that is the atmosphere we want to keep.' (Deputy head teacher). The key goal as articulated by the leadership team in this school was about not letting the 'chaos and problems of the community' spill over into the school. Other schools took a very different approach. In one school, the school was seen as having a strong role in the community: 'our role is quite varied, really, not just teachers, but sometimes social workers, adviser, so many different roles. . . . For parents, it's like their community centre, I think, not just a school.'

(Senior manager). The bond with parents, or more accurately mothers in the Asian context, was strong: 'it's like a family, I think'. The concept of the school as a family came up in quite a few of the interviews. For the head teacher, the school has a role to play in raising aspirations, but should also be the centre of the local community. 'It's got to be a place where everybody feels welcome, where everybody feels they have got a part to play in the education of the children.' These differences led to very different levels of engagement with the community and community groups. In the second school cited, which is a type III (localising cultural inclusion) school, the school works closely with community groups, such as local mosques in this predominantly Muslim community. The community appeared to take pride in the school, and parents interviewed expressed a great deal of satisfaction with it. In the first school, which is a type I (delivery focused) school, tensions were more apparent. Some community members felt and expressed at community meetings that the school excluded too many pupils, and was in that way exclusive of the community. School staff denied this, pointing to statistics showing sharply decreased exclusion rates, and claimed rumours were being spread by disgruntled members of staff of the school that it had replaced.

What is clear to see from the data highlighted above is the extent to which schools are oriented to their community is connected to their rationales re-educational equity discussed earlier. Type I (delivery focus) schools appear the least community oriented, while type III (localising cultural inclusion) schools appear most community oriented. However, it has to be pointed out that the context in which the schools worked appeared to play an important role in views on educational equity. The extent to which communities were internally coherent differed significantly between schools, and where this was the case it was inevitably easier for the school and its leadership to engage with that community than where the community was diverse and fragmented. It is important to point out here that fragmented communities were present in both ethnically homogeneous and ethnically heterogeneous areas. Parental commitment to education also differed substantially. In one school serving a homogeneous Asian community, parental involvement in the school was high, and there appeared to be evidence of parental engagement with mainstream education. This was in evidence in our meeting with parents, whose key concern was the founding of a university locally. Pupils were strongly involved in out-of-school activities organised by the school, like dance clubs, cooking clubs, football and religious activities. This was not the case in the homogeneously white school discussed above. I would describe community involvement with schooling in this area as not subscribing to what teachers and head teachers would see as being beneficial to educational attainment. There was also pathologising and deficit orientated narratives about these communities held by teachers and head teachers. Therefore, it would appear that schools' relationship to their community(ies) was influenced by both the context in which the school worked, such as community cohesion, and the values and vision of the school, in particular the rationales about educational leadership and educational equity. The exact mix of these two factors was found to largely determine any individual school's relationship with its community.

Although the study above provides an interesting array of examples of leadership rationales for educational equity what it perhaps fails to do is articulate a more coherent set of leadership values (Day *et al.*, 2000) that reflect more explicitly notions of educational equity. The work of Stevenson (2007) and Walker *et al.* (2009) focus on multi-ethnic schools and provide evidence of how head teachers can sustain a set of equity values that reflect all three rationales but with a stronger emphasis on relational justice and localising and democratic processes. In particular their work showed how school leadership for equity was demonstrated in four arenas of school activity. First was the curriculum and teaching and learning; second, the creation of inclusive organisational cultures; third, the nurturing and developing of staff; and fourth, the mobilisation of the community in support of educational goals. In each of these four domains research evidence generated by Stevenson (2007) and Walker *et al.* (2009) suggested that school leaders had the capacity to articulate their values in ways that promoted an equity agenda within multi-ethnic schools. For example, in regard to teaching and learning teachers were encouraged to develop curricula that reflected ethnic diversity and drew on the cultural background of students. In support of the creation of inclusive cultures school leaders worked hard to ensure that all ethnic groups were represented across the full range of the school's life (extra-curricular activities, student councils, governing bodies). However, according to Stevenson (2007) an absolutely key feature of these institutional cultures was the need to challenge racism and racist behaviour and to communicate a zero-tolerance attitude to all forms of racism. Stevenson (ibid.) documents how school leaders were highly effective in developing policy as operational statements of values with regard to racism and the handling of racist incidents. Student interviewees, for example, reported little racism and identified robust and well-understood policies within their schools for dealing with racist incidents. Crucially, students displayed a high degree of confidence in these procedures. They did not believe that racism would be tolerated, and when it manifested itself they had confidence the school would deal with it. This is not to assert that the schools were racism-free zones, but that the school community had confidence in the school to deal with racism and racist incidents.

With regard to the development and nurturing of staff, Stevenson's research (ibid.) suggests that school leaders often went to extra lengths to mentor and support Black and Minority Ethnic staff in order to not only advocate for individuals, but also to ensure that the ethnic profile of the school staff better reflected that of its local community. Links with the wider community were given a high priority and in the fourth domain there was also evidence that schools leaders placed considerable emphasis on developing partnerships with local community organisations and taking the school to the community, rather than expecting the community to come to the school. This was seen as particularly important in areas where language issues, for example, appeared to militate against parental engagement with the school.

Discussion

Although not representative of all schools generally, what the various research studies above demonstrate are a breadth of school leadership views about educational purpose, quality and equity and strategies for securing that equity in a variety of disadvantaged urban contexts. Where head teachers were localising in tone, in the values set for the school and in the interventions they undertook, most of these were geared towards an instrumental focus on improving educational outcomes and credentials through either enhanced delivery focused school processes or appropriate inter- or multi-agency activities to deal with barriers to learning within families and communities. It was clear that all school leaders were concerned by strand one of the EEF – the distributional inequalities of educational outcomes and experiences. Where there was a movement away from a delivery focused rationale some school leaders focused on notions of educational interventions to aid cultural inclusion that might assist marginalised students engage more successfully with a society and world as they were constituted. Once again the focus was on outcomes, but in this case on particular types of social skills and behaviours. However, there were also leadership narratives and rationales in Stevenson's and Walker *et al.*'s research that reflected the second strand of the EEF and that focused on relational and distributional educational issues that might impact on the autonomy of young people to pursue educational capabilities that they might value. The narratives in the data about barriers to learning were couched in a variety of ways that reflected discourses about barriers to succeeding in currently configured educational contexts and also about reassessing context as a way of helping to develop young people's valued educational capabilities. However, there were clearly some school leaders that focused solely on school processes. These rationales reflected Lupton and Thrupp's recent research (2012) that documented how head teachers notions of educational barriers were not part of wider distributional discourse about structural inequalities in their communities. Only some of the leadership narratives and rationales critically examined educational processes that might be silencing young people's voice and their educational trajectories. And here the focus was on school leader values that reflected notions of relational justice in the way they wanted their schools to intervene with their young people and families. However, there were also a number of school leaders that believed that educational inequalities were a result of barriers to learning that emanated from deficit families who demonstrated pathologised behaviours such as low levels of educational aspiration and poor parenting skills. Although not representative of all schools, these studies focused on schools that demonstrated an espoused commitment to notions of educational equity and therefore, one might argue, most attuned to some of the issues associated with enhancing that equity. Using critical case methodology, one might argue that if wider distributional or relational issues of justice reflected in the EEF are not attended to within all schools that are perhaps most committed to notions of educational equity, then they are even less likely to be developed within those schools that do not have such an explicitly espoused vision of educational equity and social inclusion.

Summary

The chapter examined school leadership rationales for educational purpose, quality and equity and illustrated the extent of these rationales through empirical data. Evidence suggested that school leaders ranged from a delivery focused and human capital approach to educational purpose, quality and equity to aspects of a localising, multi-agency, standards and cultural inclusion agenda and also a democratic agenda that made reference to both distributional and relational issues of equity beyond the school. Some of the narratives of equity detailed ways in which young people and their families can be marginalised or silenced through the educational processes that they experience and there were examples of how authentic educational voices might be activated and made integral to the way schools operated. In other words there was some evidence from our schools that school leaders focused on the second two strands of the EEF and in particular the process issues of equity that reflect the development of educational needs and desires of young people.

6   Educational equity and the work-related curriculum

Introduction

In the previous two chapters the book has documented various policy initiatives and school leadership rationales that have focused on combating educational inequity. While these national policy initiatives and leadership rationales have, to lesser and greater extent, received a certain amount of publicity in and around ideas of educational equity, far less attention has been given to curriculum initiatives that have attempted such a task. Much of this curriculum response in England arose out of the relaxation over the last decade of National Curriculum requirements in Years 10 and 11 (14–16 year olds). This policy of providing restricted exemption from the English National Curriculum requirements provided greater flexibility for schools to develop various curriculum initiatives to meet the differing needs of young people – particular those young people defined as being 'at risk' of gaining few educational qualifications. The purpose of this chapter is to consider the development of the work-related curriculum as one major curriculum initiative that arose from this increased flexibility. In particular the chapter focuses upon an extensive scheme entitled the Engage programme that was in a large conurbation in the North West of England to try to re-engage and re-motivate what were termed in local policy speak as 'disaffected young people' back into the mainstream curriculum.

The programme reflected distributional concerns about improving educational attainment and credentials and encouraging young people to remain in full time education and/or training post-16. Although this was the aim of the programme, what I suggest in the chapter is that within Engage, and perhaps in other such schemes, tensions exist between the distributional objectives of such policies and the simultaneous objectives of tapping into the wider socio-cultural and relational dimensions of young people's lives that influence the way they engage with such policies. One consequence of such tensions is that young people participating in such schemes may in fact become less willing to participate fully in schools' broader attainment agendas. What I will suggest is that work-related schemes such as Engage may in fact have the opposite effect to that desired in that young people are provided with a significant 'taste' of relationally just environments that go beyond school, that reflect more clearly their own valued educational capabilities and aspirations and that appear to be in contradistinction to their own experiences of school.

In developing such a perspective this chapter references ideas developed in Chapter 3 about the primacy of young people's identity and agency and those factors that appear to shape that identity and agency, including subjective dispositions created by social relations in and out of school. As such, therefore, this chapter examines how wider socio-cultural and relational factors create a culture of practice for young people that mediates their particular interactions with various significant others, including teachers, employers, family and friends, and therefore in the way they understand and interact with curriculum initiatives such as the work-related curriculum.

Engage – a work-related curriculum initiative

Engage is the name of the work-related/work based learning curriculum initiative developed by a North West Training and Enterprise Council (TEC). The specific remit of the programme, as stated by the TEC, was to cater for the differential needs of 'at risk' disadvantaged urban young people who were not getting the most out of mainstream curriculum provision. Hence at the outset the programme was developed because of distributional equity concerns over the non-participation and underachievement of young people in education and training throughout the conurbation. The project was, therefore, aimed at the 14–16 age group and in particular young people who it was felt would benefit from a programme of vocational learning that would take them out of school for part of the week. The three broad aims of the programme were:

• To increase participation in education pre-16.
• To improve achievement of recognised qualifications at 16.
• To increase participation in structured learning post-16.

The specific objectives of the programme, as stated by the TEC, were to:

• achieve National Vocational Qualification qualifications;
• increase motivation and attitudes to education;
• enhance attainment rates in GCSEs;
• increase personal effectiveness, confidence and self-esteem;
• contribute to core/key skills;
• increase standards of behaviour and attendance;
• contribute to project/assignment work in GCSEs;
• underline the relevance of the National Curriculum within the world of work;
• help increase parental support of the pupils' work in school;
• increase participation rates of young people into structured post-16 education/training and/or employment.

The programme ran in 66 schools with approximately 500 young people in Years 10 and 11 (14–16 year olds) participating. Briefing sessions were held in schools during Year 9 and young people who expressed an interest in the programme completed an application form and attended an interview during the summer term. The young people's choice of a training provider was based on the occupational area in which they wanted training and in their geographical location. Training providers had the final say on the places they allocated and they were responsible for finding the trainees a work placement with local employers. Trainees were expected to spend one day each week over the lifetime of the programme at the employers. Every 5–6 weeks, on-the-job training was replaced by a day at the training provider to carry out underpinning work. Trainees worked towards National Vocational Qualifications level 1 (an entry level occupational training qualification) units in their particular occupational choice within the following broad areas:

- Construction
- Engineering
- Manufacturing
- Transportation
- Business Administration
- Retailing and Customer services
- Hospitality and Catering
- Hair and Beauty
- Care
- Sport and Leisure.

Although at first sight this particular work-related curriculum appears to fit the stated cultural imperative of many young people from economically deprived localities – it provided them with the opportunities of gaining experience, knowledge and qualifications to enable them leave education at an early stage and to make a smoother transition into the local youth labour markets (Furlong and Biggart, 1995) – the stated equity objectives of the programme were clearly distributional and seemed to reflect a youth development perspective (Wyn and White, 1997). This perspective was about attempting to re-engage, re-motivate, and change behaviour patterns of young people in order for them to achieve within the mainstream system. As Wyn and White (ibid.) have noted, a youth development perspective has the unfortunate tendency of providing a rationale for the notion of mainstream, a majority of around 80 per cent who are on the same footing and categorising the other 20 per cent as needing remedial/special/alternative measures to re-engage them back into the mainstream.

> The young people who do not conform to the standards of this mainstream are identified as those at risk, requiring specific attention to bring them into line with the mainstream.
>
> (Wyn and White, 1997: 51–52)

Because this perspective is based on the socio-psychological concept of homogeneous age development, it fails to address wider relational and socio-cultural dimensions. Arguments documented in Chapter 3 and other youth research (Raffo and Reeves, 2000; Hodkinson *et al.*, 1996; Cohen and Ainley, 2000) would suggest that it is precisely the interaction of relational socio-cultural experiences that result in young people, at any given age, acquiring significantly different forms of practical knowledge and understanding which manifest themselves in different responses to various contextual experiences. Hence, what the implementation of work-related curriculum initiatives such as Engage appear to fail to do is to examine:

> . . . how and what and where people actually learn, in families, through friendships, in peer groups; they [are] not looking at the local situated knowledge that is acquired and transmitted through those settings, or at the kinds of identity work this entails.
>
> (Cohen and Ainley, 2000: 92)

In contrast, my approach adopted for examining how young people interact with programmes such as Engage was guided by a need to draw out the valued educational capabilities/outcomes and situated knowledge of young people that were informed by authentic social relations that make up their lifeworld. As I documented in Chapter 3, by understanding how various situated and placed based networks to which young people belong influence their norms, values, outlooks, aspirations and actions, theorisations are then better placed to appreciate the nuances that young people demonstrate in their interactions with programmes such as Engage.

Methodological issues concerning the study of young people and their experiences of the Engage programme

To achieve the aim of examining the wider socio-cultural dimensions that impact on the identity and agency of young people our research team was inspired by the methods adopted by Hodkinson *et al.* (1996) in their study of training credits. From the outset we wanted to ensure that our approach focused on the holistic experiences of young people as they moved through the two year programme and not just on specific components that were to do solely with the educational systems and mechanisms for implementing Engage. We followed this route because we wanted to examine in detail the various factors that might impact on the agency and motivation of individual young people and hence the way they viewed and experienced Engage and school more generally. In essence we wanted to be sensitive to the notion of learning as a form of cultural practice for these young people. Thus we gave primacy to the way these young people understood Engage in the context of their wider relational socio-cultural lives and experiences. Hence, we attempted to examine some of the various localised networks that made up young people's lifeworlds in order to explore how these networks created meaning for them in the context of Engage and transition. As part of this research, we examined an individual young person's potential access to intellectual, symbolic and material resources within these networks and the levels of congruence and dissonance among and between each.

We started this process by the structured questioning of 110 young people early in Year 10 about their general perceptions and experiences of Engage. This was followed by a number of focus groups, with between eight and ten young people in them, to develop themes that were emerging from the structured interviews. This data guided the development of our aide-memoires for our in-depth case studies. These cases were undertaken via a detailed 18 month longitudinal shadowing and interviewing of ten young people (with different occupational interests and atypical cases, e.g. female on a construction placement) in their placement, back at school, with friends and also through interviews with parents and other relevant stakeholders involved with that individual in the project. This approach to our research and analysis allowed us to explore more deeply the various influences on young people's attitude to Engage and schooling. Interviews were semi-structured and tape-recorded. Each researcher took responsibility for the whole network that belonged to that individual young person – his/her teachers, parents/guardians, training providers, employers and so on.

Following Hodkinson's lead our analysis was at three levels:

> We began by examining each stakeholder perspective separately. Secondly we took each trainee as the centre of a network and built up his or her [school/ Engage/family] story through a mixture of stakeholder perceptions. Analysis was done through repeated listening to tapes, to tease out harmonies and dissonances within and between perceptions. Thirdly we focused on specific issues raised by both types of story and by relevant literature, and synthesised these elements heuristically into a more comprehensive, theoretically rich picture . . .
>
> (Hodkinson *et al.*, 1996)

Although I might have shared thematic analyses of the data about how the programme impacted in general ways on the educational autonomy and agency of the various young people what I feel is more important in the context of this book and its focus is to provide in-depth narratives that pertain to the holistic experiences of educational equity for young people. For the purpose of this chapter I provide one particular case – the story of Daniel.

Moving the research focus from narrow distributional outcomes to a wider examination of agency, identity and autonomy

As I indicated earlier the official TEC policy objectives for the Engage programme were about developing a work-related curriculum experience that might enhance pupil motivation in order to then improve the distributional outcomes and experiences of behaviour and attendance, GCSE performance while in school, and staying on rates either into training or further education after school. However, as I have already indicated above, the research data strongly suggests that any attempt to create a causal link between various curriculum strategies and policy aims and improved distributional educational outcomes: (a) takes for granted the notion of motivational transfer from one educational setting to another which is highly debatable, (b) does not in any way theorise fully individual student agency, autonomy and motivation, and finally (c) does not examine the type of influences, norms and values that may reinforce or constrain that autonomy and agency. Active life choices made, and everyday tasks resolved, by young people are a consequence of an *individual* practical knowledge (both direct and mediated) and understanding of circumstances that are *situated* and *created* within *localised networks of influence.* What this suggests is that, based on the process of developing trustworthy reciprocal social relations within localised networks of influence, young people are provided with an opportunity to gain information, observe, ape and then confirm decisions and actions with significant others and peers that reflect localised cultures. Thus everyday implicit, informal and individual practical knowledge and understanding is created through interaction, dialogue, action and reflection on action within individualised and situated social contexts (Lave and Wenger, 1992; Seely Brown, Collins and Duguid, 1989; Suchman, 1987). It is this active, subjective practical knowledge, created through the situated social contexts of these constellations of people, that then enable individuals to develop autonomy and demonstrate agentic freedom to solve some of their everyday tasks and, at the same time, facilitate their development of competence, self-confidence, self-esteem and identity and what they value educationally. And in this sense my perspective can be aligned clearly to Cohen and Ainley (2000) who set out what they feel should be the main research focus for examining school/curriculum interventions on young people:

> How some young people learn to culturally labour more productively than others, why some are more able than others to turn their cultural labour into realisable forms of cultural capital, how this relates to social capital formation and peer networks thus becomes the heart of new youth policy research agenda.
>
> (Cohen and Ainley, 2000: 92)

Hence our specific research agenda for Engage became one of ascertaining how the policy aims and implementation strategies of the programme reflected young people's own individualised narratives or aspirations that arose from identity work linked to informal and formal learning as a form of cultural practice in localised and situated network contexts in urban settings. As I documented in Chapter 3, it is the combination self-interest/rational choice and the structuring influences of various individualised social networks that are comprised of school, family, friends (cf. Bourdieu's notion of 'habitus'), and work placement relations, which in themselves are structured by local cultures and the macro-social issues of gender, ethnicity and class, that provides the context for understanding agency, autonomy and motivation in relation to Engage. Before developing this analysis further I now describe in some detail the case of Daniel. Through an exploration of his experiences over the 18 month programme I attempt to develop further my theorisations of educational processes of engagement and distributional and relational impacts on autonomy that reflects ideas about learning and engagement as a form of cultural practice.

Daniel's story

Daniel is one of the ten qualitative in-depth cases that I and my research team followed over an 18 month period during the research. During that time we interviewed Daniel in his work placement setting, at school and then in college on a number of occasions. We also spoke to his teachers in school and college, his parents and his tutors from the training providers and employers. In keeping with our approach to the study we attempted to gain both a holistic and yet developing and changing understanding of Daniel as he experienced his educational and vocational provision.

In trying to make sense of the data generated, and in order to tell Daniel's story, it became apparent that a central component in our understanding was his notion of an evolving adult identity linked to his own cultural and ethical value system that was emerging out of a complex set of relationships with peers, teachers, and tutors on placement and his family and place of residence. What I attempt to do is to tell this story.

Daniel is a 15-year-old boy who at the time of the study transferred to a further education college from a special school for children with learning and behaviour difficulties. He was completing a one year course of 'Vocational Choices'. During this period, and as part of his Engage programme, Daniel spent a day a week on a work placement at a local council (entitled Millport for the purposes of this book) in its gardens and landscape works department with his mentor, Andy. He had previously been placed with another horticulture training provider (entitled placement 1 for the purposes of this book) which only lasted a few weeks.

It is clear from the outset that Daniel does not always enjoy school life.

Daniel: I do like school but I just get depressed you know. One week I'm happy, one week I'm depressed . . .

Interviewer: So what triggers that?

Daniel: It's really like in lessons, PE it gets me down. We have it two lessons a week. I heard them telling that they're gonna cut it down or something. We would have been having it now . . .

We also hear that he struggles with maths in school and that this also gets him down. In addition his peer network at school is problematic for him. He has few friends and if anything he sees himself as different to them and outside of their sphere of influence.

In contrast to his experiences of school and his problematic peer network, his experiences of the Engage programme at Millport Council and the more adult environment at college seem to fit his school-to-work aspirations and capabilities and also his emerging sense of an adult identity.

> I mean I have got bad temper problems but I've not had them since I've been here [the college] because the kids are different you see . . . cos they're dead adult here aren't they . . . being in a more grown-up environment it don't cause any problems.
>
> (Daniel)

> I'd rather be out of school and doing this all week [Engage placement] 'cos they like me being there and like they treat you dead good you know and that, they like respect you. The guys are like a bit rough and ready if you know what I mean but like they're quite fun to be with.
>
> (Daniel)

But why did the experience at Millport become so important for him? In all the interviews with, and transcripts produced on, Daniel it is clear that the Engage experience is central to his emerging views about what he values and his autonomy in engaging with those valued capabilities. His parents acknowledge this and he is particularly fearful of any incidences that might jeopardise his participation. His fear is based on the potential loss of what he sees are very important relationships that he has developed during his placement and that have enabled him to become embedded in a network of adults, develop a new sense of himself, have confidence to learn, and take advantage of an environment that provides a more appropriate learning context.

> I like Millport Council. I like it a lot because you just learn loads and I get on with all the blokes. I've seen all the managers and that and they've said when I leave school they might be able to get me a job like or something . . . I'd rather be out of school and doing this all week, 'cos they like me being there and like they treat you dead good, you know and that. They like respect you.
>
> (Daniel)

He constantly describes Millport Council as a place with masses of potential for learning:

> I'd rather go to Millport Council because I learn a lot more there. Here's a lot more things to do.
>
> (Daniel)

I've learned loads of things. I've learned block paving, like and I've just learned holes. I've learned how to flag, I've learned how to make cement and do it. I've learned how to prune trees back.

(Daniel)

In many respects, however, it is the pedagogy that Daniel experiences that allows him to 'learn loads of things', a pedagogy that reflects close contact and evolving bonds and the fact that various workers and supervisors take him through the different procedures step-by-step.

And the reason for why he has these close contacts with others at the council is because of the ever-developing trust they have in his attitude and approach to the placement and to them. Common phrases about Daniel included 'fits in', 'works hard', 'has the right attitude', 'happy to help him', 'doesn't hold us back', 'he's like one of us', 'would give him a job'.

Daniel is an exceptionally good lad, everyone likes him. I've no problems with him.

(Dave)

On Thursdays he's part and parcel of [the] workforce. He's one of Andy's gang. We've no problems with that whatsoever. He's an integrated part. All of the lads know 'im because this is the mess-room, as well as my office, for some work groups. So he meets not just David and whoever's working with him. He meets all the others. He knows all the others and they know Daniel. He gets in with all the banter and everything else that goes on. He's probably learning things he shouldn't be learning but that's the way it goes.

(Paul)

Yeah it's a very good scheme for kids to get an idea of what the working environment is. We can find it a bind if their attitude's not as good as Daniel's then they're a pain in the butt. You're chasing after them. We're not a teaching environment. The men here are earning bonus so they don't want to be dragging round after him so when we get someone like Daniel who doesn't do that, that's great for us. When we get the other end of the scale when they are a pain then it's no good to you because I'd have the men coming to me saying "this chap is affecting my bonus" and I can't blame 'em for doing that. With Daniel I don't have to do that. He works with Dave on landscape on various other jobs. It's working sound as a pound.

(Andy)

And it is quite clear from the research that Daniel, crucially, gets on with his colleagues at Millport. They have become significant in the life of Daniel and this is due, in no small measure, to the relational care, support, protectiveness and attention that he feels he has received from his work colleagues.

The paternal instinct always comes out and the men look to him but other than that he's just part of the workforce.

(Dave)

I mean I don't treat him as a kid but I'm always aware that I don't treat him as a child. It's like I said "if you can't manage it, you tell me". Even if I have to stand back and watch him. I don't go with him to the toilet but I make sure that he doesn't go to a place where he could get lost, wander off. As a child he wouldn't be allowed to go. At night when I drop him off at the main gate for his parents, if they're not there I wait till they turn up. If they don't turn up I stay with him because in this day and age you don't know who's about do you? Except for that, no because I mean he doesn't come across as a child.

(Andy)

In essence the supportive and protective approaches that colleagues take towards Daniel allow him to be more trusting in others and therefore to take more risks with things that he has, in the past, felt were his weakness, for example maths. It also provides him with the foundations on which to be more open and communicative with others even to the point of him pointing out mistakes in work carried out by his 'master' colleagues.

When it comes to the maths they'll show you how to do it 'cos like if anybody mentions maths I just like go stiff, I just get panicked but last week we were in the bottom of Vernon Park making room for some shrubs 'cause the architect drew it out and we had to like mark it and everything. I just went helping like and he didn't let me measure it because I told him I'm not good at maths. They wouldn't let a student do it just in case they made a mistake. It wouldn't be wise would it? There's this guy who's quite clever and he were measuring and I said "will you show me how you're doing it?". And he showed me and I thought he explained it better than the teachers really, although I wouldn't tell them that.

(Daniel)

And all of this relationship building, growing confidence, and the learning of new skills and knowledge has clearly impacted on how Daniel sees his school-to-work transition – planning ahead, thinking through his options, pleased that his boss at Millport has mentioned the possibility of a longer term placement. He asked his colleagues at Millport how they ended up working for the council and whether they had been to college. He respects their greater experience. He takes them seriously and they take him seriously. Pedagogical equity are reflected in the relationships that underpin the way they work together

I was havin' a word with all the fellas to see how it was they'd done it. There's a fella that's gone to Withingshawe College for gardening at Leaton Park. I were just asking how their thoughts were you know towards it because it's good if you can ask them, see how they went about it. They've got jobs with the council now. I'd like to work for the council. I know it's not always the case but I'm in it now so they know my face like for the future 'cos they've taught me what they know and they know what I'm capable and what I'm not capable of.

(Daniel)

In summary, Daniel has developed strong and effective relationships with colleagues on his work placement – relationships that are typified by high levels of trust, support and respect and which have resulted in growing levels of self-confidence, the learning of new skills, an emerging transition identity and a clear contrast to things that he did not enjoy at school, particularly his peer network.

So how do we interpret the case given some of the theoretical issues high-lighted earlier in this chapter and in chapters 2 and 3?

Applying the EEF to Daniel's story

I highlighted earlier the importance of cultural practice and localised networks of social relations as a way of theorising the contextual identity and agency of young people. Daniel's story clearly provides evidence of the importance of these factors. It demonstrate at the micro level the extent to which Daniel developed valued educational capabilities and outcomes through being embedded and then rewarded (materially and symbolically) for being part of a mutually reinforcing, complementary and trustworthy network of social relations. In addition the extent to which agency and autonomy was enhanced for Daniel can also be understood by the extent to which, at the meso level, he was positioned in those networks to acquire 'rich information' from particular 'non-redundant' (Granovetter, 1973) individuals/groups of individuals in those networks. In addition, at the macro level, it was also about the extent to which he was posi-tioned to enjoy material privilege that might be then bestowed upon Daniel because of his embeddedness in those networks. Without this multi-level analysis there was every danger of focusing on one particular aspect of autonomy and agency for Daniel without appreciating how other, wider issues at different levels of analysis might then influence the depth and effectiveness of his engagement. Hence the analysis of the data generated at one level might, for example, suggest that Daniel had become part of an effective work placement where he had devel-oped strong trust relationship and opportunities to learn informally and socially and therefore had developed valued educational capabilities to maximum effect. However, if we examine the data a little more fully at various other levels of analysis the extent of the autonomy for Daniel to chose and achieve particular valued educational capabilities and outcomes might not be quite what it seems. The nature of his position in the Engage network, the extent to which that network had something new to impart to Daniel, the complementarity of that network to other networks to which he belonged and trusted and the extent to which that network was then in a position to provide access to all the important resources for identity and transition aspirations may all have supported his agency and autonomy. Together they make up the broader and more specific factors that impact on his autonomy and agency to pursue an emerging set of valued educational capabilities. So how might we make sense of Daniel's story using the EEF?

In developing an understanding of how issues of equity inform an understanding of Daniel's evolving autonomy and agency, there is a need to explore how this autonomy and agency has been freed to engage with evolving valued educational capabilities. In many respects this agentic freedom is supported by what I have observed in other research settings (Raffo and Reeves, 2000) that is suggestive of the need for individual young persons to create equitable relationships within networks of trust and respect. In the case of Daniel we see that he developed very important trust and obligation relations during his Engage placement, relations that enabled him to become fully embedded in that network and that also freed him to develop a new sense of identity and agency. Because of the shared values and norms he has with colleagues at Millport Council, there is a sense in which Daniel has developed a compatibility with others resulting in forms of cultural practice that are manifested in particular forms of engagement and learning. Based on this emerging notion of mutuality, obligation and trust, we start to see how Daniel begins to pursue certain clear transition objectives via his work placement network that Daniel clearly values. But how do broader issues of equity impact on Daniel's ability to develop his choices in and around these emerging valued capabilities? At one level this is about the extent to which Daniel's autonomy develops in ways that enable him to gain 'information rich' resources, particularly in relation to his emerging school-to-work transition hopes of gaining an apprenticeship with Millport Council. This means examining the patterning of his ties at the meso neighbourhood level. At this level of analysis, I adopt Granovetter's description of 'the strength of weak ties' (Granovetter, 1973). Granovetter argued that access to new information is obtained through an individual's weak ties to sets of relations that are different from his/her own. For Daniel, his work placement set of relations can be classified as different or 'weak' because it is new and has the potential of being information rich since it is not based on strong localised and familiar bonds where opportunities of acquiring new information may be limited. He is confident that being 'in it now' and having his face seen and approved provides him with the autonomy and freedom to get an apprenticeship with the council. Colleagues are information rich because they know what is required to get onto an apprenticeship – a level of information that he could not have dreamt of acquiring through his school, peer and family groups that can be classified as strong and yet closed. And because he is appropriately embedded and accepted within this group and also clearly understands the vernacular of the work placement and its value system he is able to develop an educational identity and agency that furnishes him with what is culturally and socially required. The group provides Daniel with new information and new channels and links into potentially fruitful work opportunities. In addition the value of any weak tie is a function of that tie's trustworthiness and authenticity.

For Daniel, there is a clear sense in which strong trust has developed within this weak tie network at Millport – trust that provides the appropriate foundations for Daniel to take risks and attempt to obtain valuable scarce resources such as information, skills, and a work/transition identity. In summary, Daniels equitable positioning within this broader weak tie group complements the analysis of some of the more specific equitable educational processes experienced via the placement. But what do broader macro level distribution and relational analyses suggest for his agentic freedom to pursue these school-to-work transitions?

Based on the EEF, a macro level analysis requires an examination of the macro-social regimes that either enable or constrain the extent to which young people may forge ties with others, how those ties manifest themselves, and the distribution of resources that is then pertinent to that individual. Hence for Daniel, there is a need to examine what external social, cultural and economic forces resulted in Millport Council existing in the first instance and the extent to which it is well placed to access continuing or enhanced levels of resources in the future to assist with Daniel's emerging aspirations. The data suggests that Daniel has entered a domain where a working-class apprenticeships model based on time serving for the council still pervades. At the same time, however, Daniel is pursuing work/training opportunities at Millport Council that are potentially part of a bygone era – an era where local councils employed many more workers and where those types of jobs would be for life. The political value system of today and the economic realities of the area render such activity systems ever more redundant with continuing cutbacks in local council services. The opportunities that inhere to Daniel's network of colleagues are limited in the future by the fact that, at a macro-social level, this form of work organisation is no longer in the ascendancy. For Daniel this results in aspirations being unfulfilled in the longer term by the lack of a permanent work opportunity. Hence although our analysis of Daniel's emerging educational identity at the micro and meso level appeared to be strong, his ultimate aspirations in the final analysis are thwarted because of the reduced distributional opportunities at the macro level.

Other examples

In this chapter I have described how the particular configuration of social relations and values systems pertaining to a particular example of a work-related curriculum project have combined to simultaneously enhance and constrain Daniel's freedom to engage with valued educational capabilities. These have been exemplified by: (a) major levels of pedagogical and relational equity derived from his experiences at Millport Council in terms of identity work, cultural labour, autonomy and informal learning, (b) little involvement with, and hence influence from, previous school peer groups, and (c) ultimate frustrations in his aspirations becoming a reality at the distributional macro level.

However, this particular case is not representative of all other cases studied in the research. Each individual has his/her own particular notions of autonomy and configuration of valued educational capabilities and outcomes that emerge from particular networks, influences and sites for informal learning and forms of cultural practice. We have Rachel, for example, whose Engage placement provides little compatibility with her own valued educational capabilities, where school is categorised as the antithesis to her own informal networks of support and learning, that include family and friends, and where future aspirations are likely to be protracted and precarious given the lack of distributional opportunities that are currently pertaining to her experiences. Anthony's experiences demonstrate that, on the face of it at least, the distributional rationale for Engage can hold true. He has been re-motivated to succeed in school because of his experiences of Engage. However, a deeper analysis suggests that this new-found enthusiasm for school is instrumental and the result of a timely merging of wider socio-cultural factors. We see, for example, that after a rather uninspiring start to his Engage experience (that was reflected in his own views about his approach to school and life more generally), he gradually developed the type of rapport, trust and obligation relationships with his work placement colleagues that enabled him to develop a work identity and forms of cultural practice that resulted in significant levels of workplace success and ensuing desire to continue in motor vehicle maintenance, post school. He developed a new and important set of valued educational capabilities. His levels of engagement and learning within the educational processes of the work placement linked more broadly to distributional opportunities offered by the company suggested that there was every indication that a Modern Apprenticeship was about to be offered to him. Anthony's contribution to and acceptance within his placement setting had met with company-wide support. This provides him with the rationale for attempting to achieve more fully at school and for him distancing himself from a peer group that had previously furnished him with a set of values and orientations that had distracted him from mainstream educational provision. In addition his parent/relatives continued to support Anthony both at school and on his placement. For Anthony, the equitable normative and cultural influences of specific relations combined to help him to develop his autonomy to pursue valued educational capabilities at his placement and in school.

Summary

What this evidence and my theorisations suggest is that schools need to be more reflective about how the wider socio-cultural lifeworlds of young people, and particularly the various social make-up of those lifeworlds, impact on the individual identity, agency and autonomy of young people. By understanding how and why informal practical knowledge, value introjections and social relations develop for young people and how these then enable particular valued educational capabilities to be developed and enhanced, schools may be better placed to develop curricula and support systems linked to distributional opportunities that really meet young people's needs as opposed to attempting to re-engage them in standardised mainstream provision. In many respects this is what authentic personalised learning might mean – not the functional imperatives of an education system that derive from human capital imperatives of the time but instead an enriching and engaging curriculum and pedagogical experience based on mutual respect, recognition and relational equity. In that sense it is not the work-related curriculum per se that influences the engagement of young people with leaning but instead a student-centred approach that appreciates the agentic freedom and autonomy of young people to develop educational capabilities and outcomes that they value. The power of such arrangements comes about when the distribution of resources (e.g. valued work opportunities) is aligned with forms of relational justice that young people experience through non-judgemental, cultural and socially appropriate engagements with significant others. Taken together with resources that open opportunities that are then supported by social relations that make these opportunities believable and achievable are ultimately what provide an equitable approach to education. In the next chapter I examine a vocational educational project that attempted to deal with both distributional and relational issues for those young people most disadvantaged by the educational system.

7 A vocational education programme based on notions of equity

Introduction

This chapter reports on a small-scale curriculum project that I, with colleagues from the University of Manchester and with partners from across the city of 'Melville' in the North West of England developed in response to the educational disengagement of some of our young people most disadvantaged. It was a vocational education programme with a strong mentoring component that aimed to provide opportunities for creating valued educational capabilities for a group of young people (16–19 year olds) that linked to labour market opportunities reflected in emerging economic developments in the city.

In undertaking the development and implementation of this programme we, as a team, were aware of many factors that were having a negative educational impact on many young people in the city. These included:

- a lack of clear school-to-work trajectories;
- the absence of appropriately networked, labour market aware and yet culturally sensitive 'role models' within young people's localised communities;
- the personally debilitating effects of economic deprivation;
- the experience of school curricula and pedagogical approaches that were alienating and appeared irrelevant for many urban young people.

We developed an intervention programme that attempted to respond, in some small way, to some of the documented distributional and relational factors that I highlight in Chapter 3 and that were influencing young people's educational agency.

Before examining the project in any detail, I will summarise briefly the socio-economic context that our young people were experiencing in the city of Melville. In so doing I will refer back to some of the theoretical ideas developed earlier in the book.

Context: Post-industrial Melville and the challenges for disadvantaged young people

The changes in the social and economic structures of the urban landscape of Melville has seen a long-term trajectory of structural change associated with a transition from 'industrial' to 'de-industrial' and then 'post-industrial'. This has been characterised by a physical reorganisation of the city, with a shift from production and manufacturing to consumption and the service sector (O'Connor and Wynne, 1996; Zukin, 1996) and the apparent development of an information society (Zukin, 1991; Bell, 1973). At one end of the growth in the consumption and service sector spectrum are changes that have given rise to the development of design-led, information rich companies working within a new 'flexible' organisation of production (Harvey, 1989; Lash and Urry 1994). At the other end of the spectrum, however, there has also been a growth in potentially low skill service sector jobs often associated with employment in hospitality, catering, and IT clerical work. Businesses in the city operating within the first two environments depend on the generation and exploitation of new knowledge and new working methods; successful firms in these environments are R&D and innovation intensive, constantly redesigning business organisation to create the flexibility required to accommodate this. Business in the latter end of the service sector environment are competing on price and rely on cheap, flexible and efficiently used resources, including labour resources.

Reflecting both these developments, the labour market in Melville has been characterised at one level by flexibility of conditions of employment – including the growth in part-time working, non-standard employment and employment in smaller work units – and at another level the increased demand for technical skills, cultural knowledge, knowledge generation and information processing skills, collectively referred to as flexible specialisation. Both these changes to the labour market have, however, meant that for working-class 16 year olds in the city, traditional whole-scale transition into manufacturing jobs (Willis, 1977) is no longer an option.

In essence, disadvantaged young people in Mellville are facing a changing labour market scenario and a changing social context. At the same time that high-paying industrial jobs have disappeared, urban neighbourhoods in and around the city have also lost a central aspect of their identity: their affiliation with the production of a product (Aronowitz and Giroux, 1985). This has been replaced by a diffused, flexible labour market – both in terms of conditions and in skills – with, at one level, increased levels of unemployment and temporary employment and at another, the need to develop cultural capital (Bourdieu, 1986), knowledge and information processing skills, and social skills associated with working in post-Fordist business organisations. For many neighbourhoods and communities in the city this has resulted in what I described in Chapter 3 as distributional marginality that is reflected in increased unemployment and increased social instability and life insecurity; a disconnection from macro-economic trends where communities are not linked into major service sector growth of the city; isolation and stigmatisation of particular poor and excluded communities in the city; a dissolution of 'place' with concomitant reduction in feelings of home and relative security; a loss of hinterland including kin, cliques, trade unions and the church and social fragmentation. For many of our most disadvantaged young people this has meant a decline in traditional transition to adulthood trajectories. Instead they feel ever more responsible for navigating these complex trajectories. And as I outlined in Chapter 3, they do so by utilising a personal agency that arises from localised norms, values and practical everyday informal knowledge that are reflected in the networked social relations to which they belong and that in themselves also reflect the interplay of macro, meso and micro socio-economic and cultural factors of the city.

So for our young people in Melville, the scarce resource of practical and reliable everyday knowledge, such as the development of contacts and information channels for gaining local work, are in many respects conferred on the individual through the embeddedness of social relations in local networks in particular places. However, these are often mediated by the intersection of localised gender, ethnic and social class characteristics that limit opportunities to acquire material and symbolic resources required for post-Fordist employment and life-style options. Using Granovetter's notion of the 'strength of weak ties' (1973) developed in the previous chapter, I am suggesting that disadvantaged young people in Melville require opportunities to link into networks of social relations and powerful knowledge that go beyond the immediate locality and hence their immediate experiences. These ties are classified as weak because they stand in contrast to strong ties that are exemplified by strong bonds with family and friends in a locality. It is the type of tie one may have with a work colleague or a friend of a friend and is usually predicated by a lack of deep knowledge about that individual or what he/she knows. However, their strength in that access to new information can be obtained through an individual's ties to network nodes at a distance from their own local network. Local networks by their very nature can be constraining, as often they do not provide the potential for an individual to be best placed to obtain information about new developments – particularly work opportunities within emerging economic sectors. Hence it is 'weak ties' that may provide young people with pathways for learning and development that go beyond the structuring influence of locality, class, gender and ethnicity. At the same time however, what I noted in previous chapters is that young people will only access these weak tie networks if the social relations that underpin them reflect their cultural and social imperatives, resonate with educational capabilities and outcomes that they value and are just and dignified. It therefore requires an appropriate bridging mechanism to move them from having their lifeworlds recognised and respected to having those lifeworlds challenged and developed. At the same time it also requires the appropriate redistribution of resources to enable them to access these new experiences.

Programme funding and ethos

This project was funded via the European Social Fund EMPLOYMENT Youthstart programme. The programme was designed to support the development of innovative projects for accessing and then progressing disadvantaged and marginlised 16–19 year olds into further training and employment. This funding stream, therefore, allowed us to create a VET programme that was based on a model of mentoring that was designed to be both cultural sensitive and yet engaging for young people. At the same time it provided resources to enable young people to access experiences that were beyond their normal everyday lives. The project was aimed at opening up aspirations for these young people by creating authentic 'weak ties' (Granovetter, 1973), via appropriate community-based mentoring, into new and emerging business sectors associated with the creative and cultural industries[1] – industries that have become synonymous with growth in Melville's economy. The main innovative emphasis of the programme was, however, the development and implementation of our mentoring model.

The underlying philosophy in relation to mentors

In essence the role of mentors on the programme was to develop relationally just relationships with young people in order to provide the foundations for then extending opportunities into new creative/cultural industry networks. The learning and development that would then ensue was premised on notions of situated learning (Engeström, 1987; Lave and Wenger, 1992; Seely Brown *et al.*, 1989; Suchman, 1987) and Soviet activity theorists (Leont'ev, 1978; Vygotsky, 1978), where the 'apprentice' young person would work legitimately at the periphery of the work setting (cf. Lave and Wenger's notion of legitimate peripheral participation) and who would, with time, have the opportunity of moving into more core activities. The mentor was, therefore, to provide a culturally sensitive link into these new environments and provide opportunities for the young people to acquire appropriate technical and social skills required to work in the sector. During the placement the mentor would provide cognitive support through modelled behaviour and appropriate guidance and teaching. Evidence from studies carried out by situated learning theorists suggest that authentic learning in the workplace in many respects provides the most complete and deep understanding of the social and technical skills required to effectively operate in the workplace and that the enculturation process that takes place there provides the individual 'apprentice' with a vehicle for understanding the 'tools' of work within those settings (Seely Brown *et al.*, 1989). Building on these theories, our mentoring model (Raffo and Hall, 1999) had three broadly sequential stages or phases to it:[2]

1 Weak ties, liminality, risk and learning to survive In essence this phase of the mentoring would be ongoing. It was concerned with dealing with the insecurities and uncertainties of young people having to undergo, as a central difficulty, transition into an unfamiliar and uncertain post-industrial landscape – ties into various networks of social relations that are fundamentally different to those they have experienced previously. The mentor, at this point, acts as critical and knowledgeable friend. She takes the role of confidante and adviser and provides the type of guidance and support often missing for disadvantaged young people. The mentor acts as Turner's 'appropriate and aware adult guidance' (1967), appropriately impacting on the agency and identities of young people through the development of appropriate supporting, caring and equal relationships. These, in essence, provide an initial confidence for young people to start to deal with both a new liminal state and evolving and enhanced social networks. This ongoing activity then links to the next two sections in that the implicit and reflective learning that then takes place in the work setting results in diminished levels of support and guidance as the young person starts to become more autonomous and engaged.

2 Situated learning and the implicit and informal learning of flexible skills   This second phase suggests that young people will naturally learn by being part of a legitimate community of expert participation (Lave and Wenger, 1992), a 'zone of proximal development' (Vygotsky, 1978) and part of an embedded network of social actors (Raffo, O'Connor and Lovatt, 1996). By observing and aping their mentors and by solving problems with scaffolded guidance (Bruner, 1966) from mentors, they start to develop their own informal theory. In essence, and in line with the theory of social constructivism, they engage with what is around them using their current perceptions of that experience to then further their own practical understanding of living in a changing Melville. As importantly it provides them with an opportunity of working authentically in a positive setting that enables progression and development. The implications for the mentor and the work setting are therefore important and require that what the young person is offered does in fact allow for legitimate participation, even though at the start this might be peripheral in terms of what they produce and how they produce it (Lave and Wenger, 1992). It should also allow for young people to be given a 'voice' about how they understand their participation within that community.

3 Cognitive mentoring, the reflective practitioner and the engaged young person   This occurs later in the programme and commences the process of using powerful codified knowledge, where the expert mentor feels it is appropriate, as a trigger to enhance and develop the young person's informal theory. As Sixsmith and Simco (1997) suggest, this does not replace practitioner knowledge and advice but allows an additional trigger to aid self-reflection. It is at this stage that the young person becomes more autonomous as his/her repertoire expands, thus enabling the young person to deal more successfully with new or emerging problems and contexts. It is also at this point that social skills of the young person develop to a point where he/she is able to feel more confident about working more centrally in the work setting. These developments provide opportunities for reflective cognitive links to be made between familiar and unfamiliar work situations thereby enhancing the skills flexibility of young people as they deal with these situations.

What I have described is a multifaceted model of mentoring that we used as the basis for our project. However, to make this relational model of mentoring a reality we needed to think carefully about the distribution of resources that would aid young people's access and engagement. Part of this involved drawing down resources that local youth agencies could provide by involving them in both the development and the implementation of the programme.

The development of the programme

The partners in the development of the programme included the following anonymised agencies:

- Melville Youth Service;
- MEWCAT – a local further education college;
- The Well-being Film Association (WFA) – a community-based co-operative film and video production and training centre;
- Mew Sip Youth College – a 'virtual' college in the centre of Melville acting as an umbrella organisation for local initiatives working with disaffected and economically disadvantaged young people;
- A charitable housing and shelter organisation for young people with an educational dimension to their work;
- A national charitable housing and shelter organisation for young people;
- The Careers Agency – careers advice and information;
- Melville School Non-Attendance Project – voluntary sector project.

All those involved in the development of the programme were clear that the programme needed to feed into the lives and interests of young people and that at the same time the programme should also develop technical and social skills that reflected a high-skills growth sector of the local economy. In many respects the way we developed the programme reflected many of the issues/concerns highlighted by Stokes and Tyler (1997). We attempted to make project planning as inclusive and as democratic as we could and the ethos and practice of project implementation evolved organically, but was clearly rooted in our shared philosophical and theoretical position on mentoring adopted at the outset.

The programme was designed to be trainee centred and have a pedagogical style that emphasised a hands-on, practical skills development approach. The assessment and accreditation system was developed also to meet the learning needs and styles of the young people on the programme and included, for example, portfolio production assessed by the Greater Melville Open College Federation (GMOCF) and the avoidance of summative tests and exams that had historically scared young people in their experiences of schooling. It was decided that the programme should be delivered in two locations. The main location was WFA, a community-based media and cultural centre that was not only involved in commercial video, film and graphics production but was also experienced in delivering VET programmes on site. The other location was a large local further education college, which would be responsible for the delivery of a number of programme modules.

The MYCAT programme had a four week induction programme followed by seven interrelated modules, each of which lasted approximately three weeks, based on a three-day working week.

MYCAT Training Curriculum

A collaborative Technology and Creative Arts programme designed
and implemented by WFA, MEWCAT, University of Manchester,
and MYCAT Mentors via the ESF EMPLOYMENT Youthstart programme

Module 1: Research Techniques, Basic Introduction
Description – A brief introduction to research and pre-production competencies for
producing Modules 3, 4, and 5
Level: Foundation GMOCF

Module 2: Graphic Design, Basic Introduction
Description: A basic introduction to graphic design techniques using traditional media
Level: Foundation GMOCF

Module 3: Desktop Publishing (DTP), Basic Introduction
Description – A basic introduction to DTP competencies using the design brief for a
poster and a flyer/pamphlet
Level: Foundation GMOCF

Module 4: Desktop Video (DTV), Basic Introduction
Description – A basic introduction to DTV competencies using a design brief for a short
2D animation or a 2D animated sequence for a video programme
Level: Foundation GMOCF

Module 5: Video Production Techniques, Basic Introduction
Description: A basic introduction to video production competencies using a design
brief for a short programme incorporating vox pops, interviewing and V/O techniques
Level: Foundation GMOCF

Module 6: Video Post-Production Techniques, Basic Introduction
Description: A basic introduction to video post-production/editing competencies using a
design brief for a short programme incorporating professional editing principles
Level: Foundation GMOCF

Module 7: Web Page Design, Basic Introduction
Description: A basic introduction to web page design with introductory use of Java and text
based and graphic inputs
Level: Foundation GMOCF

Mentoring – Mentored placements will run alongside and between modules and
wherever possible will 'dovetail' into the module experiences. Social and technical
skills will be developed via the placements

Life Skills Management – A life skills management programme will be implemented
through the modules and via the medium of drama

Figure 7.1 The MYCAT programme.

These modules were backed up by work placements with mentors. Mentors would also work at MEWCAT and WFA with a view to both supporting the young people on the programme and ensuring greater smoothness of transition between WFA, MEWCAT and the work placement setting. Most importantly within each module young people were positively encouraged and supported to work on briefs that interested them and that were located in their experiences of neighbourhoods and city. For example in the induction programme, a number of young people decided that their video project would be on Melville street life and mentors worked collaboratively with them to create work plans, video shoots, and editing and post-production finalisation. As such the emphasis in the design of the project was on delivering aspects of a place-based curriculum that was tapping into the funds of knowledge recognisable to students and the communities to which they belong. The underpinning educational approach was student-centred focusing on constructivist interventions to learning where the young people were co-researchers with mentors in problem solving and developing media-based solutions. As such the project emphasised higher order cognitive skills of analysis, synthesis and evaluation and in addition aided the development of numerous other skills such as team work and working creatively. Having developed the framework of the programme we then needed to implement it.

The implementation of the MYCAT project

Given the multi-dimensional aspect of the project, there were a whole number of issues that we encountered during the development, implementation and review of the project that I could have reported back on in this chapter, such as the challenges of developing and implementing a multi-agency project, the use of drama in the support of life skills management for young people, and overcoming the structural constraints in the lives of young people. I will make reference to some of these issues throughout the chapter, however, since the main focus of the project was on developing relationally just ways of supporting pedagogically young people within the programme, the chapter concentrates on how the mentoring worked out in practice. In order for me to do this, I will briefly describe the research tools that we used in researching the programme.

Research tools

1 Baseline data Each mentor was interviewed and asked questions in the following areas:

- How did they come to be involved in the creative/cultural industries?
- What types of skills were required for working in the sector?
- Why were the interested in becoming a mentor and what they felt mentoring was about?

2 Ongoing reviews of mentors and trainees   Trainees and mentors were observed in training session by a researcher. Informal, unstructured interviews also took place during the training days to elucidate any observations made. These occurred approximately twice within the lifespan of the project. Mentors were also asked to keep logs of the work they did with trainees during placements.

3 Exit interviews   Through a structured interview schedule, trainees and mentors were asked about their experiences of the course and particularly about the mentoring component.

The practice of mentoring on the project – the views, attitudes and experiences of mentors

This section of the chapter makes reference to both biographical information from mentors and the evidence generated through our research. I start by examining the background of what we defined as technical mentors – those mentors from the creative/cultural industries who would be responsible for supporting social and technical skills development by the young people. I examined the skills they thought were important for access and progression into the creative/cultural industries, why they decided to get involved in the project and what their guiding views were about mentoring. This was then followed by the experiences of mentoring and what mentors felt were the most important aspects of that process. I then examined the role of what was defined as the support mentor – a mentor that was brought into the project with specific experiences of youth work and who was responsible for the affective and emotional components of working with young people and, in many respects, for introducing the project to young people. Again I examined his/her background and his/her guiding principles to what he/she did which was then followed by their experiences of mentoring on the programme. The final section then embeds the reality of mentoring from both technical and support perspectives into how young people themselves experienced the mentoring in practice.

1 Background of technical mentors   Nine technical mentors, in various ways, were involved in the project. Of those nine, four stayed with the project throughout the two years. The mentors generally were self-employed in the creative/cultural arts sector, although two worked for community-based multimedia co-operative organisations. Their arts background revolved around new technologies and image production and manipulation in, for example, digital photography, video production and projections, graphic design and virtual reality developments. The age of the mentors ranged between 25 and 40 years of age, with most completing higher education undergraduate and postgraduate courses often via non-traditional routes. There was a fairly even split between men and women and there was one male black mentor.

2 What important skills did technical mentors suggest were required for working in the creative/cultural industries sector?   In developing a technical mentoring component to the programme we needed to be clear about the type of working environments that young people might meet within the sector and also the type of skills that were viewed as essential to being able to access the sector. Our mentors provided some of this data – data which was reflected in the findings of a more detailed study on the creative/cultural industries carried out by O'Connor (1999).

Both O'Connor's findings and statements from many of our mentors suggested that the social skills of working in the sector, particularly notions of confidence and tapping into appropriate networks, were vital:

> . . . it is all about confidence. If you, as a producer, have confidence in you . . . I want to make the trainees aware of the fact that it's all about confidence and reinforcing that self-confidence. Doubt just does not come into it as it holds you back.
>
> (Mentor 3)

As well as the development of social and cultural capital through networking there was also a clear notion that working in the creative/ cultural industries sector required multi-skilling and a cross-platform synthesis of skills:

> No, I wouldn't say it was any one particular skill at all. In fact it seems to me the more varied skills you have, the more likely you are to produce something original, because you are bringing in different elements focusing it on producing some form of artwork whether 3D or virtual art.
>
> (Mentor 3)

It was our intention that both the formal training environment and the curriculum and mentoring experiences would provide young people with those relevant experiences.

3 Why did mentors get involved in the project?   Many of the mentors had had some experience of working on educational programmes and particularly with young people who had not succeeded in school. In many respects mentors saw clear parallels between their own adolescent days and the present experiences of the young people on the programme. For example nearly all the mentors described having had some problems with their secondary schooling:

> I think when I was at school I was a bit of a slow learner at times. I was not really interested in school and I was not very good at it either and I think that put me at a quite a disadvantaged position; feeling very under-confident and like not feeling very good about myself. Only since doing my MA have I felt good about myself.
>
> (Mentor 4)

> . . . throughout most of my secondary school education I was in the lower classes for a lot of stuff. From the age of primary school right up to sort of

probably about 16. I really didn't have great self-esteem about my education knowledge. Even though I was quite bright I didn't fit in with their way education should work.

(Mentor 6)

These generally poor experiences of education provided the mentors with some way of empathising with what the young people on the programme thought about their own experiences of education. For mentors, therefore, the reality of an inadequate education and a lack of an opportunity to succeed provided them with both a stimulus for getting involved and also conferred an ethos of what they wanted to create through their mentoring role.

4 What were the technical mentors' background experiences, views and philosophies that guided their understanding of mentoring?   Most of the mentors wanted young people to get on, to develop a self-awareness, to be able to stand proud and communicate effectively who they were and what they could do. They also wanted them to get involved in real projects and in real work:

I think in some ways . . . it is not so much in the skills, the experience of skills, because I honestly think they are taught and you can pick these up . . . it is not about brainwashing them. It is more that they feel that they are people who you genuinely want to see get on; for no other reason than to see them get on. I think if you do that then you are going to attract young people across the board. It's about saying . . . "it is part of your own experience and your self-awareness of who you are and if you are comfortable with that and you know what you are getting from the experience, and that there is no hidden agenda in there and that you are taking other people for who they are", then it tends to go okay. I think I would personally be happy that they got out of it would really be social skills to be honest and confidence. A lot of them that come in, you know . . . I have seen Lee and a couple of the kids that have come in and . . . they are very insular. They might have lots of friends, they are very loud outside in their own environment but take them into another one and they are very shy. They are quite happy when they are with a group, because they have got that group to support them. We have all been in gangs of friends because you feel most secure in that environment. Take them out of that and they are very insecure. When you strip down all their barriers around them, then there is themselves who feel they have got very little, they have not got the educational background maybe. They have problems. They are very quiet on their own, they don't have maybe their real identity. They have shared that with so many other people, so I think to put them with people they have never met before of their own age, maybe from different areas, different experiences; they are coming into a place like this where there is lots of people about, there is all sorts going on, you know they were quite happy that someone from MTV was doing a video right now, who loves to talk to them so it was all that and they could see where other people work. I mean for me if I had just come here at that age I would never have known anything like this existed at all, I would not have known anything about this video. It has just opened a whole door and it is really allowing them to experience I think other avenues, other things in life, other experiences rather than maybe going to school having a joint, having a drink, bunking off school, girlfriends, boyfriends, family. There are other things out of the very important structure that they are in right now. So it is really social skills if they pick skills on the computer that is brilliant and I think they are going to do that anyway. I have got no problems with them doing that, you know it does not come down to their sort of level of education, it is just common sense and most of them have got that. They wouldn't survive where they are without it, so I have got no problems with that. I think they are going to get more from that actual social interaction from a lot of other people and for me that is the main point of doing this project. [It] is that they gain confidence in themselves and hopefully they are going to think about things a little bit differently, maybe go to college. Why not? You know it is not that far-reaching for them, maybe not but at least they have experienced something else in life, they might keep links with some of their mentors, with some of the people they meet here. For me that is valuable. I think all young people need that.

(Mentor 5)

In addition mentors wanted more for young people than the confining prescriptions that class-based structures seemed to create in terms of expectations and aspirations. Mentors talked about mentors in their own lives that provided ties into other experiences, ties that would enhance opportunities for developing 'other' forms of capability for themselves and which enabled them to be in the position they were now in.

Coming back to the young people, all through school they are trained to work for somebody and now, having contact with them, I want them to know they are not destined to work at Tesco's. I want them to look at other more creative things and look at their own creative aspects and culture. [For me] it was Rosemary, a colleague of mine. When I was at a women's meeting, Rosemary happened to be working there as a volunteer then, she was actually a writer and she was doing watercolours and was a social worker. I couldn't believe she was doing all this stuff. She actually started talking to me about Australian artists and an exhibition that was coming over here. She asked me if I wanted to go, it was Aboriginal paintings. So I went and she started talking about art over there and how she was getting involved over here. I just found her the most fascinating women I had ever met. My normal conversations were like "are you going to the pub tonight?" or "who's your boyfriend?", no one ever asked my opinion about anything. I was only seventeen at the time, so for anyone to ask my opinion about anything was unknown and when she asked me to go to the gallery, because I had never been to one before, so I spent a lot of time with Rosemary. We started to go to plays and things, so she was a big influence on me. It wasn't that I wanted to be like her. I respected her. She was an independent woman. I thought she's thirty and not married, she's happy and all the things she's done. So yes, Rosemary, and also I think at the time my mother had died, so at seventeen I was on my own, so maybe that is what it was. I made that almost maternal link with her and still do in some ways. I suppose for the want of a better word she was like my mentor, she helped a lot in my development.

(Mentor 5)

There was also a clear notion that part of the mentoring role was not only about developing social skills but also about getting young people to appreciate all the different aspects of putting together a piece of creative/cultural work. This would provide them with a multi-dimensional understanding of working within the field:

Interviewer: Are there any sort of particular skills or ideas that you share with the trainees that you might think would help the trainee in the future?

Mentor 4:   I think I could show them about organisation and showing them why it is important not just telling them and about how ideas can be put into practice.

Interviewer: What sort of learning do you think you would be aiming for or the project could be aiming for?

Mentor 4:   I see the trainee being able to . . . from A to Z how to put a project on like all aspects of it. Like the idea has already been invented but say, going out to the river, positioning projectors, trying it out on the river at different points, see what works, different images . . . to technical things like finding out where to get power points and waterproofing cables, to marketing things about how do you get publicity and working with the H2000 environment you know, take them to the offices to get a sense of what they do.

Interviewer: Sort of getting a whole sense of all the different aspects of cultural work.

These background perceptions on mentoring were not too dissimilar to our own model highlighted above and with appropriately grounded training, mentors made clear links between their own views and perceptions and the sequential stages in the model.

5 The reality of technical mentoring on the programme   It is clear that the views and philosophies about mentoring linked to the grounded training programme played an important part in the way mentors approached their work with young people, particularly in the time spent developing trusting relationships that were the basis to the first stage in our model. Time and effort was dedicated to what might be termed as anthropological work – trying to get to know young people as individuals, to find out what interested them and then to support them appropriately. It was very much about relationship building. In many cases the role initially was much more one of supporting them personally and in providing some form of continuity for them:

> I think it provided "continuity" for the trainees especially when modules were being run at different sites. I think it was also useful in encouraging, supporting trainees to attend, get in on time, link up with each other.
>
> (Mentor 9)

Some mentors were more involved than others in the project. Where mentors were involved with young people during the induction period, and then at MEWCAT and WFA and on external projects, there was a clear notion that they were effectively working with trainees. For example they had provided the young people with opportunities for achievable skills development that were appropriately structured, and that linked clearly into the interest of young people. For those mentors less involved in the mentoring process, the rapport developed along more traditional lines, with a clear distinction being made between trainee and mentor and with a more detached style of interaction. Trust relationships were not developed in the same way and there was clearly a less authentic feel to the way mentors worked with their trainees. In addition the 'message' being delivered by these latter mentors on how certain skills were important for the creative/cultural business sector was less readily accepted and internalised by the young people. For those mentors in the early part of the programme that had invested time in developing effective social relations, advice given to young people seemed to be more readily accepted. For example, one of the young people took up further training in the creative arts after the course had finished because the advice given by the mentor was trusted and had been internalised as a realistic option for that individual.

In many respects, although the technical skills development was important, most of the mentors suggested that their supportive work as a significant other in the lives of the young people was even more important. They felt that the technical skills part of their mentoring would look after itself, as long as the young person had developed a confidence and trust in working with them. It was also this aspect of their work that provided them with the greatest sense of fulfilment. However, the negative aspect to this was that, in developing a deep interest in the individual young person, there was a risk that mentors would become emotionally involved in the external lives of young people in a way that was not sustainable in the longer term. It was because of this issue that we recruited a support mentor who had had experience of working in this capacity. In addition we decided to also include a life skills management through drama component to the programme that allowed young people to role-play and express their feelings about various issues that were impacting on their everyday lives.

In terms of technical skills mentoring, most of this was done at WFA and in reality we only touched on the third part of the cognitive mentoring model highlighted above. We decided that, given the importance of known stable environments, for developing confidence and trust relationships, to include further aspects of mentoring experience away from the security of WFA would overly complicate the issue, create instability and potentially result in problems with attendance and motivation. This issue was particularly reinforced when we had problems of attendance once trainees were asked to follow some of their modules at MEWCAT. In essence what the project at its inception had underestimated was the time needed to get young people to feel confident about coming onto a course and then of developing authentic relationships with significant others in a work/educational setting that was unfamiliar to them.[3] Our technical mentors had appreciated this factor and had in some respects become more support oriented than skills oriented in their work.

6 The notion of a support mentor and the reality of support mentoring   We defined the role of support mentor as an individual who provided personal support to young people and intervened on their behalf with programme staff, family and other outside agencies as and when young people felt they needed this. This role, taken on by a single individual, was incorporated into the programme in order to minimise any potential social, emotional or cultural barriers to participation a young person may have been experiencing. This would also provide the young person with authentic opportunities for informal social learning, particularly as the support mentor would be seen by the young person as representative of his/her culture and locality and someone who could therefore effectively relate to young people.

The requirement for a support mentor arose early on in the project when it became obvious that we did not have the capability of dealing with the many issues that young people were bringing into the project from outside. It was clear that both technical mentors and trainers, although clearly wanting to develop effective and authentic one-to-one relationships with their young people, could not fully cope with all the issues confronting them. The support mentor's role became one of trying to understand some of the external forces impacting on the young person, supporting them where necessary and communicating these issues, where appropriate, to both training staff and technical mentors.

Interestingly, although the support mentor was there to provide this personal support, it soon became apparent that he was also becoming more and more interested in what the MYCAT course had to offer young people and his role was not only one of supporting young people with their personal and social issues but was also providing the practical and emotional support for the development of their technical and social skills needed for working within the creative/cultural sector.

Experiences of the young people working with technical and support mentors

There were five trainees between the ages of 16 and 19 who were enrolled on the project. Two were female and two of the young men were black.

It was clear through focused observations and discussion with trainees that working with mentors at WFA and MEWCAT had provided them with insight and skills. They talked about understanding the process of doing graphics or producing a video because mentors had helped them understand that process by demonstrating those skills via their own work. And by understanding the process, often through working on real projects with mentors, the young people had developed practical skills that they could apply themselves to their own projects. The notions of copying, aping, applying and modifying – the second stage in the mentoring model – were clearly evident and the development of these skills via authentic work settings also influenced how some of the young people then perceived taken for granted images outside of their training environment. For example, one of the trainees, when she now watches television, is continually looking at the types of camera shots that were used in the images and then reflecting on her own experiences of film production.

Working with mentors also resulted in young people starting to develop self-confidence, proving to themselves that they could learn and could develop skills – both of which had been highly problematic for most of them at the beginning of the project:

> . . . more motivated, positive, big confidence boost, like nothing can stand in my way.
>
> (Trainee 1)

> . . . everything from confidence to using equipment I've never used before.
>
> (Trainee 3)

> I've now seen that there is something I can do . . . I got a lot out of the mentor.
>
> (Trainee 4)

They were also much clearer about the types of work that could be found in the high-tech creative/cultural industries sector in Melville:

> There is such a wide range of areas whether its TV, radio, photography, funded projects, design, video editing and production. I want to do them all! It's given me a great insight as to where I want my future to go. It has put me on the path to the career I want.
>
> (Trainee 1)

> I've learned that there are jobs out there.
>
> (Trainee 4)

But in many respects the important aspect of the programme was about the way mentors related to young people and the way the young people felt authentically valued by mentors through their actions and work. This mutuality provided the young people with a confidence that they, themselves, could in fact work in these types of sectors and that they did not have to resign themselves to employment in the low skills sector:

Well I like the attitude from everyone. They really helped me, plus showed me a lot of respect and I've given them a lot back . . . talking to adults who listen to you and don't judge you because of where you live or might have a dodgy background. [They] encourage you to set your sights higher than working for Burger King.

(Trainee 3)

Martin [the support mentor] . . . he helped sort out my problems and you knew you could just ask without feeling intimidated or stupid.

(Trainee 1)

In some respects the informal comments from one trainee to a mentor about the whole project seemed to summarise how young people felt about the project. He suggested that more projects like MYCAT needed to be implemented. He also recognised that he had needed someone to point him in the right direction because he had been into petty crime and his mum had threatened to throw him out of the house. Working on this project had helped him with his relationship at home because he and his mum could talk to mentors and she could see that he was taking things seriously. More importantly he felt that he could now take himself more seriously.

Conclusion – a relationally just mentoring relationship

The project had had a clear notion of mentoring from the outset. However, the reality of implementing and monitoring the project suggested that the balance of the mentoring role needed, in the first instance, to emphasise the first stage – the supportive role – where appropriate relationships based on trust and mutual respect could be developed. These initial relationships then allowed young people to take the potential risk of attempting to learn and develop new skills. They reflected the importance for young people of being treated like an adult, respecting their viewpoints and backgrounds, understanding them as individuals. The programme was therefore about building authentic relationships linked to the notions of mutuality. In many respects these relationships created increased opportunities for young people to demonstrate agentic freedom and autonomy. This freedom and autonomy was reflected in how young people were learning practical knowledge and technical skills through new networks of social relations. Mentors had authentically created weak ties for young people into a different world of high-skills work that provided greater distributional opportunities. The result was that these young people now confidently thought that there was more to life and work than being an unskilled employee.

Although the MYCAT project was small-scale and in no way provides generalisable evidence, there may be certain messages from the project that mainstream, formal education systems could examine in order to develop more equitable educational policy and practice.

As I documented in Chapter 3, the first message that our research supports is that schools/colleges may need to appreciate more fully that young people are not passive recipients as they move through school. The evidence above suggests that the agency of young people is informed by a practical informal knowledge that is situated and developed through the authentic social relations that individuals have with significant others, often place-based and that create opportunities for agentic choice about valued educational capabilities. The problem is that schools and the staff within them, through their values, actions and curriculum structures often and, perhaps unintentionally, misrecognise and misunderstand young people's identities. To avoid this problem, evidence in this chapter suggests that schools may need to reflect carefully on the following:

- Authentic listening to the holistic lives and experiences of young people and more genuine attempts at individual and systemic relationship building – i.e. young people developing confidence in the system through developing a confidence in the relationships with representatives of that system.
- Inclusive curriculum and pedagogical style that both reflects and furthers young people's aspirations/interests and choices (e.g. opening up authentic horizons for young people by creating 'weak ties' to emerging sectors via relationships with socially and culturally sensitive technical and other mentors).
- The use of professionals who have a clear understanding of the identities and types of agency being demonstrated by young people and who can then provide non-threatening mediating facilities and personal support (personal, career based, guidance to other agencies) when required. This is about equitable relationship building with young people.

Although not intended as a panacea for all problems associated with educational disengagement, what I hope this project demonstrates is how educational policy and practice can develop more equitable ways in which professionals in schools are recruited, trained and deployed and also the way curricular initiatives are developed and then implemented. Perhaps more importantly what the project summarises are the important equitable distributional and relational aspects of curriculum and pedagogy that clearly impact on the autonomy and agency of young people to develop and then engage with valued educational capabilities.

Notes

1 The term creative/cultural industries is necessarily wide and covers such areas as non-subsidised arts, audio-visual recording, publishing, broadcasting, applied arts, design (including graphic, furniture, interior), and sites of cultural consumption such as cafes, restaurants, clubs and associated micro-fashion businesses.
2 For a more detailed explanation of how we derived our model of mentoring see Raffo and Hall (1999).
3 See Raffo and Reeves (2000) about the importance of locality in terms of security, confidence and identity for young people.

8 An educational equity toolkit

Before outlining the educational equity toolkit that is suggested by the title of this chapter I will synthesise the main arguments and evidence from the preceding chapters in the book in order to build an appropriate foundation on which to develop my toolkit.

National and international data about educational inequalities are clear about the link between poverty and educational attainment. In most internationally developed country contexts the geographical concentrations of educational disadvantage correlate almost exactly with urban areas or neighbourhoods of greatest economic disadvantage. In many countries the main policy response to such problems have been loosely located around notions of improved educational credentials (a proxy for human capital acquisition) and a narrowing of the gap in the attainment of those credentials that are then linked to commensurate levels of enhanced social mobility. The practice vehicle for such a policy response has tended to focus around a set of school effectiveness/improvement strategies that reflect some of the following ideas:

- The 'most effective' schools in challenging contexts are those with the strongest forms of educational leadership that are delivery focused and are both transformative and distributive depending on the particular stage of the improvement life cycle of the school.
- School-to-school collaborations can drive up performance, particularly when beacon schools are matched up with those schools that are less capable/ successful.
- The meticulous use of pupil achievement data can aid streaming, banding, differentiation of curriculum and goal setting that, taken together, can drive up student performance and educational outcomes.
- Inspection frameworks aid the accountability of schools and will continue to drive up school performance.
- New school organisation and governance systems, freed from the strictures of national agreements and agendas can drive up performance. These schools are best exemplified in England by academies and Free schools.
- Improved pedagogical practice based on developed notions of direct instruction, enhanced challenge and assessment for learning will improve

the educational outcomes of those students most disadvantaged and disengaged.

- School choice and educational markets will continue to drive up performance of those schools in most challenging contexts.
- The loosening of National Curriculum with more vocational choices at Key Stage 4 will help 'personalise' the curriculum for those least inclined to an academic curriculum.
- Enhanced early years education will continue to provide appropriate educational support for parents and the building blocks for disadvantaged children to engage in successful educational trajectories in the future.
- New powers to enable teachers to effectively develop and implement behaviour policies will constrain unhelpful and disruptive students and therefore improve educational attainments for the majority.
- Training of new teachers and the continuing professional development of current teachers that focuses on those technical standards highlighted above will continue to improve student attainments.

Such technical school improvement approaches have enhanced the quality of the school system as a whole as measured by particular educational outcome indicators. However, although such improvements have been made, the closing of the educational gap between the most and least advantaged groups of young people (the educational equity indicator from a human capital perspective) has not materialised. As I have articulated throughout the book, part of the reason for such equity failure is that these strategies, both separately and taken as a whole, have struggled to recognise the scope of the challenge, and hence the systemic level of resource that might be required to improve the situation, both within and beyond schools. Perhaps more worryingly, however, is that such approaches have often lacked both theoretical and empirical coherence as to how and why disadvantaged young people might or might not engage with the educational project. These approaches have generally failed to recognise that educational equity requires a strong focus on the personal educational development and rights of young people that reflect their educational autonomy and freedom to aspire to educational capabilities and outcomes that they value. In addition, these strategies have made little reference to notions of power in education and in particular how the educational project might be changed and reconfigured to facilitate more fully the articulation of an authentic voice of disadvantaged young people and their families and communities. In summary, the technical list of improvements essentially fail to engage with the symbiotic relationship between the material and relational injustices that young people experience and, in particular, how together they constrain young people's engagement with schooling practice. What I hope the book has done is provide some important philosophical argument and empirical evidence for thinking differently and more systematically/ rigorously about such things. However, what I do recognise is that school improvement strategies, if coherent, appropriately scoped and embedded in appropriate normative equity principles, can assist schools become more effective in the delivery of educational quality and equity. I develop some of these ideas later in the chapter

To recap my argument, in Chapter 2 I reviewed some of the literatures about equality, equity and justice and developed an Educational Equity Framework (EEF). This framework guided my review of some of the macro, meso and micro educational equity policy and practice developments that I have researched over the last ten years. Central to this framework have been notions of distributional and relational equity and the importance of attending to both equally if disadvantaged young people are to be given the opportunities to develop appropriate levels of autonomy in educational settings. What this meant specifically was the need to examine the distributional inequalities of educational outcomes and how they could be related to both the broader and more specific distributional and relational inequities of educational process. As I stated, knowing about distributional inequalities in educational outcome does not, in itself, provide explanations for why these inequalities occur, nor for what policy is trying to improve. In many respects the second two strands of the EEF attempted to provide answers to these questions. In developing these two strands of the framework I made reference to the central importance of young people's individual agency and autonomy in converting educational resources into valued educational capabilities and outcomes. The central concern for educational equity therefore becomes one of enabling young people to demonstrate the autonomy to aspire and then choose and pursue educational capabilities and outcomes that they value and are valued more generally in society. Central to this enabling is a fair allocation of resources. At the same time I argued that young people need to experience relational equity in their lived worlds both outside and inside schools for them to be able to symbolically, culturally and cognitively engage effectively with the material opportunities of educational provision. This means educational institutions recognising, respecting and representing what is valued culturally, socially and educationally by their young people, families and communities. It means schools, teachers and policy makers explicitly working against the way young people and their families and communities are often pathologised in morally negative ways as deficient in terms of their values, behaviours, orientations and approaches to education. It also means fighting against the way these very same disadvantaged constituents often have their voice silenced or marginalised through the educational process. It is therefore about opening up appropriate dialogues of engagement that demonstrate 'heartwork' (Hogan, 2010) by teachers and schools in the way that educational opportunities are made visible, enticing and achievable for young people. It is what Swann and her colleagues document in the remarkable story of Wroxham School where the school community attempt to create an approach to learning that is transformative and without limits for all its students (Swann *et al.*, 2012).

Based on these theorisations and conceptualisations of education and equity I then reviewed educational equity research that I, and colleagues from the University of Manchester and beyond, have been involved with over the last ten years. Based on this evidence I signalled what I considered to be a number of important insights. Firstly, as stated above, that the main policy focus in most affluent countries re- educational purpose and quality is about improved levels of human capital acquisition. Strategies for enhancing human capital acquisition have focused on raising educational outcomes across the system as a whole and by improving the distribution of such outcomes. In England, as I have noted, this has included the development of a powerful mix of target-setting, national curricula and pedagogical development, and high stakes accountability. However, the continuing distributional difficulties that schools in poor urban contexts face in improving educational outcomes for all students has resulted in these schools and their contexts being provided with additional compensatory resources – an approach that reflects what Fraser terms 'affirmative redistributional strategies' (1996). Additional funds have been provided to schools and areas through area based initiatives (ABIs) to help narrow the attainment gap between more and less disadvantaged groups of young people. Criticisms of these approaches have forked along two main lines of argument. Firstly, too much emphasis in ABI policy and practice has been placed on redistributive measures resulting in too little focus on the relational equity issues that young people, families and communities experience in their particular contexts. Secondly, the redistributive measures needed to make real improvements in the educational lives of young people in disadvantaged communities are inadequate. Funds need to go beyond schools and be more transformative of local neighbourhood infrastructures and employment opportunities. In summary ABIs, although often directed at those neighbourhoods most in need, often develop a contextual rhetoric of improvement in disadvantaged neighbourhoods that underemphasises the important cultural, social and economic factors at play in those areas. Policy makers appear to lack an understanding of how macro, meso and micro level factors intersect in disadvantaged urban locations to create structuring influences in the way young people, families and communities engage with education. In addition, my review of ABIs suggested that there was little evidence of these policies delving into issues of relational equity that reflect the funds of knowledge or assets of communities. More often than not the narratives and language of policy point to the deficits of young people and families – including, material, cultural and aspirational deficits – that need overcoming. In such discourses the educational project is not seen as the problem. It is disadvantaged young people and their families that need to change (Gewirtz, 2001). This cultural change is about young people and families becoming aspirational vis-à-vis the education system as currently constituted. To bring about this change, policies have provided additional, targeted resources to such young people and families to help them access education in ways that reflect the priorities of the system. Hence within many of the ABIs reviewed there were examples of initiatives to support 'at risk' young people engage more effectively with education in a variety of ways that included breakfast and after-school clubs and parenting classes that would provide 'correct' child rearing strategies to support young people make the most of education.

To compliment my review of educational policy strategies directed at improving educational equity I also provided examples of school leadership perspectives on educational equity. Evidence from school leaders pointed to three leadership rationales for equity. Many head teachers extolled what might be termed an instrumental, delivery focused rationale for educational equity that focused on enhanced educational attainments delivered through a school improvement/ effectiveness agenda. For other head teachers the focus was much more on a localising rationale that recognised the need to go beyond the school gates to try and reduce barriers to engagement that emanated from outside of the school. Often this approach was articulated as extended school provision that incorporated appropriate multi-agency/inter-agency working and that brought educational advice and resources to those families most in need. Examples of extended school provision included better crèche facilities, parenting classes, IT for the community, parents and children curriculum projects, opening up school facilities to the community, recruiting school governors with knowledge of neighbourhood needs and issues, etc. For a minority of head teachers, although educational attainment was central to their thinking, there was also a focus on the importance of the cultural diversity of students. In these situations school leaders recognised the potential diversity of students but at the same time stressed the importance of schools as socialising agents for minority groups to be better prepared for the different cultural landscapes of mainstream society. Taken together these equity rationales pointed to equipping young people with the right levels of educational credentials that would enable them to access mainstream jobs. In addition, there was a recognition by some head teachers that issues of disadvantage may influence their work as school leaders. These head teachers were willing to focus on issues of relational educational equity – in other words how schools might represent, respect and work with the students and the families and communities to which they belonged. A comparison of this evidence with my EEF developed in Chapter 2 would suggest that head teachers appeared to be clearly concerned by strand 1 of the framework that focuses on the distribution of educational outcomes and experiences. In contrast there were only some school leader narratives and rationales that suggested the importance of students' autonomy and engagement with valued educational capabilities.

As well as examining leadership strategies for educational equity, I was also keen to focus on curriculum development projects that aimed to meet the needs of the most disadvantaged and disengaged students. In examining curriculum design programmes for 'at risk' young people I was reminded that policy and practice perspectives and approaches in this area had a long track record of classifying disadvantaged young people as not being best placed to make the most of an academic curriculum. In making such judgements there has often been an essentialising discourse by policy makers and practitioners about the educational culture and talents of disadvantaged young people. The narrative associated with this discourse has generally focused on the merits of a vocational work-related curriculum for innately less academically capable working-class/disadvantaged students. Within such a narrative, the argument often made is that such young people would naturally thrive in more practically oriented environments and would thus be motivated to develop their educational talents more broadly. Both my evidence, and evidence about developments in the work-related curriculum more generally, have suggested that although the vocational can often provide a link into educational arenas that young people value, there is no guarantee that it will always do so. What the evidence documented in the book suggests is that the vocational experience can be valued in its own right but that perhaps what is more important is the way many vocational educational experiences are often embedded in informal, equitable and relationally just social relations between young people and their trainers/mentors/teachers. My research pointed to those successful pedagogical interventions when mentors, trainers and teachers clearly located themselves within the value system of young people and provided them with the respect to pursue their valued educational and vocational aspirations, an approach that reflects Bernstein's argument (1970) that effective pedagogy demands that the 'culture of the child must first be in the consciousness of the teacher'. However, this did not necessarily lead to a general motivational transfer to school and the school system. My research pointed perhaps to the very opposite occurring. Given the liberating and engaging experiences of a different, culturally relevant and more valued and relationally just pedagogy, many of the young people involved in work-related projects became ever more antagonistic to a traditional curriculum delivered within institutional authority and power structures that often silenced their concerns and aspirations, and labelled them as less capable. However, I also stated that a relationally just pedagogy was not sufficient in itself to bring about educational equity for young people. Young people needed to be provided with a distribution of resources that would allow an appropriately accredited outcome from this pedagogy to hook into the opportunities beyond school and in particular the evolving world of education, training and work that they valued. One might argue that educational equity for those most disadvantaged only really occurs when distributional and relational concerns work in tandem. In many respects the MYCAT project documented in Chapter 7, was a small-scale project that attempted to bring about this ideal. It did this by: (a) creating opportunities for young people to engage in a growing sector of Melville City Centre economy, and (b) developing a curriculum, pedagogy and assessment system that focused on young people's valued educational capabilities and on building just social relations with trainers and mentors. It was a curriculum that attempted to build and accredit the valued capabilities of young people by linking them into their experiences of localised place. And yet at the same time the curriculum enabled a sophisticated development of funds of knowledge and skills of these young people that went beyond the local and became pertinent to their futures in the post-industrial city of Melville and perhaps to a more globalised economy.

So what do the EEF and my summary of the book suggest for improving educational equity, particularly in disadvantaged urban contexts? How do the main messages translate into an equity toolkit that might guide policy and practice in such contexts? Let me start with the first question.

What the EEF and my review of policy and practice at various levels of analysis and in various contexts suggest is that to develop an educational system that is equitable requires a focus on the broad issues of scope, coherence and power. In terms of scope and coherence, my argument is that education policy and practice needs to examine the interpenetration of the macro, meso and micro realities of the lived experience of young people and how these factors impact on their autonomy and agentic freedom to both aspire and engage with valued educational capabilities. At the macro level I have suggested that increased levels of globalisation has had deleterious impacts on many urban communities, particularly in relation to high levels of family and environmental poverty. As I argued in previous chapters, this poverty has indirect influences on educational outcomes because of the way factors such as low levels of economic resources, inadequate housing and estate designs, noise pollution, environmental pollution and dirty living conditions, inadequate local resources and infrastructures mediate young people's identity and engagement with educational processes. The impact of these economic and environmental factors suggests the need for educational policy at the macro level to be aligned with general redistributive public policy on poverty eradication. Brady (2009), in his international comparative analysis of welfare reform, suggests that poverty eradication is most successfully brought about through focusing on the widespread improvements in welfare benefits and the structural improvements in employment and urban renewal. This therefore means that educational policy, and in particular educational ABIs, need to be more clearly integrated so that the distribution of additional educational resources is embedded into broader policies for improved housing, employment, transport and other public services as well as to welfare reforms that might reduce poverty. In other words that educational policy becomes part of a more general macro policy exercise for equity. In locating themselves in these broader equity considerations, educational policy makers and practitioners will therefore understand more fully some of the dynamics that have historically created educational disadvantage and challenge in the first instance.

Although appropriately conceptualised distributional analyses are a necessary precondition for improved educational equity they are not sufficient in their own right. What I have argued throughout is the need for policy makers to recognise that ABIs also need to focus on others aspects of the EEF, and in particular the relational justice that give primacy to the values, orientations and identities of families and communities to which young people belong. This means ensuring that places, families and young people are not stigmatised by poverty but instead are provided with the assets and resources to help engage in civic aspects of life, including education, with dignity and pride.

So what would meso school leadership rationales and narratives look like if they reflected a more comprehensive area based strategy that reflected a coherent view of educational equity documented in the EEF – one that was both distributional and relational in its recognition of young people's educational autonomy? As I argued in Chapter 5, relational notions of educational equity require educational leadership to give an authentic voice to students and their families and communities. As Smyth (2010) notes it is a leadership that builds social relations and that is based on respect, trust and care. It is also about head teachers developing schools that are flexible, student focused and supportive and that also work with the community in an inclusive way that value the full resource of the community. The narratives about educational change and improvement should move beyond a focus on managerial values and organisational systems and change approaches that reflect instrumental and utilitarian concerns about the distribution of prescribed educational outcomes and instead should be reflective of a critical leadership stance. This stance should be about questioning educational policy and its impact on school life, and about developing alternative, more relationally just approaches to educational equity. The stance should also be about being critical of taken for granted approaches to hierarchical school organisational structures and leadership approaches that are focused on delivering particular types of educational outcomes. The starting point may be about distributional educational equity but the fundamental and core component of leaderships should be about what ought to be done to generate autonomy and agentic freedom for young people that reflect more relational forms of educational experience and outcome. It is, therefore, about the head teacher understanding how the school might inform and support the valued educational capabilities of its students and provide educational processes that personalise the experience for young people in terms of their interests and capabilities. Fielding (2006) develops this form of argument and, in his attempts to radicalise debates about the personalisation of education, articulates the need for education, and particularly the management and leadership of that education, to be concerned first and foremost with the personal and relational and then to examine the functional and distributional as a way of maximising the former. He sees the personal as being manifested in fulfilling interpersonal relations, social justice and in pursuit of 'the good life'. The functional are all the resourcing, administrative, curricular, management and leadership and teaching arrangements within schools that are put into place to achieve the personal. In terms of possible actions to achieve the personal he recommends two requirements:

> [T]he first is that they have within them, individually or in combination, reference to normative structural and organisational change that insists not only on the integrity of the ends and means, but also on the actual experience of persons in community as the ultimate arbiter of their legitimacy; the second is that their advocacy of personal and interpersonal flourishing not only acknowledges and understands the persistence of power, but also sets in place arrangement that guide its egalitarian realisation.
>
> (Fielding, 2006: 8)

In articulating such a position I agree with Fielding about the need for school leadership to develop opportunities in schools for authentic student voice that might enable staff and students to work and learn in partnership; for schools to provide 'discursive and dialogic spaces' for staff, students and the wider community to discuss and develop practice; for the emergence of democratic public spaces in schools where teachers can derive mutually supportive engagement, companionship and enquiry, and to problematise the inevitability of school leadership and hierarchical systems of control, power and authority. It is a school leadership that is focused on developing a relationally just curriculum and pedagogy. But what would this sort of curriculum and pedagogy look like?

As I have argued, a micro level focus on the coherence of school curricula and pedagogy should start by reflecting on the nature of young people's educational identity and agency and the freedom to pursue educational processes and outcomes that they value and are valued. As suggested in Chapter 3, the nature of this identity and agency reflects the intersection of space and place with issues of class, ethnicity and gender and schooling. In order to develop the ability to recognise young people's autonomy and agency schools, colleges and other educational institutions need to understand in a detailed anthropological way the manner in which educational identities of young people are relationally formed and developed. In practical terms it might mean that schools and teachers need to engage in the development of area or placed based curricula that reach out and enable the different types of area expertise of young people and communities to be respected and utilised in schools. This is not without precedent in the UK and other countries and there are examples of schools, local authorities and charities working together to engage and develop this type of work. For example, the Carnegie Trust has sponsored projects and conferences dedicated to developing and delivering examples of place-based learning in the UK. The Royal Society of Arts (RSA) in England has supported the development of area based curricula where the emphasis is on the curriculum being co-owned by schools and the community that surrounds them. It is a curriculum that uses the surrounding area and its resources as a framework for its development. It takes into account a variety of views about what it is important to know, and is taught by teachers and community members together, inside school and in other locations in the local area. The RSA's work in this area suggests that area based curricula need to respond to the following challenges and questions:

1   The people involved: re-imagining who can be involved with education, and in what ways, by engaging a wider community in curriculum development.
2   The places where learning happens: re-imagining the role of a place in educating young people by establishing the whole area as a learning environment.
3   What it is important to know: re-imagining where knowledge is created and found by exploring the context of a place.

If a relational curriculum is about focusing on giving back to young people and their communities opportunities of engaging with contexts that are meaningful to their identities, then Pat Thomson (2002) speaks of the need for a commitment to a pedagogic process which creates opportunities for learning and for individuals and communities to 'answer back' through the development of critical literacies as a means of enabling them to defend and develop their localities.

And part of this pedagogy is also about ensuring that teachers move beyond a 'pedagogy of indifference' (Lingard, 2007) in order to create appropriate bridges from young people's narratives and informal learning experiences into the codified 'powerful' curriculum knowledge of schools and the wider experiences of life. This will enable young people to acquire skills and capabilities to operate effectively and appropriately at both the global and within the local (Gruenewald and Smith, 2008; Raffo, 2006).

If notions of scope and coherence provide challenges to educational policy across the world, then issues of power may be even more difficult to confront. The book has made it abundantly clear how power manifests itself in the processes of autonomy and freedom for young people. The power to invest or disinvest in urban communities, at both macro and meso levels, can have devastating consequences on the environmental, economic, social and cultural life of these communities, its families and in particular to what young people can aspire and then do. The power to make policy decisions about the levels of welfare to support the poorest of families have key ramifications for the life experiences of families and young people and the way they are able to engage with education. In addition I have argued how the power of particular educational processes can marginalise young people's autonomy, constrain their sense capability and silence their identities within schools. Throughout the book, a strong message emanates that suggests the need for a shift in the axes of educational power from national and local policy makers and professional practitioners to community representatives, families and young people that recognises hybrid forms of co-construction and co-production in teaching and learning. National policy can then provide a supporting framework for local policy makers and professionals to work alongside the community in a way that enables the development of localised practice that recognises the different needs and aspirations of diverse cohorts of young people (Smyth, 2010). Although the challenges of scope, coherence and power highlighted throughout this book are great, it is difficult to see how systemic improvements will be made in educational equity in the urban without a concerted effort from policy makers to deal with the entirety of this agenda.

And so to the second main question for this chapter; how do I take these general points about scope, coherence and power and develop a set of questions that ask teachers, head teachers, governors, and local authority and national policy makers to reflect on educational equity in the way I have documented in this book? The educational equity toolkit is therefore my next challenge.

At the outset I need to state that in developing the incipient ideas for the toolkit I am eternally grateful to a number of academic and professional colleagues currently in the field who have worked with me. At one level I am particularly grateful to Mel Ainscow, Alan Dyson and Sue Goldrick and Mel West's (2012) work on developing equitable education systems. In the final sections of their book they document a set of conditions that are central to fostering educational equity. These include:

- Schools needing to collaborate in ways that create a whole-system approach.
- Equity focused school leadership that assists in collaborative action.
- Schools being linked to wider community efforts to tackle inequities experience by children.
- National policy being formulated in ways that enable and encourage local actions.
- Moves to foster equity in education must be mirrored by efforts to develop a fairer society.

In addition I have been guided by the work of Bernard Barker and his book *The Pendulum Swings* (2010) where he documents a whole number of recommendations for reforming educational reform. In particular his qualitative strategic priorities focus on rebuilding communities; creating the conditions for worth, growth and achievement for young people; engaging school leaders and teachers; and overcoming disadvantage. My toolkit builds on these conditions by documenting specific educational equity concerns that reflect a set of interrelated questions that teachers in schools located in communities made poor, principals of the same schools, district leaders with responsibilities for schools in those districts, district leaders responsible more generally for the well-being of those communities/districts, and national educational policy makers need to answer.

At a different level I am also particularly grateful to the professional work of Patsy Hodson and Lynne Heath at Manchester Communication Academy (MCA) who have provided me with practical exemplification of my ideas about educational equity through their experiences at the academy. I use the work that they, and their colleagues, have developed at the academy as a way of demonstrating a localised 'policy enactment' (Ball *et al.*, 2012) of the educational equity toolkit.

Let me now expand a little more on my ideas about the educational equity toolkit. The toolkit is located in an ecologically nested approach that starts with micro proximal classroom experiences of young people, moves through to general experiences of everyday school policy and practice and then, at the meso level, examines ways schools relate to parents and communities. These analyses are further complemented by questions about poor places and spaces and how they impact educationally on young people and their families. At the macro level the toolkit asks questions about how those places and spaces and corresponding educational systems are a reflection of more general social, economic and cultural policy and practice. So what types of equity questions at various levels of analysis would the toolkit ask?

The educational equity toolkit

Below are listed a number of equity questions at different levels of analysis that provide the basis to the toolkit.

Micro level
The classroom

To what extent do young people's classroom experiences reflect the principles of effective pedagogy (e.g. the ten principles articulated by the Economics and Social Research Council sponsored Teaching and Learning Research Programme (James and Pollard, 2011)) and in particular those that focus on affective, social/emotional and cognitive domains that are inclusive, appropriately pitched, respectful and underpinned by an engagement with authentic student voice that is reflected in a genuine co-construction of learning?

School level

To what extent, and in what ways, are individual student's learning maximised through school organisation that is reflective of an ethos of learning without limits and ideas of transformability?

To what extent are curriculum choices made available to young people that develop aspiration and enable valued educational capabilities to be achieved?

To what extent are curriculum choices bridged into appropriately codified powerful knowledge domains that are pertinent to young people's future lives as citizens and producers?

To what extent are young people engaged in the development of school policy and practice, particularly in relation to pedagogy, curriculum and the behaviour policies of the school?

To what extent does the school utilise its resources to meet the diverse social, cultural and cognitive pedagogical needs of young people in a personalised way?

Meso level

In relation to schools and the community, to what extent are families and communities invited into schools as partners in learning?

To what extent are the interests of families and communities represented in the governance of schools?

To what extent are schools part of the asset base of communities and, in particular, how do they develop social capital for communities and engage in local enterprise that support families and local communities economically?

To what extent is collaboration between schools and between schools and other public service providers in neighbourhoods enabled that meets the holistic needs of young people and families in such neighbourhoods as they state them?

Macro level

To what extent has educational policy been formulated that enables and encourages equitable local actions?

To what extent have general welfare and taxation policies helped those families and communities who experience the greatest levels of poverty engage with education?

To what extent has both national and local government economic policy brought investment and jobs to disadvantaged communities that, together, provide a platform for young people and families' engagement with education?

An important aspect to reflect on in developing such a toolkit is that there is little expectation that schools, educational policy and economic and social policy more generally will operate at the maximal level of equity for each question/concern. In addition I recognise that certain equity indicators are more amenable to change than others, with those most proximal to young people perhaps seen as most amenable. However, the need to develop and integrate congruently all appropriate sub-systems of educational activity, both within and beyond the school, is vital to the overall improvement in educational equity in disadvantaged urban contexts. Importantly, therefore, it is the scope, coherence and power of equity questions taken together that will provide the evidence of the extent to which the education system is journeying along a continuum of equity. At the same time the equity toolkit is not the only toolkit that policy makers and practitioners will need to develop and operationalise. Although the book's focus is not specifically about school organisation and delivery toolkits or strategies, there is a clear sense that such toolkits are essential, in practical terms, for bringing about improved levels of educational equity. I would therefore argue that many school improvement/effectiveness approaches, such as those documented at the start of the chapter, might be relevant to an equity project so long as they were subsumed within the normative values of the EEF and equity toolkit. By being orientated to issues of equity these toolkits have the possibility of enabling both 'excellence' and 'effectiveness'.

Perhaps one of the most important longitudinal studies that has focused on such a systemic improvement endeavour is that provided by the Consortium on Chicago School Research (Bryk *et al.*, 2010). The Consortium collected and analysed data, visited schools and engaged in discussions with Chicago educators, policy makers, reformers and other scholars about the practical implications of the Chicago Reform Act of 1988, and in particular the way the Act took educational power from central bureaucracy and instead chose democratic localism as a lever for educational change. Beginning in 1990, the Consortium initiated an intensive study of the internal workings and external community conditions that distinguished improving elementary schools from those that failed to improve. Over a 15 year period they developed, tested and validated a framework of five essential supports – or essential technical toolkits if you like – for school improvement. These supports or toolkits included:

- Coherent instructional guidance – this toolkit provides, in general terms, the 'what' and 'how' of pedagogy in schools that teachers can individually adapt.
- Professional capacity – this toolkit reflects the school's ability to recruit and retain capable staff and also directs attention to the efficacy of performance feedback and professional development, and the social resources within a staff to work together to solve local problems.
- Strong parent–community ties – a toolkit that focuses on strengthening these ties as a multifaceted resource for improvement. The quality of these ties links directly to students' motivation and school participation and can provide a critical resource for classrooms.
- Student-centred learning climate – a toolkit to support all adults in the school community forge a climate that enables students to think of themselves as learners. At a minimum level this is about safety and order but also includes the endorsement of ambitious academic work coupled with support for each student.
- Leadership drives change – a toolkit for school leaders that helps them to engage in the dynamic interplay of instructional and inclusive-facilitative leadership.

The important finding in the research, however, was that for school improvement to occur (defined narrowly as the improved attainment of maths and English test scores) required that each one of these toolkits was proactively and positively attended to by the school and that clear integration between the toolkits was in evidence (for example, that the leadership toolkit enabled the development of student-centred learning, strong parent–community ties, improved professional capacity and enhanced coherent instructional guidance). However, the main measure of success for improved school organisation throughout the project was enhanced educational outcomes – success criteria that, although important, are secondary in relation to notions of educational equity that I have articulated. What I have argued throughout the book is that although technical school improvement toolkits are important to school development they should be consistently utilised in relation to the normative values and ethics of the EEF and equity toolkit that, when taken in its entirety, should provide the overall process aims for the educational project. Normative notions of equity, as developed in this book, therefore act as moral values and ethical foundations on which to build education systems and through which to develop appropriate and technically effective school organisation. Without these equity foundations in place what results is what, in many respects, we experience now in many education systems. A whole set of various and at times distinct and inchoate educational strategies that make little reference to issues of coherence, scope and power and have little appreciation about how issues of equity are connected to the autonomy and agency of young people and the way they engage with education.

As importantly, although the equity toolkit is directed at schools, families, communities and society more generally, it should also act as a moral and ethical compass to the way professionals work together. This suggests that there is no room for developing equitable processes and practices for young people, parents and communities that in their development are inequitable for those involved in their core production and delivery. Issues of voice, representation, recognition and democratic processes are as important for the processes of professional practice between educational stakeholders as they are in the practice of working with young people, families and communities. These processes also reflect the Chicago's Consortium's research focus on the importance of relational trust between different stakeholders involved in the educational project (Bryk *et al.*, 2010).

Let me now provide you with the case study of the MCA. The idea of the case study is not to provide a blueprint for action – each school can only develop its own localised response – or a perfectly articulated notion of educational equity as, in many respects, it does not focus on broader societal processes of injustice. What it does do, however, is provide an example of professionals, organisations, young people, families and communities attempting to work together in equitable ways to make things educationally better and fairer in their communities. In so doing, however, it points to the particularities of the school, its context and history and the key players involved in its development. In other words it is an example that reflects a particular policy enactment (Ball *et al.*, 2012) of educational equity.

Manchester Communication Academy (MCA) case study

MCA was established as one of the key educational components of the transformational agenda for education in Manchester. What MCA articulates in its strategy, mission statement and practice is a clear notion of a purposeful quality education linked into equitable educational processes and outcomes for all its students. Perhaps most importantly it understands that to achieve such processes and outcomes requires relational trust between stakeholders and a framework of essential supports/toolkits embedded in equitable micro level pedagogical and schooling processes that are complemented and supported by meso level community engagement and multi-agency and multi-school working, all of which need to be located in fairer macro level structural, economic and cultural policy. What, therefore, does educational equity look like at MCA and how is it implemented?

With regards to micro level classroom and schooling processes the principal of the academy was clear that the school needs to recognise and respond to what was deemed 'the failings of traditional curriculum offers and pedagogy'. The vision of the school was, therefore, to create a student-centred learning climate that was wherever possible adaptable, challenging and inspiring to the needs and aspirations of its student body, with a balance between the courses and qualifications offered to the students, allowing individuals to choose the opportunities that best suited them. Educational capabilities and outcomes that are valued to students and society more generally are taught and applied through areas of academic study. The focus of the curriculum, therefore, attempts to be both innovative and creative and the emphasis is on pedagogy that is varied and challenging to maximise engagement and relevance to the learner. Coherent instructional guidance focuses on curriculum design that links subjects together to promote an interdisciplinary approach to learning and the pedagogical needs of young people are met through a range of organisational interventions. These include a screening process to identify the learning needs of individuals that uses prior attainment data, reading tests, cognitive ability testing and interviews with parents – a range of data that enables students to be placed in groups that provide appropriate support and resources to enable them to make progress. However, these groupings are flexible and the nature of the learning environment, with the integrated practice of teachers, teaching assistants and technicians working together, ensures that these groupings do not become fixed labels of ability. Pedagogical interventions are geared to all abilities and reflect the learning barriers experienced in the 'here and now' so that progress can be made.

However, the senior leadership team also recognises that it is impossible to ignore the reality of judgements made about the school and its accountability to outside agencies such as the Office for Standards in Education (OFSTED). In response to these challenges the principal talks about the 'unrelenting and unapologetic focus on progress and achievement in order for students to achieve their ambitions and the need to be able to demonstrate this to OFSTED. The last thing a disadvantaged community needs is a school at its heart that is labelled "inadequate" or "requiring improvement" and it is incumbent on us to be judged as good or better in the inspection process. If we have to take account of cognitive scores to succeed then we do but we do not have them as the only indicators of success. Ultimately our goal is reflected in the words of Haim Ginnott – "When all is said and done, we want children to grow up to be decent human beings, a 'mensch', a person with compassion, commitment, and caring".' In order to facilitate this 'unrelenting focus on progress and achievement', the principal drives change in terms of pedagogy and in particular aims for a staff:student ratio of 1:20 on average however, the system of team teaching in large groups of up to 120 students means that interventions can be multiple and diverse in any one session. For example, in Science and Technology students plan their learning activities within a prescribed framework. In any two hour session an individual student will participate in a formal seminar, a small tutorial, personalised learning through the interactive subject website, witness a demonstration, take part in a practical experiment and observe their computer-aided design being manufactured in the technology lab. During this process students will encounter a whole range of staff including technicians, teaching assistants, volunteers, and teachers. In addition the structuring of the day minimises movement around the building thereby helping to promote extended learning sessions to enable research, reflection and investigation as part of the learning process.

The principal and her staff have also developed what is termed a 'blended' or 'flipped' approach to learning, which can be described as a formal education programme in which students learn at least part of the time through online delivery of content and instruction, with an element of student control over time, place, path and pace. However, a focus on teacher empathy, experience and interpersonal relationships with students also remains core component of the affective and social domain of the pedagogical approach with cognitive aspects promoted through dialogue and discursive learning. The learning climate of the school suggests that the learning of individual students is, therefore, maximised through an ethos that puts no limits on learning and achievement. Although curriculum planning is outcome focused and related to subject-specific knowledge, skills and cognitive process and capabilities, the processes by which each student is enabled to engage with those outcomes relate to issues of student recognition and representation and also the material resources required to support learning. For example, in cooking, students are given a list of ingredients that are available on the day, have access to all equipment and resources and choose what their product will look and taste like. In English the outcome may be a piece of poetry that requires the use of convention, but the subject and genre is a matter of individual choice that reflects young people's aspirations, lifeworlds and valued capabilities. Giving young people the confidence to make such decisions and the resilience to try again when things do not work out as planned is a major aspect of the learning at the academy. The curriculum also reflects strong community ties through developments in place-based topics particularly around the humanities subjects. These include the history of Monsall, developed in conjunction with community representatives and the University of Manchester and the Asset Languages route that recognises and accredits skills in community languages. In addition, Year 9 students work on a series of projects linked to product design supported by business partners such as Salford University, Manchester College, BT, LBM, HMG Paints, Mann Diesel and Vex. A group of Year 9 students have also set up their own production company called 'Bright Sparks' and have written and produced a play about the Manchester riots which was performed at Greater Manchester Police Headquarters.

Teaching and learning within school is also supported by instructional activity undertaken at home. However, the academy is mindful that the environment at home for students may not always be conducive to learning. Constrained access to technology and resources, overcrowding, noise and domestic distractions may all combine to make off site learning challenging. Therefore much of the desired off site or home learning actually still takes place within the academy buildings, before after and during the extended school day. In addition, the academy building has been designed both as a learning and community facility and it prides itself in providing a welcoming, safe and practical environment for all those who use it or work within it. It contains large open learning spaces, and uses technology to support independent learning. Social media is used as a means of connectivity with the cultural world of young people while also recognising the need for safeguarding and encouraging responsible use of mobile phones, messaging services and the Internet.

Curriculum choices available to young people at MCA are bridged into appropriately codified and powerful knowledge domains through the use of individual learning portfolios that identify and evidence the evolving educational capabilities and outcomes of individuals. The learning is validated and extended through dialogue with teaching staff and accredited through a range of systems. Students are encouraged to apply the learning and knowledge in different contexts and across different disciplines, all underpinned by an emphasis on collaborative working, interpersonal and communication skills. These so called 'soft skills' are also evidenced and accredited so that each students builds up a skills set to support their future aspiration, whether it be further or higher education, apprenticeship, employment or training routes. In engaging in such work one key policy aim of the academy is to transform the relationship between aspiration and opportunity for young people. Low aspirations have traditionally been used in schools in disadvantaged contexts as a reason for low educational and work outcomes. Young people have aspirations but, as evidence suggest, these aspirations can harden around a set of expectations that reflect limiting inequitable cultural and economic discourses that come to prevail in their lives. The academy therefore attempts to provide route maps for young people that connect aspiration to a wider set of opportunities. Part of this work is distributive and economic and includes working with employers to ensure alignment between the curriculum and the requirements of the economy, at local regional and global level. For example the academy has worked with BT, their main sponsor, to identify their criteria for recruitment of Openreach apprentices. The company is currently planning to set up a recruitment hub at the academy as part of their national programme, and the staff and students will be integral to this process. Part of the work is also relational and cultural and as such attempts to address inequitable processes of recognition and representation for MCA students. For example, to avoid processes of stigmatisation and other barriers to participation students are provided with free uniforms, free PE kit and free cookery ingredients. In addition students are also provided with free trips, heavily subsidised holidays and residential experiences, and after-school, weekend and holiday activities. A focus on democratic principles and social cohesion is delivered via its citizenship programme that brings together the various sections of the community, helping people to build relationships beyond their natural kinship groups, and building the social capital that is a key feature of thriving communities.

Democratic principles and civic engagement also underpin the way staff, student and community voice is integrated in the development of curriculum and pedagogy. For example, the Peoples Voice Media was a project developed with a local charity that trained 18 ten year olds from local primary schools as community reporters. They interviewed and filmed adults and young people in the local market, supermarket, library, colleges and in their own schools and gathered a wealth of intelligence which were used by the academy to shape their community offer. In addition the academy's interactive website and various 'talking head' cameos by local people illustrated numerous needs expressed by the community and the academy's response to them. For instance a major issue was the lack of activities for local young people and the consequent anti- social behaviour that this occasionally engendered. The response was to put in place a longer teaching day, an extensive range of after-school learning at which attendance was compulsory at least once a week, a significant holiday programme which is open to all young people in the area, and a major community programme in the evenings and weekends, involving a wide range of health related, sporting and social activities for young people and adults. This in turn necessitated an enhanced professional capacity that resulted in the change of teachers terms and conditions of employment so that support for after-school activities became contractual; the employment of support staff on 52 week contracts so that they could support holiday clubs; the appointment of a full time Community Outreach Manager and site staff to enable the extended use of facilities; and financial negotiations that produced a range of fees favourable to community groups so that they could take full advantage of facilities at minimal cost. In addition the academy has developed a toolkit that focuses on the voice of all its stakeholders, including students, parents and community. This is used to identify areas for development and the key priority is to move from just speaking to the stakeholder base to developing an active and equal dialogue[1]. However, the student voice component is still relatively underdeveloped and is in part due to the recent opening of the academy with only one year group and relatively small numbers of students currently in attendance at the school. At this early stage of implementation the academy feels it has been successful in establishing a dialogue around emotional and social areas but less so with the co-construction of the curriculum.

In terms of governance of the academy as a company the governing body is legally charged with realising the core objectives articulated in the company's memorandum and articles in addition to the traditional roles and responsibilities of a school governing body. The professional roles held by governing body members not only facilitate this dual mandate but also represent the interests of the local community and its residents. These roles currently embrace senior responsibility at a local and global level in BT, Manchester Council, Northwards Housing and Manchester College. The governing body not only evaluates the school's impact on disadvantage on the families of the community but also focus on integrating strategy between member organisations, their community strategies, their networks and experience. The governing body is relatively small and only has one parent governor but community representation is secured to a certain extent through the academy's co-sponsors. Manchester City Council is represented on the governing body by the deputy chief executive responsible for neighbourhoods. The Manchester College is also represented through a vice principal with responsibility for Employability and Adult Learning. In addition the academy has a co-opted governor who is chief executive of the biggest social housing organisation in North Manchester.

At the meso level the academy clearly has a strong focus on developing strong parent–community ties. One of the key features of the memorandum and articles of the academy as a company is the assertion that the academy will combat the impact of disadvantage in its locality, in order to gain the best opportunities for its students and their families. This, therefore, is not just a school with an emphasis on community involvement, but an organisation driven by the campaign for educational equity for young people and their families and community.

The extent to which the academy, families and the community work in partnership is determined by how collaborations can create a more equitable outcome for local stakeholders. Although the school opened its doors two years ago, the strategic vision and planning began some years before. The community development strategy is organised into nine distinct focus areas, each of which detail a vast range of targeted community activity. The focus areas are: research; global; enterprise; partner schools; adult services; preschool services; MCA facilities; MCA student attainment and MCA pastoral care. An example of how the partnerships work together is in the MCA community college. Here adults, largely from the academy's immediate community attend a number of courses throughout the day and into the evening. In an area where 53 per cent of the adult working population has no qualifications at all, this is a significant provision. LBM, a local company and contact centre is working closely with the school to offer work placements to the students' parents and family members. This is made easier by a number of factors including; greater governance and management freedom; the extensive facilities at MCA; the educational co-location of family members; the corporate social responsibility commitment of LBM and BT; the support of community partners such as Manchester Adult Education Services, North Manchester Regeneration and Jobcentre Plus and the school's capacity to lever in additional funds, in this case the Neighbourhood Learning in Deprived Communities fund.

Part of the regeneration of the area has been the building and development of MCA and in many respects the MCA facility is regarded as an asset by the community – as one community member stated: 'The academy has put the heart back into Collyhurst.' The facilities are available to the community every day of the week throughout the year. In 2011–2012 54,000 community sessions were enjoyed by individuals, over 80 per cent of whom lived in the immediate locality. In addition to the variety of activities undertaken in the school, the buildings are used for 1,000 extended school activities per week attended by MCA students. The academy also regularly hosts local, regional and national conferences, training and meetings. Currently it is the home of Manchester Football Association and the Key Stage 2 of a local primary school.

Becoming a community asset is a key part of the community development strategy and goes beyond the use of the facility to the development and implementation of a number of vibrant community projects. The list below indicates the investment of the academy into its community:

- BfL: Behaviour for Life is a programme to encourage the development of vital 'soft skills' essential for successful and happy lives.
- BT Legacy Project: A software solution to ensure a legacy from the Paralympic movement for young people in Manchester with disabilities.
- EarlyBird: A drive to support young people to gain appropriate qualifications as early as possible.
- MCA Cinema: The opportunity to watch film together in state-of-the-art facilities.
- MCA Community College: Adult learning opportunities offered by MCA and Manchester Adult Education Services (MAES).
- MCA minischool: Preschool learning opportunities for 0–4 year olds.

- MCA Restaurant: Themed dining events with live music performances.
- MCA Theatre: Performances and workshops including a project based on the Augusto Boal – Theatre of the Oppressed model.
- North Manchester Business School: An enterprise centre offering business incubators to young people with good business propositions in North Manchester.
- Once Upon a Time: A limited company established to gather, document, celebrate and share memories using a multimedia approach. There are already 500 members.
- Project 10: A multi-agency research project conducted by a new company of professionals seeking a better understanding of disadvantage.
- Scene@MCA: MCA facilities.
- Schools Out There: A national forum of schools working together on community development.
- The Brainhouse Academy: A working partnership with a school in one of the largest slums in Nairobi.
- The Urban Crew: A citizenship project in collaboration with Northwards Housing and partner primary schools, culminating in the ASDAN Key Steps Award for 100 pupils each year.

However important the process of becoming a community asset has been, there has been an ongoing attempt by the staff at the academy to also recognise the assets already present in the area. Initially there was pressure to adopt a deficit approach to community involvement and to attempt to develop solutions to well-rehearsed problems. The advantages of excellent resources, a greater degree of autonomy, strategic support, and a staff team chosen for shared values and vision has made it easier to see the possibilities and strengths of the community of which the school is already an integral part.

Collaboration between schools and between other public sector providers in the neighbourhood that meets the holistic needs of young people and families in such neighbourhoods is perhaps best exemplified by Project 10 which is a genuine example of provision beyond the academy, but driven by it. It involves work with a range of other services and organisations in order to understand and address community needs more fully. In particular, it works very closely with the local authority regeneration team. The academy has taken a lead in setting up a social enterprise as a limited company. The company has three directors, each from a different partner organisation. The wider group of partners effectively forms an executive committee and together they agree on and monitor the company's activities at a strategic level. The company's activities are undertaken by an operational working group, made up of those partners who are best placed to take action in the local community. The partner organisations all contribute resources in-kind by committing time to the company's activities. The fact that the company is an independent entity that is not owned by any one service provider or organisation, is seen as important in ensuring that area issues, rather than particular service agendas, drive its actions. It also allows the company to secure funds and commission activities in its own right when its activities extend beyond its 'in-kind capacity'.

In order to develop an advocacy role in its local area and to inform its future activities, the new company is currently undertaking research and consultation in its local community. This involves exploring different perceptions about what is good about living in the area, what local people would like to change about the area, and what it might be possible to do. Eleven of the company's partner organisations are actively involved in the research: the academy, the local further education college, the police, the area's social housing provider, Sure Start, Jobcentre Plus, the local church, the local tenants' association, members of a local community-led oral history project, the primary care trust's school health adviser, and the local authority adult education service. Each has committed to undertake five interviews with families in the area with whom they already have established relationships.

At the macro level, the educational policy of the local authority of Manchester, in conjunction with national educational policy incentives, has resulted in the Manchester Model of academies. The city identified the economic growth sectors in Manchester and then looked at key corporate players who could help to generate wealth for the city. In addition they looked at the deprivation statistics and the areas of low educational attainment and widened their search for potential partners to include those organisations with a strong corporate social responsibility agenda. Based on this work the authority recruited six organisations, all of which were new to the world of academy sponsorship, to act as lead sponsors for the programme. These organisations are: BT, the NHS, Laing O'Rourke, The Cooperative, Manchester Airport and Manchester College. The council also nominated themselves as a co-sponsor for each of the academies and were able to lever in government funding through the Building Schools for the Future programme to provide the required capital investment.

This model brings together public and private academy sponsorship and has sent a clear message about the purposes of the new academies – they are not just about education but about community engagement and regeneration. The governance models within the academies also reflect this commitment to mitigate the impact of deprivation, and to make the academies the hub of their communities. There is a genuine attempt by local government to bring investment to disadvantaged communities and provide a platform for young people to engage with education. However, this citywide approach has not been sustained and much of the impetus to achieve this transformational change has been left to individual academies and their sponsors and partners. However, the role of MCA and other academies have had a major role in providing stability in what are often chaotic circumstances. The scale of current welfare reforms and the cuts in public spending which have desta-bilised inner-city communities will inevitably impact on young people, who require continuity of care and provision in their lives. Increasingly MCA have found them-selves in demand as partners by a number of local welfare organisations in an attempt to launch a joint offensive on poverty in the area.

Some of these partnerships have proved particularly beneficial, such as that with MAES which led to the development of our community college. The college has now enrolled over 400 adult learners in the last 18 months onto award-bearing courses that reflect the demands of the local labour market. In addition, there has been additional funding to support short-term courses aimed at increasing the confidence and skills of adults in the workplace.

The picture of equitable educational approaches developed by MCA and partners is one that focuses on both broad and specific educational processes that might engage young people, their families and communities in things that they value and that are valued. It is a story about pedagogy and curriculum, partnerships and ethos, scope and coherence in a school's attempt to deal with complex economic, cultural and organisational issues. Perhaps a central component in making this programme of activities happen is the development in the professional capacity of school and in particular the way MCA staff have been recruited and supported in their work. At interview stage prospective candidates are asked the same questions which expose their equity value set. Once in post, staff's commitment to such values is reinforced by the schools performance management system that requires all staff to evidence how they have demonstrated core equity values in their work. In addition, terms and conditions of employment require all staff to commit to community involvement through the provision of after-school and holiday clubs, and in some cases through teaching in our community college and involvement in community projects. Procurement principles of the school are also underpinned by an equitable community-oriented ethos that commits the school to local suppliers who are involved in providing training for local people and use locally sourced materials. The academy recognises its responsibility as a large local employer and advertises all vacancies in local jobcentres, the community college and in local media, with a view to employing local people. This includes employing young local people as apprentices with a view to permanent placements at the organisation.

Conclusion

The MCA, I feel, provides an appropriate conclusion to my book. In many respects it represents an attempt to engage with what Gerald Grace has described as complex hope that reflects 'an optimism of the will that recognises the historical and structural difficulties which need to be overcome' (Grace, 2004: 59). In the intellectual journey that various stakeholders have taken in setting up the academy there is a detailed appreciation of the challenges in making education more equitable in their neighbourhoods. In responding to the challenge there has also been a recognition of the need to work at numerous levels of analysis in an integrated and trusting way – a recognition based on an understanding of the intersectionality of variables impacting on disadvantaged young people and their families. But there is also an optimism of spirit that recognises the importance of young people's localised agency freedoms to develop educational capabilities that are valued. The MCA story is an unfolding story and in undertaking such dedicated work there will always be issues that will need to be examined and further developed. There is, however, one major caveat to this story that the school recognises is beyond its control and beyond the control of many of its partners and stakeholders. It is a caveat that recognises the challenge of scope highlighted above and in particular issues of macro policy related to poverty in urban contexts. It is the issue of scope that the American scholar Jean Anyon argues is central to what policy might mean in relation to tackling the poverty–education link:

> Policies such as minimum wage statutes that yield poverty wages, affordable housing and transportation policies that segregate low-income workers of color in urban areas and industrial and other job development in far-flung suburbs where public transport does not reach, all maintain poverty in city neighborhoods and therefore the schools. In order to solve the systemic problems of urban education, then, we need not only school reform but the reform of these public policies. If, as I am suggesting, the macro-economy deeply affects the quality of urban education, then perhaps we should rethink what 'counts' as educational policy. Rules and regulations regarding teaching, curriculum, and assessment certainly count; but, perhaps, policies that maintain high levels of urban poverty and segregation should be part of the educational policy panoply as well . . .
>
> (Anyon, 2005: 2–3)

Although the details of Anyon's argument relate to the US urban context, the wider point she makes holds good in any situation where policy makers take seriously the need to tackle the poverty–education link. To be successful, policy interventions need to have a sufficiently wide *scope*. Specifically, while they need to address the response of the education system to the academic challenges posed by learners living in poverty, they also need to tackle what she calls the 'macro-economy'. MCA in many respects is working hard to be more equitable in what it does for its young people, families and communities. But it cannot do it alone. Nor can it do it with its partners. In a situation where educational inequalities are a manifestation of deep structural inequalities that reflects a policy process characterised by power asymmetries, there is a limit to what schools like MCA can do. In developing the arguments in this book I have adopted a critical stance to such challenges. Throughout I have attempted to expose the limits of policy action, and the failure of policy makers to push sufficiently hard at those limits. And yet at the same time, the book recognises that issues of educational equity are complex and that there are ways of working equitably that can be inserted into educational policy and practice that might enable change and improvement to occur over time. My hope is that in detailing arguments about what improving educational equity might mean in the context of our poorest urban contexts, policy makers and practitioners can develop a set of appropriately scoped, coherent and just set of interventions that improve the educational lives of those young people for whom too often education has provided very little.

Notes

1 See Appendix: MCA Toolkit – Schools speaking for themselves.

Appendix: MCA toolkit – schools speaking for themselves

Schools speaking for themselves: Student voice 1

	'A school where adults and young people work together so as to ensure the safety, security, and emotional well-being of pupils.'		
	Beginning	Developing	Embedding
1 Every young person has an identified and trusted point of contact within the school.			
2 Pupils understand the systems and procedures operating in the school.			
3 Young people feel safe and secure in school.			
4 Pupils have a sense of ownership and identify positively with the school.			
5 Pupils trust the school to listen to their concerns and views.			
6 Pupils are confident about disclosing information and receiving an appropriate response.			
7 The learning environment actively promotes and ensures the well-being and safety of young people.			
8 Pupils are able to access additional services from school to support them and their families.			

Key questions	Sources of evidence
1 **How does the school ensure that every young person has an identified and trusted point of contact?** • Is there a mentor for every pupil in school? • Are young people able to identify their preferred point of contact? • How regularly are formal meetings available to discuss concerns? • What procedures and training does the school provide for mentors? • Does the school provide peer mentors? • How does the school monitor the effectiveness of its approach?	Policy documents School mission statement Audits Job descriptions Training records and courses
2 **In what ways are pupils helped to understand the systems and procedures operating in the school?** • What information is included in pupil planners? • Do pupils have access to the school's website and intranet? • How does the school communicate changes in procedures to young people? • What input do young people have into the systems and procedures in the school? • How are lines of communication between young people and adults clear and responsive to need?	School reception area School environment Website Notice boards Use of form tutor period Newsletters
3 **In what ways does the school ensure that young people feel safe and secure in school?** • How does the school communicate its commitment to safety and security? • How often are pupils consulted about their views? • How accessible and visible are staff during breaks and lunchtimes? • How does the school demonstrate partnership working with other agencies?	School documents and policies Display Security measures Staff presence Pastoral systems
4 **How do pupils show a sense of ownership and identify positively with the school?** • Do pupils respect the school buildings and environment? • Are pupils prepared to report incidents of damage and vandalism? • Do pupils participate in school events and promotional activities? • Do pupils present a positive image of the school to others in the local community?	Maintenance costs Security reports Pastoral records Feedback from parents and community Levels of pupil mobility Display work

5 **Do pupils trust the school to listen and how are they able to express their views and concerns?** • Is the school usually made aware of issues from pupils? • What evidence is there to show that pupils are confident about disclosing information to staff? • Are pupils familiar with school policies? • Does the school have clear procedures for handling complaints from pupils? • To what extent are pupils engaged in their own assessment and reports?	Pastoral records Referral procedures Student Council minutes
6 **In what ways are pupils confident about disclosing information and receiving an appropriate response?** • Is there clear guidance to staff with regard to sensitive information? • How does the school record and safeguard private and sensitive information? • Are pupils made aware of Child Protection policies and procedures? • Does the school have clear policies and procedures around conflict resolution? • What follow-up procedures does the school have to ensure responses are appropriate?	Pastoral records School policies Staff handbook Staff training records
7 **How does the learning environment actively promote and ensure the well-being and safety of young people?** • Is the ECM agenda clearly communicated in school? • Are policies and procedures clearly signposted to pupils? • How are pupils kept informed about developments and changes in school? • Is the school website regularly accessed by pupils? • Is there a feedback process to school from pupils? • Is the school a 'Healthy School'?	Displays Schemes of work SEF Tutorial procedures Newsletters
8 **Are pupils able to access additional services from school to support them and their families?** • Does this school see itself as a link to other services? • Are mentors aware of the available support? • Does the school provide a drop-in centre for pupils? • Are pupils given access to other support agencies? Does the PHSE programme provide information about agencies and support?	Pastoral records Lunchtime and after-school activities Schemes of work Multi-agency involvement

Schools speaking for themselves: Student voice 2

	'A school whose culture and structures promote articulate and autonomous learners.'		
	Beginning	Developing	Embedding
1 The Student Council influences the learning environment of the school.			
2 Students form part of the school self-evaluation process.			
3 Students are able to initiate research and lead change.			
4 Students construct, use and articulate their own individual learning plans.			
5 Students are involved in the co-construction of the curriculum.			
6 Students are trained in Assessment for Learning Strategies and use them in lessons.			
7 Information for learning is provided and accessed by students.			
8 Students regularly engage in learning conversations with adults and peers.			

Key questions	Sources of evidence
1 How is the Student Council used to influence the learning environment of the school? • Are students empowered to make decisions? • How are their views communicated and to whom? • What areas of school life are they encouraged to debate? • What aspects of school life are most commonly discussed? • Is learning a regular agenda item? • Does the Council make decisions and recommendations? • How is the Council kept informed of school priorities? • Does the SIP include student-generated priorities? • Is funding available to support student proposals? • Is there any evidence of change to the learning environment initiated through student voice?	Constitution and terms of reference for Student Council Agendas/Minutes of Council meetings School SEF School Improvement Plan
2 Do students regularly engage in school self-evaluation processes? • Are students consulted about the school SEF? • Do departments consult students in their evaluation process? • Do students have a role in reporting processes to governors? • Does the school encourage Student Learning Walks? • Is there a forum for students to discuss learning? • Are students involved in the identification of school priorities? • Do departments have strategies for the development of student voice? • Is there evidence of student involvement in these processes? • Is there a formal system of student evaluation? • What training has been given to students to support this involvement? • Do individual teachers seek student feedback on teaching and learning? • Do student questionnaires and surveys focus on learning? • Do students evaluate their own and others learning outcomes? • Is student feedback used to change practice?	School and departmental monitoring systems Classroom evaluation techniques Student questionnaires SEF School and departmental plans

Key questions	Sources of evidence
3 Do students construct, use and articulate their own individual leaning plans? • Do students have a Learning Journal? • How frequently does the school provide student reports? • Do students assess their own progress? • How are they made aware of their own learning styles? • Do teachers respond and adapt to different learning styles? • What data is accessed by students? • Are students engaged in target setting and review processes? • Do students have access to a Learning Guide?	Student profiles and reports Learning Journals Student planners Lesson observations Student learning profiles ILPs
4 What opportunities does the school provide for students to initiate research and lead change? • How are students able to voice concerns and raise issues? • How does the school respond to these issues? • Are solutions mainly teacher generated? • Are students trained in research techniques? • What training does the school offer to develop student leadership skills? • How are these skills used in the school? • Are there specific projects led by students?	Student questionnaires and interviews Leadership programmes SEF School Improvement Plan Student research activities
5 To what extent are students involved in the co-construction of the curriculum? • Do students engage in curriculum audits? • Does the curriculum reflect personalised learning opportunities? • How are groups of students organised and do students have any input? • Do student interests or preferences influence the curriculum provision? • Do students have a free choice from a range of curriculum options? • What has changed in the curriculum as a response to student voice?	Curriculum plans Student planners Option booklets and pathways SEF Student surveys

6 **Are students trained in Assessment for Learning (AfL) techniques and can they use them in lessons?** • Are students setting targets and reviewing their progress? • Are students aware of AfL and what it means for them? • Are students able to recognise AfL techniques and do they record their use? • Do teachers make learning objectives explicit? • Are clear criteria for progress and success made explicit in lessons? • Are students able to use AfL techniques in group and paired work? • Do teachers model AfL in lessons? • How do students assess their own learning in lessons?	Student planners Lesson observations Departmental plans Student surveys
7 **How much information for learning is provided and accessed by students?** • Does the intranet provide access to lesson plans and resources? • Are students able to email work to teachers? • Do students share ideas and learning through the intranet? • Is there a virtual learning environment (VLE) in school? • Is the use of the intranet monitored? • Do students have access to online learning and revision packages? • Do student planners contain schedules for projects? • Is there a 'Learning to Learn' opportunity for students? • Do departments provide access to resources and teachers beyond the school day? • Is the use of the library monitored? • Does the school provide study support programmes and after-school learning clubs?	School intranet Study Support programmes Website use VLE Student planners Homework monitoring
8 **To what extent do students regularly engage in learning conversations?** • Do departments provide opportunities for debate and discussion? • Are students taught how to develop a learning dialogue? • Is oral work accredited equally with written work? • Does the school culture promote effective conversation? • Do teachers initiate and engage in learning conversations with students? • Do students initiate learning conversations with peers? • How is student conversation monitored? • Is the impact on attainment evaluated?	Schemes of work Cultural surveys Student questionnaires OFSTED report SEF Data analysis Lesson observations

Schools speaking for themselves: Parent voice 1

	'A school where parents and carers work together as equal partners to ensure the emotional and social well-being of young people.'		
	Beginning	Developing	Embedding
1 Parents and carers are respected as equal partners in the education of their child.			
2 Parents understand the way the school day and curriculum are constructed.			
3 Lines of communication between school and home are clear and responsive to need.			
4 Parents and carers feel welcome and have access to appropriate people.			
5 Parents and carers trust the school to listen and respect confidentiality.			
6 Parents and carers are able to initiate conversation with the school.			
7 Parents can rely on fast, frequent and accurate information from school.			
8 Parents know that schools can access additional services on their behalf.			

Key questions	Sources of evidence
1 **How does the school demonstrate that parents and carers are respected as equal partners in the education of their child?** • Do vision and policy statements refer to parents and carers? • Is the school prospectus readily available? • Is it easy to read and understand? • Is there a parent focus group that scrutinises documentation? • Are local language needs and context taken in to account?	School prospectus Mission statement Constitution of governing body
2 **How do parents show an understanding of the school day and curriculum requirements?** • Do parents support the school's attendance and punctuality procedures? • What are the levels of unauthorised absence in schools? • Are students equipped for lessons? • Do parents support extra-curricular activities? • Does the school offer preschool and after-school care?	Attendance records Letters to parents School monitoring records Extra-curricular registers
3 **Are lines of communication between school and home clear and responsive to needs?** • How does the school ensure that parents receive key information? • What type of communication is sent to parents? • Does the school have co-ordinated and quality assured procedures for home–school communications? • Are mechanisms for response made clear and used? • What actions has the school taken in response?	Letters to parents Newsletters School quality assurance procedures SEF School Improvement Plan

Key questions	Sources of evidence
4 How are parents and carers made to feel welcome and given access to appropriate people? • Is there a clearly indicated and welcoming parent reception area? • Is there a private interview room for parents and teachers? • Do parents know who the first point of contact is in school? • Is there a fast response system to parental concerns and queries? • Is there an open door policy for parents and carers? • Does the school record and monitor levels of parental satisfaction?	School reception area School plans Parental handbook Parental questionnaires and surveys SEF Complaints procedure
5 How does the school ensure parental trust? • Is there clear guidance to staff with regard to sensitive information? • How does the school record and safeguard private and sensitive information?	Child protection procedures Inter-agency contacts Parental surveys
6 In what ways are parents and carers able to initiate conversation with the school? • How frequently do parents initiate contact with the school? • What role is played by parent governors? • Are parents confident about approaching staff with concerns and queries?	Attendance at meetings SEF
7 Are parents able to rely on fast, frequent and accurate information from school? • How often are student reports sent home? • How are parents kept informed about the school? • Is the school website accessed by parents? • Is there a feedback process to school?	Parental surveys School reporting procedures Monitoring of school Website
8 Do parents know that schools can access additional services on their behalf? • Does this school see itself as a link to other services? • Is there a parent mentor in school? • Does the school provide a drop-in centre? • How often are inter-agency meetings arranged? • Are parents given access to other support agencies?	Records of multi-agency meetings Extended school provision Staffing structures and role descriptions Drop-in centre facilities

Schools speaking for themselves: Parent voice 2

	'A school which regards parents and carers as key to student success.'		
	Beginning	Developing	Embedding
1 Parents and carers know that the school meets the needs of students as individual learners.			
2 The school provides the support that parents and carers need to help students with their learning.			
3 Parents and carers are clear about who can help with student learning problems.			
4 The school incorporates parents/ carers knowledge into personalised learning programmes.			
5 Parents and carers are confident about approaching the school with issues affecting student performance.			
6 The school promotes the value of lifelong learning.			
7 The school provides a platform for parent/carer participation in learning and teaching.			
8 Parents and carers understand and share the ethos of the school.			

Key questions	Sources of evidence
1 How do parents and carers know that the school meets the needs of students as individual learners? • Do all relevant staff have knowledge of individual student learning? • How do the school's structures and systems enable personalised learning? • How is this communicated to parents? • In what ways do teachers show knowledge of learners as individuals?	Policy documents School mission statement Curriculum structures Options and pathways Student reports
2 How does the school provide the support that parents and carers need to help students with their learning? • Is information accurate and accessible in terms of both location and language? • How are parents kept informed about learning in terms of curriculum content, pedagogy, progress? • What type of support is given to parents to ensure access and inclusion? • How does the school know what support is required by parents?	Website Notice boards Newsletters Parental learning resources Contact with other agencies
3 How does the school ensure that parents and carers are clear about who can help with student learning and progress? • Are lines of communication clear and accessible? • How does the school monitor feedback from parents? • Is there evidence of improved performance as a result? • Do staff job descriptions reflect this as a priority?	Information sites Lines of communication Prospectus and newsletters Questionnaires and surveys Progress monitoring
4 In what ways does the school incorporate parents/carers knowledge into personalised learning programmes? • What mechanisms exist to find out parents knowledge? • Do personalised learning programmes take account of the student's home environment? • Do review meetings record parents' opinions about progress and ability? • How does the school culture encourage a learning dialogue with parents?	Curriculum planning Individual Education Plans Record of review meetings Data monitoring Parent focus group Parent emails

5 **In what ways do parents and carers demonstrate confidence about approaching the school with issues affecting student performance?** • Are a range of teachers and mentors trained in responding to concerns? • Is there a suitable location for interviews? • How does the school encourage parental visits and involvement? • How does the school judge its response to parental enquiries?	Parent focus groups Parent emails Induction programmes for parents Training plans
6 **How does the school promote the value of lifelong learning?** • Does the website direct parents towards learning opportunities and other services? • Is there a thriving adult education programme? • Does the school provide family learning activities? • Is there a training programme for adult workers in school? • How are aspirations and success celebrated and communicated? • Does the school support and provide access routes to FE and HE for adults?	Extended school provision Drop-in centre facilities Adult education Parental presence in schools NEET figures
7 **In what ways does the school provide a platform for parent/carer participation in learning and teaching?** • Do parents access the learning resources on the school website? • Do parent focus groups review teaching and learning? • Does the school provide information events for parents on innovation and changes in learning? • How does the school ensure inclusion and access for parents to engage in dialogue about learning?	Culture surveys Parent emails Progress monitoring Parental requests for support
8 **In what ways do parents and carers understand and share the ethos of the school?** • Is this reflected in home–school contracts? • To what extent is there parental support for cultural activities, trips, etc? • Do the school PTA and governors model the values of the school? • Are parents and carers used as ambassadors for the school? • How does the school know about parental commitment to the ethos of the school?	Questionnaires and surveys Parent focus groups Recruitment and retention of students Publicity

Schools speaking for themselves: Staff voice 1

	'A school where the social and emotional needs of staff are understood and staff well-being is a priority.'		
	Beginning	Developing	Embedding
1 Staff are knowledgeable about the structures and systems operating in the school.			
2 Staff model the values and vision of the school.			
3 Staff feel that they are made welcome and inducted into school life.			
4 Staff trust that the school is committed to their personal and professional well-being.			
5 Staff believe that their views are respected and listened to.			
6 Staff feel that the school is committed to ensuring a healthy work–life balance.			
7 Staff believe that the school promotes positive and equal relationships amongst staff.			
8 Staff are given sufficient opportunities to enhance their personal effectiveness.			

Key questions	Sources of evidence
1 Are staff knowledgeable about the structures and systems operating in the school? • Is there a clear and updated staff handbook? • How are job descriptions publicised and made available? • How are staff informed about the staffing structure? • How are staff updated and informed about procedures? • What opportunities are there for staff to contribute to the development of structures and systems?	Staff handbook School intranet OFSTED SEFs Staff briefings
2 How do staff model the values and vision of the school? • How do departments demonstrate their commitment to the school's values and vision? • How are the values and vision of the school communicated? • What opportunities are available for staff to share in the development of institutional values? • How do individual staff demonstrate their commitment to the values and vision of the school?	Departmental handbooks SEF IIP Portfolio and reports Staff questionnaires
3 In what ways do staff feel that they are made welcome and inducted into school life? • What information is provided to new and temporary staff? • How does the school ensure access to professional mentors for new and visiting staff? • How is the induction programme quality assured? • Does performance management reflect a requirement for staff well-being? • What do exit interviews tell you about the reasons for staff turnover? • Is there a performance review system for new and temporary staff?	Performance management records Retention and staff turnover rates Exit interviews Induction programmes
4 Do staff trust that the school is committed to their personal and professional well-being? • What systems are in place to gather evidence about staff well-being? • How is information about staff handled and communicated? • What type of support is offered to staff facing personal or professional challenges? • How are staff able to access appropriate personnel? • How does the school ensure confidentiality?	Staff retention IIP Questionnaires Staff absence rates Policy documents Cultural surveys Case studies

Key questions	Sources of evidence
5 In what ways are staff views respected and heard? • How does the school encourage staff participation in school life? • How are staff views gathered and used? • What impact has resulted from staff views? • What opportunities are there for staff to initiate dialogue? • How are focus groups and working parties organised and recruited?	Staff voice Training plan INSET records SEF Minutes of meetings
6 How does the school demonstrate a commitment to work–life balance? • What opportunities are there for flexible working arrangements? • How do school leaders monitor work–life balance? • How does the school demonstrate its commitment to work–life balance? • What training and activities are provided to enable staff to improve their own effectiveness around work–life balance?	IIP Meetings schedule Monitoring records Staff training plan Staff evaluations
7 How does the school promote an ethos of positive and equitable staff relationships? • How does the school enable equal access to decision-making processes? • How is participation in school development enabled? • What leadership opportunities exist for staff and how are they accessed? • How does the school demonstrate that status is no barrier to effectiveness? • How does the school encourage a culture of influence and positive engagement amongst staff?	Minutes of meeting Policy statements Staffing structures SEF Evaluations
8 What opportunities exist for staff to enhance their personal effectiveness? • How is team work and team leadership enabled by the school? • What opportunities exist for project management? • How does the school promote an innovative culture? • What opportunities are there for staff to engage in research? • How does the timetable allow staff time for reflection and sharing of best practice? • Does the school provide opportunities for professional coaching? • How is the school able to demonstrate distributed leadership?	Performance management records SIP Research journals Engagement in professional learning Timetable

Schools speaking for themselves: Staff voice 2

	'A school whose culture and structures demand continuous professional development.'		
	Beginning	Developing	Embedding
1 The school promotes a climate of sharing and collaboration to improve.			
2 The school has clear systems and structures to support professional development.			
3 The school measurers the impact of professional development.			
4 The school actively works with external partners to bring additional capacity to school improvement.			
5 The school ensures that there is equality of access to professional development opportunities.			
6 The school values and accredits all types of staff development.			
7 The school listens and responds to initiatives and ideas generated through staff voice.			
8 The school has an established and resourced practitioner research programme.			

Key questions	Sources of evidence
1 **How does the school promote a climate of sharing and collaboration to improve:** • decision-making and participation? • communications? • focus groups? • discussion forums? • learning walks and time to share? • peer monitoring and mentoring? • database of best practice? • twilight training?	School reception area School environment Website Notice boards Use of form tutor period Newsletters
2 **What systems and structures exist to support professional development?** • Performance management • Staffing structures • Identification of training needs • Website links • Secondment and leadership opportunities • Membership of networks.	School documents and policies
3 **How does the school measure the impact of professional development?** • Training needs analysis • Data trails • Career progression • Attainment • Staff feedback.	
4 **In what ways does the school actively work with external partners to bring additional capacity to school improvement?** • Local and regional networks • Business partners • Community programmes • Extended schools • Cultural links and visits • HE – student associates, ITT.	Learning walks Induction

5 **How does the school ensure that there is equality of access to professional development opportunities?** • Policy and procedure • Tracking the involvement of staff • Performance management reviews • Training plans.	Records of multi-agency meetings Extended school provision Drop-in centre facilities
6 **In what ways does the school value and accredit all types of staff development?** • Communication of success • Database of best practice • Dissemination of ideas • Leadership pathways • Showcasing.	
7 **How does the school listen and respond to initiatives and ideas generated through staff voice?** • Is there a staff voice? • Staff forums and focus groups • Funding mechanisms to support ideas • Formal feedback systems • Disagreement and disaffection • Stakeholder scrutiny • Evidence of change.	
8 **How has the school established and resourced a practitioner research programme?** • Links with external networks • HE support • Research journals • Feedback • How do staff access funding and time? • Value placed on research • Evidence of impact.	

Schools speaking for themselves: Personal communication competencies

	'A school where young people are helped to develop the qualities and skills of effective personal communication.'		
	Beginning	Developing	Embedding
1 Students are able to articulate their learning needs in discussion with each other and their teachers.			
2 Students understand how to make a contribution to the emotional well-being of their classes.			
3 Students have an understanding about different kinds of communication.			
4 Students understand about contexts in communication.			
5 Students learn about different kinds of self-presentation.			
6 Students know how to develop confidence in articulating and presenting ideas.			
7 Students are at ease with visitors to the school and understand about corporate responsibility.			
8 Students understand the need to present opinions courteously and to listen with respect to others.			

Key questions	Sources of evidence
1 **How do students demonstrate the ability to articulate their learning needs and learning outcomes?** • What evidence is there that students in classes are seen to discuss work with each other and with their teachers? • How do students respond to challenging questioning from teachers and learning assistants? • How are student journals used to show thoughtful responses? • In what ways is peer and self-assessment encouraged? • Do students realise the importance of independent study?	Observation in class by colleagues and student-researchers Review of classwork and portfolios
2 **How do students demonstrate understanding of emotional well-being?** • How are students made aware of the concept of citizenship? • What evidence is there of student willingness to take part in school activities? • How do older students interact with younger students? • In class, do students respond thoughtfully to the contributions of others?	Observation in classroom and corridors Focus group interviews
3 **How do students show understanding of different kinds of communication?** • How are students encouraged to use appropriate language within the classroom? • How do students show awareness of when it is appropriate to change register from informal to formal communication? • How are students helped to be clear about the different ways to present ideas in writing – e.g. from memos to synopses to essays and PowerPoint? • In what ways do students interact positively with peers during lessons?	Observation in specific sessions across the curriculum Portfolio reviews Focus interviews
4 **How do students demonstrate understanding of context in communication?** • How are positive contributions to classroom discussion recorded and evaluated? • Is there evidence that students are prepared to volunteer questions and answers in teacher-led sessions? • Is there evidence that students are prepared to gather information for the School Council and to contribute ideas for discussion there? • What opportunities does the school provide for students to present ideas to audiences beyond the school? • How do students respond to challenging questions?	School Council minutes Observation by peers and by staff Evaluative responses from school external partners

Key questions	Sources of evidence
5 Are students learning how to present themselves and their ideas within the school context? • What opportunities are there for students to learn about presenting material to others, e.g. as PowerPoint presentation? • How are students taught about the importance of clear articulation when addressing large groups? • How are students made aware of the varying needs of audiences, e.g. do they use visual back-up when presenting information? • What opportunities are provided for students to take the lead in small group discussions? • How well do students cope with challenge from peers in discussion?	Evidence as above with specific focus on presentations and group discussion with cross section of students
6 Do students know how to develop confidence in articulating and presenting ideas? • In what ways are students enabled to consider practising the presentation of ideas? • Is there evidence that students understand the need to join in discussion in order to grow in confidence? • How are students made aware of the impact of body language on communication?	As above
7 Are students at ease with visitors and able to respond corporately? • How are students helped to understand the concept of corporate responsibility? • Is there evidence that students respond helpfully to visitors to the school? • In what ways are students prepared to volunteer to represent the school on public occasions?	Focus group interviews with selected representatives of student group Observations on school open days Evaluations from external partners
8 Do students understand the need to present opinions courteously and to listen with respect to others? • How do students demonstrate listening skills in their interactions with teachers or peers? • In what ways are students encouraged to respond politely even when they disagree with the opinions of others? • How are students helped to present a controversial view while having regard to the feelings and beliefs of others?	Classroom observations Evaluative reports from staff Evaluative reports from peer group

Schools speaking for themselves: Communication with the local community

	'The school has a wide range of confident and capable partnerships.'		
	Beginning	Developing	Embedding
1 There is an ongoing and effective commitment to community engagement.			
2 Partnerships are established which have a shared understanding of purpose.			
3 Partners are fully satisfied with the benefits and achievements of partnership working.			
4 The school is recognised as taking a leading role in the development of community provision.			
5 Partnership planning responds to local needs and is cognisant of personal and cultural contexts.			
6 The local community values the school as a provider of learning.			
7 The school uses the wider community to enhance student learning.			
8 The school contributes effectively to local networks.			

Key questions	Sources of evidence
1 How does the school demonstrate commitment to developing confident and capable partnerships? • How does school documentation reflect a range of partnerships? • To what extent is documentation referring to partnerships co-authored by community partners? • Is there a community focus group which has oversight of partnership contracts and relationships and how does it operate? • In what ways are local language and cultural contexts taken into account? • Is there evidence the school has structures in place for response to community concerns, issues and needs? • How does the school respond to community initiation of change or modification to provision?	Specialist School Community Plan Prospectus Letters to parents Partnership agreements
2 How do the school/community partnerships demonstrate a shared understanding of purpose? • How are committees established to scrutinise partnership activity and develop effective evaluation strategies? • How are partners informed about the role played by specific partnerships and about their purposes?	Policy statements Minutes of meetings Letters and briefing papers Evaluations and surveys
3 How is the partners' level of user satisfaction demonstrated? • How is the level of user engagement in partnership activities identified? • How does the evaluation process monitor progress of partnership engagement? • Do evaluations indicate that users of partnership services are satisfied by specific provision and how is this recorded? • How does the school ensure that increasing numbers of community partners are engaging with the school?	Surveys and questionnaires Monitoring
4 How is the school recognised as taking a lead in community provision? • What evidence is there to show that the school engages with other schools to share knowledge of partnership working? • Is there evidence that the school has initiated partnerships? • Is the community's use of school premises regular and sustained and how is it monitored? • What type of community activities which include a teaching and learning focus are provided by the school?	Community plans LIG plans EiC plans External evaluations OFSTED

5 How does partnership planning respond to local context and needs, including cultural and personal contexts? • In what ways does partnership provision reflect local cultures? • What mechanisms exist to enable the school to gauge local needs? • How does the school use surveys and evaluations to reflect community confidence that provision meets needs? • What mechanisms are in place for individuals to comment on partnership provision?	Community plans LIG plans EiC plans External evaluations OFSTED
6 How does the local community indicate the value it places on the school as a provider of learning partnerships? • What is the range of learning opportunities offered to the community? • What take up is there of school provision? • Does the school attract additional funding through the provision it offers the community and how is this used for the benefit of all? • How do community participants demonstrate learning as a result of engagement in schools community programmes? • How do a range of community partners demonstrate confidence that the school makes a positive difference to community well-being? • How does the school demonstrate its commitment to regeneration of the community?	Evaluation of training Recruitment and retention rates Learning outcomes Lifelong learning opportunities Community projects
7 How does the school use the wider community to enhance students learning? • What type of community service programmes exists in the school? • How are students used to coach, mentor and tutor other students? • How are community partners welcomed into and used by the school to lead student learning? • In what ways is the local community used by the school as a learning resource?	Schemes of work Community links Monitoring reports
8 How does the school demonstrate its contribution to local networks? • What evidence exists of a planned programme by the school for network activities? • How does the school evidence robust collaborative working? • How do students engage with peers from other schools? • What evidence is there to show that partners benefit from the school's contribution to networks? • Does the school provide facilities for co-located services?	SIP Training plans LIG and LA evaluations OFSTED

Schools speaking for themselves: National communication

	'A school which improves learning outcomes through collaboration and innovation.'		
	Beginning	Developing	Embedding
1 The school is recognised nationally for innovative practice.			
2 The school provides opportunities for staff to engage with, and influence national practice.			
3 The school has an ongoing and effective commitment to collaborative practice.			
4 Student learning is enhanced by connecting to the national learning community.			
5 The school is 'research engaged' and encourages reflective practice.			
6 The school provides opportunities for students to engage with the national learning community.			
7 The school contributes directly to the learning of others nationally.			
8 The school ensures that all stakeholders are informed of national initiatives and strategies.			

Key questions	Sources of evidence
1 How is the school recognised nationally for innovative practice? • What type of practice is recognised nationally? • Which national organisations and agencies does the school engage with? • To what extent does documentation refer to national partnerships? • What awards does the school have to exemplify national recognition?	Awards, e.g. IIP, International Schools Award Presentations at national conferences, e.g. SSAT Publications Engagement with government agencies Website hits and links Involvement in national pilots
2 What opportunities are provided for staff to engage with the national learning community? • How are staff encouraged to develop national links? • Are staff able to access national leadership and CPD programmes? • Does the school have ASTs or Lead practitioners who work at a national level? • What evidence exists of a planned programme by the school for staff network activities?	School training plan Staff CPD records
3 How does the school demonstrate its commitment to collaborative practice? • Does school documentation reflect a range of partnerships? • Does the school commit resources to collaborative practice? • What evidence is there to show that the school engages with other schools to share knowledge of partnership working? • Is there evidence that the school has initiated collaborative partnerships? • Does the school enable the dissemination of best practice through webstes, training, etc? • How does the evaluation process reflect the impact of partnership engagement?	School Improvement Plan Staff training plan Membership of collaborative group Publications and websites Participation in national strategies and pilots School reviews and SEFsOFSTED reports
4 How is student learning enhanced by connecting to the national learning community? • Does the school implement national initiatives and monitor their impact on earning? • Are staff encouraged to take informed risks and challenge orthodoxy? • Does the school have evidence of improved standards as a result of change? • How does the school respond to student ideas about change? • How are students used to coach, mentor and tutor other students?	OFSTED SEF Raise Online Data analysis Departmental reviews Student Council minutes

Key questions	Sources of evidence
5 **In what ways is the school 'research engaged' and how does it encourage reflective practice?** • What mechanisms exist to enable the school to gauge national priorities and initiatives? • How does the school demonstrate its commitment to research and reflective practice? • Do students and staff regularly engage in school-based research? • How does the school measure the effectiveness of research? • What level of resource is committed to research and reflection? • What training is provided by the school?	OFSTED Partnership reports Publications School reviews SEF Access to training
6 **How does the school ensure that students connect to the national learning community?** • What type of learning activities are provided by the school to encourage student engagement with national forums? • How are students supported and advised about connecting to national learning organisations? • How does the school measure the impact of this engagement? • How do students engage with peers from other schools? • What opportunities does the school provide for students to interact with peers nationally?	NAGTY membership Internet and email links National student voice organisations Youth Parliaments Provision of internet accounts Website activity Student evaluations Publications
7 **How does the school contribute directly to the learning of others nationally** • Is there evidence of the school demonstrating its practice in national forums? • How does the school enable effective dissemination of its practice? • Is the school approached by other schools for support and advice? • What evidence is there to show that partners benefit from the school's contribution to networks? • Does the school commit resources to dissemination and support of others?	Partnership agreements Conference publicity Visits to school Showcase activities Staff training plans
8 **How does the school ensure that all stakeholders are informed of national initiatives and strategies?** • What methods does the school use to inform stakeholders? • How is the effectiveness of this evaluated? • How involved are governors in formulating the school's response to national priorities? • Does school documentation reflect national issues and future thinking?	SIP Governors reports and minutes Newsletters Websites Family Learning Workshops OFSTED SEF

Schools speaking for themselves: Global communication

	'The school has strong international links that enhance communication and global citizenship.'		
	Beginning	Developing	Embedding
1 There is an ongoing and effective commitment to international links.			
2 Global partnerships are established which help to develop citizenship and cultural understanding.			
3 Partners are fully satisfied with the benefits and achievements of partnership working.			
4 The school is recognised as taking a leading role in the development of international provision.			
5 Partnership arrangements are cognisant of personal and cultural contexts.			
6 The global community values the school as a provider of learning and resources.			
7 The school uses the international community to enhance staff and student learning.			
8 International partnerships make a significant contribution to the communication competencies of students.			

Key questions	Sources of evidence
1 How does the school demonstrate commitment to international partnerships? • How does school documentation reflect a range of global partnerships? • To what extent are partnerships co-authored by international partners? • In what ways are different language and cultural contexts taken into account? • How does the school respond to initiation of change or modification to provision from its international partners? • What resources does the school commit to international links?	Specialist School Community Plan Prospectus Letters to parents Partnership agreements Staffing appointments Training plans Website
2 Global partnerships are established which help to develop citizenship and cultural understanding. • How extensive are the school's international links? • What type of partnership agreements does the school have? • What types of communication are used? • In what ways do partners contribute to the development of global citizenship? • How does the school measure the effectiveness and impact of cultural links?	Evaluations Cultural surveys Schemes of work Policy documents OFSTED reports
3 Partners are fully satisfied with the benefits and achievements of partnership working. • How is the partners' level of user satisfaction demonstrated? • How does the evaluation process monitor progress of partnership engagement? • How does the school ensure that partnership activities are disseminated and valued? • How are the achievements of partnership working recorded and evaluated?	Surveys and questionnaires Monitoring Partnership communications Websites Newsletters CPD opportunities
4 How is the school recognised as taking a lead in developing global links? • What evidence is there to show that the school engages with other schools to share knowledge of international partnership working? • Does the school have external recognition of its work? • Do prospective partners approach the school as a result of its reputation?	School plans Language College plans iNet membership Student exchanges and trips External evaluations External awards OFSTED

5 How does partnership planning respond to local context and needs, including cultural and personal contexts? • In what ways does partnership provision reflect local cultures? • What mechanisms exist to enable the school to gauge local needs? • How does the school use surveys and evaluations to reflect community confidence that provision meets needs? • What mechanisms are in place for individuals to comment on partnership provision?	Community plans LIG plans EiC plans External evaluations OFSTED
6 How does the global community show that it values the school as a provider of learning and resources • What take up is there of school provision? • Does the school attract additional funding through the provision it offers the community and how is this used for the benefit of all? • How do community participants demonstrate learning as a result of engagement in schools community programmes? • How do a range of community partners demonstrate confidence that the school makes a positive difference to community well-being? • How does the school demonstrate its commitment to regeneration of the community?	Evaluation of training Recruitment and retention rates Learning outcomes Lifelong learning opportunities Community projects
7 How does the school use the international community to enhance staff and student learning? • What type of international learning programmes exist in the school? • How are international partners welcomed into and used by the school to lead learning? • What opportunities are there for staff exchanges and international placements? • In what ways is the international community used by the school as a learning resource? • Do students recognise and respect the international ethos of the school? • How does the school measure the impact on learning outcomes?	Schemes of work Community links Monitoring reports
8 In what ways do international partnerships make a significant contribution to the communication competencies of students • What evidence exists of a planned programme by the school for global network activities? • What methods of communication do students use to engage with international partners? • Is there a planned programme of student exchanges? • How do students access additional language learning to enable global communication?	SIPTraining plans LIG and LA evaluations OFSTED

References

Ainscow, M., Dyson, A., Goldrick, S. and West, M. (2012) *Developing Equitable Education Systems*. London, Routledge.

Anyon, J. (1997) *Ghetto Schooling*. New York, Teachers College Press.

Anyon, J. (2005) *Radical Possibilities*. New York, Routledge.

Aronowitz, S. and Giroux, H. (1985) *Education Under Siege: The Conservative, Liberal and Radical Debate*. South Hadley, MA; Bergin and Barvey.

Aspden, J. and Birch, D. (2005) *New localism – citizen engagement, neighbourhoods and public services: evidence from local government*. London, Local and Regional Government Research Unit, ODPM.

Ball, S., Bowe, R. and Gewirtz, S. (1995) Circuits of schooling: a sociological exploration of parental choice of school in social-class contexts, *The Sociological Review*, 43: 52–78.

Ball, S., Maguire, M. and Braun, A. (2012) *How Schools do Policy*. London, Routledge.

Barker, B. (2010) *The Pendulum Swings: Transforming School Reform*. Trentham Books, Stoke on Trent.

Bauder, H. (2002) Neighbourhood effects and cultural exclusion, *Urban Studies*, 39(1): 85–93.

Bell, C. (2007) Space and place: urban parents' geographical preferences for schools, *Urban Review*, 39(4): 375–404.

Bell, D. (1973) *The Coming of Post-industrial Society*. Basic Books, New York.

Bell, D. (2003) Access and achievement in urban education: Ten years on. Speech given to the Fabian Society by David Bell, Her Majesty's Chief Inspector of Schools. London, Ofsted.

Benadusi, L. (2001) Equity and Education – A critical review of sociological research and thought, in (eds) Walo Hutmacher, Douglas Cochrane and Norberto Bottani, *In Pursuit of Equity in Education – Using International Indicators to Compare Equity Policies*. New York, Kluwer.

Bentham, J. (1789) *An Introduction to the Principles of Morals and Legislation*. Oxford, Payne; also Clarendon Press, 1907.

Bernstein, B. (1970) Education cannot compensate for society, *New Society*, 15, 387: 344–347

Biesta, G. (2011) *Learning Democracy in School and Society: Education, Lifelong Learning, and the Politics of Citizenship*. Rotterdam, Sense Publishing.

Blanden, J. and Machin, S. (2003) *Educational Inequality and the Expansion of UK Higher Education*. London, London School of Economics, Centre for Economic Performance.

Bourdieu, P. (1986) The Forms of Capital, in J. E. Richardson (1986) (ed.) *Handbook of Theory of Research for the Sociology of Education.* Greenwood Press.

Bourdieu, P. (1998) *Practical Reason: On the theory of action.* Cambridge. UK, Polity.

Bourdieu, P. and Passeron, J. (1977) *Reproduction in Education, Society and Culture.* London, Sage.

Bowles, S. and Gintis, H. (1976) *Schooling in Capitalist America.* London, Routledge.

Boyle, B. and Charles, M. (2011), Education in a multicultural environment: equity issues in teaching and learning in the school system in England, International Studies in Sociology of Education, 21(4): 299–314.

Brady, D. (2009) *Rich Democracies, Poor People: How Politics Explain Poverty.* Oxford University Press, US.

Brighouse, T. and Fullick, L. (eds) (2007) *Education in a Global City: Essays from London.* London, Bedford Way Papers 32.

Broadfoot, P. and Nisbet, J. (1981) The impact of research on educational studies, *British Journal of Educational Studies,* 29(2): 115–122.

Brown, P. (1999) Globalisation and the political economy of high skills, *Journal of Education and Work,* 12(3), 233–252.

Bruner, J. S (1966) *Towards a Theory of Instruction.* Harvard, Belknap.

Bryk, A., Bender Sebring, P., Allensworth, E., Luppscu, S. and Easton, L. (2010) *Organising Schools for Improvement – Lessons from Chicago.* Chicago and London, The University of Chicago Press.

Burchardt, T. and Vizard, P. (2009) *Developing an equality measurement framework: A list of substantive freedoms for adults and children.* Research Report 19, Equality and Human Rights Commission: equalityhumanrights.com

Bynner, J. and Joshi, H. (2002) Equality and opportunity in education: evidence from the 1958 and 1970 birth cohort studies, *Oxford Review of Education,* 28(4): 405–425.

Byrne, D. (2005) *Social Exclusion.* Berkshire, Open University Press.

Campbell, C. and Whitty, G. (2007) Urban Education in the United Kingdom, Section Editors' introduction, in W. Pink and G. Noblit (eds) *International Handbook of Urban Education.* Dordrecht, Springer, 929–942.

Carr, D. (2006) Professional and personal values and virtues in education and teaching, *Oxford Review of Education,* 32(2): 171–183.

Cassen, R. and Kingdon, G. (2007) *Tackling Low Educational Achievement.* York, Joseph Rowntree Foundation.

Chitty, C. (2002) Education and social class, *The Political Quarterly,* 73(2): 208–210.

Cohen, P. and Ainley, P. (2000) In the country of the blind?: Youth studies and cultural studies in Britain, *Journal of Youth Studies,* 3(1): 79–96.

Corver, M (2005) *Young Participation in Higher Education* (HEFCE, 2005/03).

Creemers, B.P.M. and Kyriakides, L. (2012). *Improving Quality in Education: Dynamic Approaches to School Improvement.* London, Routledge.

Cummings, C., Dyson, A., Papps, I., Pearson, D. and Raffo, C. (2005) *Evaluation of the Full-service Extended Schools Initiative: End of first year report.* London, DfES.

Day, C., Harris, A., Hadfield, M., Tolly, H. and Beresford, J. (2000) *Leading Schools in Times of Change.* Buckingham, Open University Press.

Dean, C., Dyson, A., Gallannaugh, F., Howes, A. and Raffo, C. (2007) *School, Governors and Disadvantage.* London, Joseph Rowntree Foundation.

Demie, F., Butler, R. and Taplin, A. (2002) Educational achievement and the disadvantage factor: Empirical evidence. *Educational Studies* 28, no. 2: 101–10.

Deneulin, S., Nebel, M. and Sagovsky, N. (2006). Transforming unjust structures: The capability approach. In S. Deneulin, M. Nebel and N. Sagovsky (eds), *Transforming Unjust Structures—The capability approach* (pp. 1–16). Dordrecht, Springer.

DfEE (1997) *Excellence in Schools.* London, The Stationary Office Limited. Cm 2681.

DfEE (1998) *Teachers: Meeting the challenge of change.* London, DfEE. Cm 4164.

DfES (2003) *Every Child Matters.* London, The Stationery Office. Cm. 5860.

DfES (2004) *Five Year Strategy for Children and Learners.* London, DfES. Cm 6272.

DfES (2005a) *Higher Standards, Better Schools for All, More Choice for Parents and Pupils.* London, HM Government. Cm 6677.

DfES (2005b) *Extended Schools: Access to opportunities and services for all. A prospectus.* London, DfES.

Dobbie, W. and Fryer, R. (2010) *Are High-Quality Schools Enough to Close the Achievement Gap?* NBER Working Paper 15473, National Bureau of Economic Research, US.

Dyson, A., Kerr, K., Raffo, C. and Wigelsworth, M. (2012) *Developing Children's Zones for England.* Save the Children Fund.

Engeström, Y. (1987) *Learning by Expanding: An activity-theoretical approach to developmental research.* Helsinki, Orienta-Konsultit.

Field, S., Kuczera, M. and Pont, B. (2007) *No More Failures – Ten steps to educational equity.* OECD Training and Education Policy, www.oecd.org/publishing/corrigenda

Fielding, M. (2006) Leadership, radical student engagement and the necessity of person-centred education, *International Journal of Leadership in Education*, 9(4): 299–313.

Fielding, M. and Moss, P. (2011) *Radical Education and the Common School.* London, Routledge.

Foster, P., Gomm, R. and Hammersley, M. (1996) *Constructing Educational Inequality.* London, Falmer Press.

Foster, W. (1989) Towards a critical practice of leadership, in J. Smyth (ed.) *Critical Perspectives on Educational Leadership.* London, The Falmer Press.

Foucault, M. (1975) *The Birth of the Clinic: An archaeology of medical perception.* New York, Vintage.

Fraser, N. (1996) Social Justice in the Age of Identity Politics: Redistribution, recognition and participation, *The Tanner Lectures on Human Values.* Stanford University, May 1996.

Freedman, S. and Horner, S. (2008) *School Funding and Social Justice: A Guide to the Pupil Premium.* Policy Exchange.

Furlong, A. and Biggart, A. (1995) Social Reproduction in an Urban Context: Neighbourhoods, Labour Markets and Discouraged Workers, *British Sociological Association Annual Conference*, Leicester.

Gandin, L. and Apple, M. (2002) Challenging neo-liberalism, building democracy: creating the Citizen School in Porto Alegre, Brazil, *Journal of Education Policy*, 17(2): 259–279.

Gardner, P., Dillabough, J. and McLeod, J. (2004) *Disenfranchised youth, class conflict and educational exclusion.* Social Sciences and Humanities Research Council Grant.

Gewirtz, S. (1998) Conceptualising social justice in education: mapping the territory, *Journal of Education Policy*, 13(4): 469–484.

Gewirtz, S. (2001) Cloning the Blairs: New Labour's programme for the re-socialization of working-class parents, *Journal of Education Policy*, 16(4): 365–37.

Gewirtz, S. and Cribb, A. (2006) What to do about values in social research: The case for ethical reflexivity in the sociology of education, *British Journal of Sociology of Education*, 27(2): 141–155.

Gonzales, N., Moll, L. and Amanti, C. (2005) *Funds of Knowledge*. Mahwah, New Jersey, Lawrence Erlbaum.

Goodson, I. (2008) Schooling, curriculum, narrative and social future, in C. Sugrue (ed.) *The Future of Educational Change: International perspectives*. London, Routledge.

Gottfredson, L. (1981) Circumscription and compromise: a developmental theory of occupational aspirations, *Journal of Counseling Psychology* 28(6): 545–579.

Gottfredson, L. (2002) 'Gottfredson's Theory of Circumscription, Compromise, and Self-Creation', in D. Brown (ed) *Career Choice and Development*. San Francisco, Jossey-Bass.

Gove, M. (2010) *Speech to Westminster Academy*, 9th September 2010, http://www.michaelgove.com/content/michael_gove_speech_westminster_academy

Grace, G. (ed.) (1984) *Education and the City – Theory, history and contemporary practice*. London, Routledge & Keegan Paul.

Grace, G. (2004) Urban education and the culture of contentment: the politics, culture and economics of inner-city schooling, in N. Stromquist (ed.) *Education in Urban Areas: Cross-national dimensions*. Westport, Praeger.

Granovetter, M. (1973) The strength of weak ties, *American Journal of Sociology* 78: 1360–1380.

Gruenewald, D.A. and Smith, G. (2008) Making room for the local, in D.A. Gruenewald and G. Smith (eds) *Placed-based Education in the Global Age. Local Diversity*. Mahwah, New Jersey, Lawrence Erlbaum.

Guinier, L. 2003. The Supreme Court, 2002 Term: Comment – Admissions rituals as political acts: Guardians at the gates of our democratic ideals. Harvard Law Review, November.

Gulson, K and Symes, C. (2007) Knowing one's place: space, theory, education, *Critical Studies in Education*, 48(1): 97–110.

Gunter, A. and Watt, P. (2009) Grafting, going to college and work on road: youth transitions and cultures in an East London neighbourhood, *Journal of Youth Studies*, 12(5): 515–529.

Gutman, L. M. and Akerman, R. (2008) *Determinants of Aspirations*. London, Centre for Research on the Wider Benefits of Learning.

Harlen, W. and Malcolm, H. (1999) *Setting and Streaming: A Research Review*. SCRE Publication, 143,

Hart, S., Dixon, A., Drummond, M. J. and McIntyre, D. (2004) *Learning Without Limits*. Maidenhead, Open University Press.

Harvey, D. (1989) *The Condition of Postmodernity*. Oxford, Blackwell.

Hatcher, R. (1998) Class differentiation in education: rational choices?, *British Journal of Sociology of Education*, 19(1): 5–24.

Hattam, R., Brennan, M., Zipin, L. and Comber, B. (2009) Researching for social justice: contextual, conceptual and methodological challenges, *Discourse: Studies in the Cultural Politics of Education*, 30(3): 303–316.

Hodkinson, P., Sparkes, A.C. and Hodkinson, H. (1996) *Triumphs and Tears: Young people, markets and the transition from school to work*. London, David Fulton Publishers.

Hogan, P. (2010) *The New Significance of Learning: Imagination's Heartwork*. London and New York, Routledge.

Hollands, R. G. (1990) *The Long Transition: Class, culture and youth training*. Basingstoke, Macmillan.

James, M. and Pollard, A. (2011) TLRP's ten principles for effective pedagogy: rationale, development, evidence, argument and impact, *Research Papers in Education*, 26(3): 275–328.

Keddie, A. (2012): Schooling and social justice through the lenses of Nancy Fraser, *Critical Studies in Education*, DOI:10.1080/17508487.2012.709185

Kendall, L., O'Donnell, L., Golden, S., Ridley, K., Machin, S., Rutt, A., McNally, S., Schagen, I., Meghir, C., Stoney, S., Morris, M., West, A., and Noden, P. (2005) *Excellence in Cities: The National Evaluation of a Policy to Raise Standards in Urban Schools 2000–2003*, DfES *Research Report RR675A*, (Nottingham: DfES), available at http://www.dfes.gov.uk/research/data/uploadfiles/RR675A.pdf [accessed on 26/04/06].

Lareau, A. (1987) Social class differences in family–school relationships: the importance of cultural capital. *Sociology of Education*, vol. 60 (April): 73–85.

Lash, S. and Urry, J. (1994) *Economies of Signs and Space*. London, Sage.

Lave, J. and Wenger, E. (1992) *Situated Learning: Legitimate Peripheral Participation*. Cambridge, Cambridge University Press.

Lawson, M.A. (2003) School–family relations in context. Parent and teacher perceptions of parent involvement, *Urban Education*, 38(1): 77–133.

Lebfevre, H. (1991) *The Production of Space*. Oxford, Blackwell.

Lee, J.S. and Anderson, K.T. (2009) Negotiating linguistic and cultural identities: theorising and constructing opportunities and risks in education, in V.L. Gadsden, J.L. Davis and A.J. Artiles (eds) *Review of Research in Education: Risk Schooling and Equity, Vol. 33*. Thousand Oaks, Sage.

Leont'ev, A. N. (1978) *Activity, Consciousness and Personality*. Englewood Cliffs, Prentice-Hall.

Levin, B. (2003) *Approaches to Equity in Policy for Lifelong Learning*, a paper commissioned by the Education and Training Policy Division, OECD, for the Equity in Education Thematic Review (OECD).

Lingard, B. (2007) Pedagogies of indifference, *International Journal of Inclusive Education*, 11(3): 245–266.

Lipman, P. (2004) *High Stakes Education*. London, Routledge Falmer.

Love, J., Kisker, E.E., Ross, C.M. Schochet, P.Z., Brooks-Gunn, J., Paulsell, D., Boller, K., Constantine, J., Vogel, C., Fuligni, A.S. and Brady-Smith, C. (2002) *Making a difference in the lives of infants and toddlers and their families: The impacts of Early Head Start. Volume 1: Final Technical Report*. Princeton, NJ, Mathematica Policy Research Inc., available at: http://www.mathematica-mpr.com/PDFs/ehsfinalvol1.pdf

Lucas, S.R. and Beresford, L. (2010) Naming and classifying: Theory, evidence, and equity in education, *Review of Research in Education*, 34: 25.

Lupton, R. (2010) Area-based initiatives in English education: what place for place and space?, in C. Raffo, A. Dyson, H. Gunter, D. Hall, L. Jones and A. Kalambouka (eds) *Education in Affluent Countries*. New York, Routledge, 111–123.

Lupton, R. and Thrupp, M. (2012) Headteachers' readings of and responses to disadvantaged contexts: evidence from English primary schools, *British Educational Research Journal*, DOI:10.1080/01411926.2012.683771

Lynch, K. and Lodge, A. (2002) *Equality and Power in Schools: Redistribution, recognition, and representation*. London, RoutledgeFalmer.

Mac an Ghaill, M. 1988. *Young, Gifted and Black: Student–teacher relations in the schooling of black youth*. Milton Keynes, Open University Press.

MacIntyre, A. (2001) *Whose Justice? Whose Rationality*. London, Duckworth.

Massey, D. (1993) Power geometry and progressive sense of place, in J. Bird, B. Curtis, F. Putnam, G. Robertson and L. Tickner (eds.) *Mapping the Futures: Local cultures, global changes*. London, Routledge, 59–69.

Massey, D. (1994) Double articulation: A place in the world, in A. Bammer (eds) *Displacements: Cultural identities in questions*. Bloomington, Indiana University Press.

McDermott, R., Raley, J.D. and Seyer-Ochi, I. (2009) Race and class in a culture of risk, in V.L. Gadsden, J.L. Davis and A.J. Artiles (eds) *Review of Research in Education: Risk Schooling and Equity, Vol. 33*. Thousand Oaks, Sage.

McDowell, L. (1996) Spatialising feminism: Geographical perspectives, in N. Duncan (ed.) *Body Space*. London, Routledge: 28–44.

Melhuish, E., Belsky, J. and Leyland, A. (2005) *Early Impacts of Sure Start Local Programmes on Children and Families: Report of the Cross-sectional Study of 9- and 36-Month Old Children and their Families*, DfES Research Report NESS/2005/FR/013. London, DfES.

Meuret, D. (2001) A System of Equity Indicators for Educational Systems, in Walo Hutmacher, Douglas Cochrane and Norberto Bottani (eds), *In Pursuit of Equity in Education – Using International Indicators to Compare Equity Policies*. New York, Kluwer.

Micklewright, J. (1989) Choice at sixteen, *Economica*, 56, 25–39.

Miles, M. and Huberman, A. (1994) *Qualitative Data Analysis*. Thousand Oaks, CA, Sage.

Mirón, L.F. and St. John, E.P. (2003) Introduction: rethinking urban school reform, in L.F. Mirón and E.P. St. John (eds) *Reinterpreting Urban School Reform: Have urban schools failed, or has the reform movement failed urban schools?* Albany, NY, State University of New York Press.

Morris, J.E. (2004) Can Anything Good Come From Nazareth? Race, Class, and African American Schooling and Community in the Urban South and Midwest, *American Educational Research Journal*, 41(1): 69–112.

Mortimore, P. and Whitty, G. (1997) *Can School Improvement Overcome the Effects of Disadvantage?* London, Institute of Education, University of London.

Muijs, D., Ainscow, M., Dyson, A., Raffo, C., Goldrick, S., Kerr, K., Lennie, C. and Miles, S. (2010): Leading under pressure: leadership for social inclusion, *School Leadership and Management: Formerly School Organisation*, 30(2): 143–157.

Noguera, P. (2003) *City Schools and the American Dream*. New York, Teachers College Press.

Nussbaum, M. (2000) *Women and Human Development*. Cambridge, Cambridge University Press.

O'Connor, J. (1999) *Cultural Production in the City*. Manchester, Manchester Institute of Popular Culture.

O'Connor, L. and Wynne, D. (eds) (1996) *From the Margins to the Centre: Cultural Production and Consumption in the Post-industrial City.* Aldershot, Arena.

OECD (2008) Education at a glance, available at http://www.oecd.org/dataoecd/21/15/41278761.pdf

Office of the Deputy Prime Minister (2005) *Mainstream Public Services and their Impact on Neighbourhood Deprivation,* London, ODPM, available at http://www.neighbourhood.gov.uk/document.asp?id=1044

Parsons, T. (1961) *Theories of Society: foundations of modern sociological theory.* New York, Free Press.

Perrenoud, P. (1998) From formative evaluation to a controlled regulation of learning processes. Towards a wider conceptual field, *Assessment in Education: Principles, Policy and Practice,* Vol. 5, No. 1: 85–102.

Pink, W. and Noblit, G. (eds) (2007) *International Handbook of Urban Education.* Dordrecht, Springer.

Popkewitz, T., and Lindbland, S. (2000) Educational governance and social inclusion and exclusion: some conceptual difficulties and problematics in policy and research, *Discourse: studies in the cultural politics of education,* 21(1): 5–44.

Power, A. (2007) *City Survivors – Bringing up children in disadvantaged neighbourhoods.* Bristol, Policy Press

Power, S., Edwards, T., Whitty, G., and Wigfall, V. (2003) *Education and the middle classes.* Buckingham, Open University Press.

Raffo, C. (2006) Disadvantaged young people accessing the new urban economies of the post-industrial city, *Journal of Education Policy,* 21(1): 75–94.

Raffo, C. and Hall (1999) Mentoring Urban Youth in the Post-Industrial City: some guiding principles based on developed notions of situated learning and a cognitive mentoring model of Initial Teacher Education, *Mentoring and Tutoring: Partnership in Learning,* 6(3): 61–75.

Raffo, C., and Reeves, M. (2000) Youth transitions and social exclusion – developments in social capital theory, *Journal of Youth Studies,* 3(2): 147–166.

Raffo, C., O'Connor, J. and Lovatt, A. (1996) Modernist 16–19 business education in a postmodern world – critical evidence of business practice and business education in the cultural industries, *British Journal of Education and Work,* 9(3): 19–34.

Raffo, C., Dyson, A., Gunter, H., Hall, D., Jones, L. and Kalambouka, A. (2007) *Education and Poverty: A critical review of theory, policy and practice.* London, Joseph Rowntree Foundation.

Raffo, C., Dyson, A., Gunter, H., Hall, D., Jones, L. and Kalambouka, A. (2009) Education and poverty: Mapping the terrain and making the links to educational policy, *International Journal of Inclusive Education,* 13(4): 341–358.

Raffo, C., Dyson, A., Gunter, H., Hall, D., Jones, L. and Kalambouka, A. (eds) (2010) *Education and Poverty in Affluent Countries.* New York, Routledge.

Ranson, S. (2000) Recognizing the pedagogy of voice in a learning community, *Educational Management and Administration,* 28(3): 263–279.

Rawls, J. (1972) *A Theory of Justice.* Cambridge, MA, Harvard University Press.

Reay, D. and Lucey, H. (2000) "I don't really like it here but I don't want to be anywhere else": children and inner-city council estates, *Antipode,* 32(4): 410–428.

Rees, G., Power, S. and Taylor, C. (2007) The governance of educational inequalities: the limits of area-based initiatives, *Journal of Comparative Policy Analysis,* 9(3): 261–274.

Riddell, R. (2005) Government policy, stratification and urban schools: a commentary on the five year strategy for children and learners, *Journal of Education Policy*, 20(2): 237–241.

Riddell, R. (2007) Urban learning and the need for varied urban curricula and pedagogies, in Pink, W. and Noblit, G. (eds) (2007) *International Handbook of Urban Education* (Dordrecht, Springer), 1027–1048. Rogers, S. (2012) *An Investigation Into New Labour Education Policy: Personalisation, Young People, Schools and Modernity* (unpublished PhD thesis, University of Manchester).

Sanchez-Jankowski, M. (2008) *Cracks in the pavement: social change and resilience in poor neighborhoods*. California, University of California Press.

Schools Analysis and Research Division, Department for Children Schools and Families (2009) Deprivation and education: the evidence on pupils in England, Foundation Stage to Key Stage 4. London, DCSF.

Seaman, P., Turner, K., Hill, M., Stafford, A. and Walker, M. (2006) *Parenting and Children's Resilience in Disadvantaged Communities*. York, Joseph Rowntree Foundation.

Seely Brown, J., Collins, A. and Duguid, P. (1989) Situated cognition and the culture of learning, *Educational Research*, American Educational Research Association, 18(1): 25.

Sen, A. (1985) *Commodities and Capabilities*. Amsterdam, North-Holland.

Sen, A. (1992) *Inequality Re-examined*. Oxford, Clarendon Press.

Sen, A. (1999) *Development as Freedom*. Oxford, Oxford University Press.

Sen, A. (2000) Social Justice and the Distribution of Income, in Anthony B. Atkinson and Francois Bourguignon, eds., *Handbook of Income Distribution*. Amsterdam, North-Holland.

Seyer-Ochi, I. (2006) Lived landscapes of the Fillmore, in G. Spindler and L. Hammond (eds) *Innovations in Educational Ethnography: Theory, methods and results*. New Jersey, Lawrence Erlbaum Associates.

Sibley, D. (1995) *Geographies of Exclusion*. London, Routledge.

Sixsmith, C. and Simco, N. (1997) The role of formal and informal theory in the training of student teachers, *Mentoring and Tutoring: Partnerships in Learning* 5(1): 5–13.

Smith, G. (1987) Whatever Happened to Educational Priority Areas?, *Oxford Review of Education*, 13(1): 23–38.

Stevenson, H. (2007) A case study in leading schools for social justice: when morals and markets collide, *Journal of Educational Administration* 45(6): 769–781.

Smyth, J. (2010) Inclusive school leadership strategies in disadvantaged schools based on student and community voice: implications for Australian educational policy, in C. Raffo, A. Dyson, H. Gunter, D. Hall, L. Jones and A. Kalambouka (eds) *Education and Poverty in Affluent Countries*, New York, Routledge.

Smyth, J., Down, B. and McInerney, P. (2010) *Hanging in with Kids' in Tough Times: Engagement in Contexts of Educational Disadvantage in the Relational School*. New York, Peter Lang.

Social Exclusion Unit (1998) *Truancy and School Exclusion*. London, HMSO.

Spicker, P. (2001) Poor areas and the 'ecological fallacy'. *Radical Statistics*, 76, Winter, available at http://www.radstats.org.uk/no076/spicker.htm

Spindler, G.T. (1997) Why Have Minority Groups in North America Been Disadvantaged by their Schools? In Spindler, G.T. (ed.), *Education and Cultural Process. Anthropological Approaches*. Waveland Press, Prospect Heights.

Stokes, H. and Tyler, D. (1997) *Rethinking Inter-agency Collaboration and Young People*. Melbourne, Language Australia: Youth Research Centre.

Stoker, G. (2006) *Why Politics Matters*. Basingstoke, Palgrave MacMillan.

Subrahmanian, R. (2002) Engendering education: prospects for a rights based approach to female education deprivation in India. In Molyneux, M. and Razavi, S. (eds.), *Gender Justice, Development, and Rights*. Oxford, Oxford University Press.

Suchman, L. (1987) *Plans and Situated Actions*. New York, Cambridge University Press.

Swann M., Peacock A., Hart, S. and Drummond, M.J. (2012) *Creating Learning without Limits*. Maidenhead, Open University Press.

Taylor, C. (2009) Towards a geography of education, *Oxford Review of Education*, 35(5): 651–669.

Teese, R. and Polesel, J. (2003) *Undemocratic schooling: equity and quality in mass secondary education in Australia*. Carlton South, Australia, Melbourne University Press.

Terzi, L. (2008) *Justice and Equality in Education*. Continuum Books.

Thompson, J.B. (1995) *The Media and Modernity: A social theory of the media*. Cambridge, Polity Press.

Thomson, P. (2002) *Schooling the Rustbelt Kids – Making the difference in changing times*. Trentham Books.

Thomson, P. (2007) Leading schools in high poverty neighbourhoods: The National College for School Leadership and beyond, in W. Pink and G. Noblit (eds) (2007) *International Handbook of Urban Education*. Dordrecht, Springer, 1049–1077.

Thrift, N. (1997) "Us" and "them": Reimagining places, reimagining identities, in H. MacKay (Ed.) *Consumption and Everyday Life*. London, Sage: 159–212.

Tikly, L. and Barrett, A. (2011) Social justice, capabilities and the quality of education in low-income countries, *International Journal of Educational Development*, 31, 3–14

Turner, V. (1967) *The Forest of Symbols*. Ithaca, NY, Cornell University Press.

Unterhalter, E. (2007) *Gender, Schooling and Global Social Justice*. London and New York, Routledge.

Unterhalter, E. (2009) What is equity in education? Reflections from the capability approach, *Studies in the Philosophy of Education*, 28: 415–424.

Valverde, L.A. (1988). The coexistence of excellence and equality. *Education and Urban Society*, 20: 315–318.

Vizard, P. (2006). *Poverty and Human Rights: Sen's 'Capability Perspective' explored*. Oxford, Oxford University Press.

Vygotsky, L. (1978) *Mind in Society*. New York, Wiley.

Wacquant, L. (2007) *Urban Outcasts: A comparative sociology of advanced marginality*. Polity Press.

Walker, A., Dimmock, C., Stevenson, H., Bignold, B., Shah, S. and Middlewood, D. (2009) *Effective Leadership in Multi-Ethnic Schools*. National College for School Leadership, www.ncsl.org

Walker, M. (2006) Towards a capability-based theory of social justice for education policy making, *Journal of Education Policy*, 21(2): 163–185.

Wasser, J.D. and Bressler, L. (1996) Working in a collaborative zone: conceptualizing collaboration in qualitative research teams, *Educational Researcher* 25(5): 5–15.

Webber, R. and Butler, T. (2007) Classifying pupils by where they live: how well does this predict variations in their GCSE results? *Urban Studies*, 44(7): 1229–1253.

Wheeler, B., Shaw, M., Mitchell, R. and Dorling, D. (2005) *Life in Britain: Using millennium Census data to understand poverty, inequality and place*. Bristol, Policy Press.

White, J. (2011) *The Invention of the Secondary Curriculum*. New York, Palgrave Macmillan.

Whitehurst, G. and Croft, M. (2010) *The Harlem Children's Zone, Promise Neighborhoods, and the Broader, Bolder Approach to Education*. Brown Center on Education Policy at Brookings.

Wilkinson, R. and Pickett, K. (2009) *The Spirit Level – Why More Equal Societies Almost Always Do Better*. Allen Lane.

Willis, P. (1977) *Learning to Labour*. Farnborough, Saxon House.

Wyn, J. and White, R. (1997) *Rethinking Youth*. London, Thousand Oaks, New Delhi: Sage.

Young, J. (1990) *Justice and the Politics of Difference*. Princeton, Princeton University Press.

Young, M. (2008) *Bringing Knowledge Back In: From Social Constructivism to Social Realism in the Sociology of Education*. New York, Routledge.

Zukin, S. (1991) *Landscapes of Power: From Detroit to Disney World*. Berkeley, Berkeley University Press.

Zukin, S. (1996) *The Cultures of Cities*. Oxford, Blackwells.

Index